BEST OF FRIENDS

Best of Friends

THE BRENAN—PARTRIDGE LETTERS selected and edited by XAN FIELDING

Chatto & Windus LONDON

Published in 1986 by Chatto & Windus Ltd
40 William IV Street, London WC2N 4DF

British Library Cataloguing in Publication Data

Brenan, Gerald
    Best of friends: an exchange of letters between
    Gerald Brenan and Ralph Partridge.
    1. Brenan, Gerald—Biography
    2. Authors, English—20th century—Biography
    I. Title   II. Partridge, Ralph
    III. Fielding, Xan
    828'.91409   PR6003.R3513Z/

ISBN 0 7011 3028 8
Copyright © Gerald Brenan and Frances Partridge 1986

Notes and linking passages copyright © Xan Fielding 1986

Photoset by Rowland Phototypesetting Ltd
Bury St Edmunds, Suffolk
Printed in Great Britain by
Redwood Burn Ltd
Trowbridge, Wiltshire

CONTENTS

In 1918 Gerald Brenan started a correspondence with Ralph Partridge which only ended with the latter's death in 1960. Nearly 500 of his letters have been preserved. Of Ralph's letters to Gerald during the same period, only 127 are extant. This disproportion prompted me at first to concentrate on Gerald's letters alone; but on second thoughts I decided to include some of Ralph's as well, not only on account of their merit but also because they contribute to the narrative.

In a private correspondence which was not intended for publication, slips of the pen are inevitable and grammatical errors and spelling mistakes and oddities of punctuation are bound to occur. Rather than copy them all down and add in every case a parenthetical *sic* (a practice I have always thought pedantic and invidious) I have simply corrected them as I saw fit. For a similar reason I have indicated excised passages by three dots, without specifying – for it seemed to me of no particular interest – the number of words or lines omitted. I have also availed myself of an editor's privilege to re-organise some of the paragraphs, since unbroken blocks of hand-writing on a sheet of paper, however they may delight the recipient, will not necessarily have the same effect on the reader when transposed in print on the page of a book.

Some of the letters are undated; I have marked these 'n.d.' and placed them where they seemed to belong. Others bear only the day of the week or of the month. But the text usually affords a clue to the year, which I have therefore taken it upon myself to inscribe, wherever possible, without further explanation.

The letters speak for themselves. Though neither of their authors was a typical Bloomsbury figure, they are suffused with the intellectual integrity which has come to be associated with that coterie. They are also a tribute to a generation, perhaps the last, which believed in the charm and power of the written word. All that remains for me is to thank Ralph's widow Frances and Gerald himself for entrusting me with the rewarding task of editing them.

X.F.

PART ONE   1919–1924

Born in Malta in 1894, into a well-to-do army family, Gerald spent his early years in South Africa and India before being sent to Radley, one of the most traditional of English public schools. At the age of seventeen he reacted against this background and, disguised as a gas-fitter and with £16 in his pocket, set out to walk to the East. He got no further than Bosnia. Caught up in the First World War, he returned to the caste he had rejected and served with distinction as an officer at the front, winning the Croix de Guerre. It was in the army that he met the man who was to become and remain for forty-five years his closest friend.

Ralph was born in the same year as Gerald and likewise abroad – in India, where his father, who came from Devonshire, was a civil servant. He too was sent to England for his education, first at a preparatory school and then at Westminster, where he rose to be head boy and from where he won a scholarship to Christ Church, Oxford. A fellow undergraduate described him as 'one of the best brains of the year'. He too had a brilliant war record, was awarded the Military Cross and the Croce de Guerra, and became a major at the age of twenty-three. There was an element of hero-worship in Gerald's liking for him: 'I admired his sexual prowess and . . . found his rollicking high spirits and zest for life irresistible . . . A Roman rather than a Greek by temperament, he called up – or so I then thought – Plutarch's portrait of Mark Antony.'

On home leave in the summer of 1918, Ralph met Dora Carrington – 'a painting damsel and a great Bolshevik,' he wrote to Gerald, 'who would like me to strike a blow for the cause.' Carrington – she was never known by her first name – lived in a converted mill near Pangbourne with the writer Lytton Strachey, with whom, for all his homosexuality, she had fallen violently in love three years before. Ralph's good looks and dashing manner delighted her and, with Lytton's approval, she invited him down to Tidmarsh Mill House. The visit was not a success. Ralph was prejudiced against his host for his 'billowy beard and alternating basso-falsetto voice' and he described him to Gerald as 'of a surety meet mirth for Olympus'. Lytton was dismayed by the militaristic views of his young guest and referred to him in a letter to Clive Bell as 'some Major Partridge or other'. And Carrington, out of loyalty to Lytton, was angry with Ralph and gave a disdainful account of him to her brother Noel, who had introduced him to her. Yet beneath the clash of opinions and contrast of personalities there was a latent mutual attraction.

After being demobilised, Ralph returned to Oxford. He was supposed to be completing his law studies, but would bicycle over to Pangbourne every week-end to see Carrington; for he was now deeply in love with her and she to some extent responded, not only because she found him irresistible but also because, to her joy and surprise, Lytton too had fallen under his spell. It was not long before the three of them decided to set up house together.

Soon Gerald, too, came home and in April 1919 he in his turn was demobilized. At loggerheads with his father as to what he should do with himself, with no money apart from his army gratuity of £250, he decided to find a cottage in the south of Spain, which he thought would be the cheapest country to live in and also one of the most congenial because it had escaped the war. There he would settle down in

peaceful, peasant surroundings to read the thousands of books he had already begun
to collect. After a farewell visit to Tidmarsh, he left England in September and Ralph
heard from him a few weeks later.

GRANADA, 10 NOVEMBER 1919

Cher Partridge,

I have long owed you a letter; here is at least a sort of scribble, all that I
can manage just now. I came here about a month ago and then set out on
foot to look for a house . . . I went by the sea coast to Motril and then
inland to the Alpujarras country, which lies between the main snow
range and some high bare coastal mountains. The Alpujarras contains
every climate from oak and chestnut forests and alpine pastures down to
groves of orange and pomegranate. It is a large area, with two small
towns (Órgiva and Ugíjar) and some fifty villages. It is in places very
beautiful . . . Órgiva lies in a high broad valley among wonderful groves
of olives, the most ancient and shady one could see, beneath which the
grass is long and green and the water channels always flowing.

I visited almost every village in this country and I have settled on the
Ugíjar area to live in. There are three or four houses in the villages there
which I have seen. I return tomorrow and within a week or so will have
chosen one of them[1] . . .

My books are, I hope, already on the way to Almeria. I returned here
for my bag and have stayed a week, resting, as for the last month I have
been unwell and suffering from a vague sort of dysentery which some
days recedes altogether and other days makes me feel so languid that I
can scarcely walk and gives me a thirst that no rivers can quench. It gets
no better, I find, and also no worse, and I am getting accustomed to it . . .

The rest of the letter is missing.

MALAGA, 5 JANUARY 1920

Dear Partridge,

I owe you many humble apologies for not having written to you more
often; you must forgive me. I am contending on this expedition of mine
with no less a person than God, who puts in my way every obstacle that
he can think of. He is chastening me and I think he even expects me to
kiss the hand that smites.

1. His choice fell on a large rambling house in the village of Yegen, which he rented for 120
pesetas – £6 – a year.

I have been in this town for a fortnight, as it were in the pound. I haven't been able to leave because I hadn't any money. All my letters went astray. Till today (when money and letters arrived) I had been without news for three weeks . . . The reason for my ever coming here, you may wish to know. On my return from buying furniture at Almeria some 3 or 4 weeks ago, I found my landlord still installed in the house and repairs going on. He said, 'Come in by all means – the house is yours.' After a great deal of polite conversation I found out that he and all his family and furniture intended to remain there till the New Year. I had to submit and, though he offered me the use of a room, I thought best to spend my time travelling about until the coming of the New Year. One lives cheaper on the roads, and so I set out for Malaga and Ronda.

But like that famous medium of Sir Oliver Lodge,[2] I am 'followed by spirits wherever I go' – strange malignant spirits that inflict torments and divert letters and weave melancholic spells. Before getting to Velez Malaga, my old disease came on and I could hardly drive one leg in front of the other. I arrived here rather ill, unable to do anything more, and I took a bedroom and bought butter and tea and porridge and the landlady cooked for me. And all day I spent reading and contrived to forget my deplorable situation . . . For lack of money I could not move. Then I got a letter which informed me that two large cases of books had been left in England, perhaps lost, and that the others had been sent off two weeks before to Almeria. They will arrive there and the Customs will break open the locks and rob and steal, and a million other misfortunes will come upon me.

So I felt. But now the money has come I am free, and tomorrow I set off to put all things right again. I shall deal terrible strokes to right and left with my sword and chase my enemies across the Alpujarras with the speed of Alexander pursuing the Persians. I have enough energy pent up in me to overcome them all. Tomorrow I go by train to Granada, taking some things I have bought with me. There I must buy some pottery and send it off by carrier, and the next day will see me climbing the high passes of the Sierra Nevada by a new track to Yegen. There I must defeat my landlord, turn out his furniture, move mine in, set carpenters to work, make contracts, annihilate the cheating innkeeper at Ugíjar, and then set off to Almeria to fetch my books and buy a lot more furniture . . .

2. The distinguished physicist was also a firm believer in spiritualism and a leader in psychical research.

Meanwhile I do not live in the present, which is full of sound and fury, but in the world to come at Yegen. The past two months have been a sad time for me – illness, extravagance, money flowing like water. I lost about £7; I have been robbed of much more. The consequence is that, though I am furnishing the house fairly completely, I shall be terribly poor afterwards. I shall have to live on a monthly salary of £3-10-0 until next winter. That will make me learn to be ascetic.

Write to me at Ugíjar and tell me your news. The most important things cannot be written, but I am very glad to know that everything is well with you. Do not let yourself be worried into professions or honours or serious occupations or art. You have something better than all these. Being in love is a terrible thing, bringing in the end far more unhappiness than happiness, but whilst one is like that it is wisest, I am sure, to live for the moment, to get all the happiness one can while it lasts, to try and do nothing that may injure it or bring it to an end. Any considerations of prudence become an impertinence.

My thoughts are turning more and more away from such things and toward ideal things. I suppose that is wisdom and I shall earn the usual rewards of wisdom – a bald head and spectacles. I sit at my window here every evening and marchionesses and countesses and, they tell me, even a duchess roll past in their victorias. They are some of them beautiful and yet such is my indifference that I have not yet seduced one of them. And yet it were a noble ambition, I think, to seduce a duchess – a strange and exotic achievement, like eating strawberries at Christmas . . .

Vaya Vd. con dios.[3]

G.B.

In April 1920 Carrington, Ralph and Lytton went out to Yegen to stay with Gerald for a few days. The visit was something of a strain for everyone. Carrington and Ralph were in a state of acute tension all the time, and Lytton was upset by the food and exhausted by the journey – 'it was death,' he later told Virginia Woolf. Gerald was sad, but at the same time relieved, when they left.

YEGEN, 17 APRIL 1920

Dear Ralph,
. . . Since you left there has been silence in Heaven, or rather in that little caricature of it called Yegen. The whole house is still and silent and empty. Your going has left me rather sad, but that cannot be helped.

From all sides come in reports of the 'guaposity'[4] of D.C[arrington].

3. Go with God.
4. i.e. 'beauty'.

Maria,[5] 'when my sister[6] turned at the door to kiss her,' noted that her skin was like velvet, or even like that mysterious cloth which they use for petticoats. And everyone says the same. She is all the rage and the young men swear that were she not married already they would have no *novia*[7] but her. This praise is extended to you and Lytton and myself, but lest I should shock your sense of propriety I will not repeat what they said . . .

You seem to have come only that you might go again. Yet it was good seeing you all. I was gloomy, I am afraid, and dull. I should apologise, but it was your fault; your going cast a certain gloom, and then I was not feeling well . . .

Report well of Yegen to H.-J.[8] and others. You carry much of her *terra sancta* with you (chestnuts and peaches grow out of the soil, pigs eat them, and you have eaten prodigiously of the pig; one of the blessings of Yegen will thus abide with you some considerable time).

I have written enough rubbish for one letter. *Vayan Vds. con Dios.*

G.B.

YEGEN, 3 MAY 1920

Querido cuñado mio,[9]

I take this opportunity of a letter to my brother to save 2½d. Do not blame my stinginess, as you roll past in your millionaire's trappings, for at Yegen 2½d. means three large breakfast eggs, and I, though hereditary prince of my own castle, am become in these democratic days somewhat impoverished, and must keep my eggs where I find them.

I wrote to you at Madrid – did you get my letter? – such a plaintive letter, for you left me with 5/– in the world and seemed to have forgotten me. Alas, poor Geraldo! For seventeen days passed, days of hideous nightmare anxiety, before he touched those 80 pesetas.

At first I said, 'He has forgotten me,' or else, 'he had not time to visit the bank.' But as days wore on, the horrid truth became more and more clear and, like those unwary prophets of Baal, I saw that the god I prayed to would send me no rain, since he was either hunting or sleeping or

5. Gerald's maid.
6. Carrington had been introduced as Gerald's sister to the villagers, who understood family connections more than friendship.
7. Girlfriend, fiancée.
8. John Hope-Johnstone, Gerald's oldest friend. A picturesque but unreliable character, he figures prominently in both volumes of Gerald's autobiography, *A Life of One's Own* (CUP, 1962) and *Personal Record* (CUP, 1974).
9. 'Dear brother-in-law' – a common term of endearment, here used with playful 'literality' since Carrington was Gerald's 'sister'.

perchance (and this soon amounted to deadly certainty) *he was eating ham*. Forthwith I abandoned my ham-eating Protector and broke into a thousand pieces the image of this unrighteous idol. How did I not, in my ignorance, heap curses on his unoffending head, long complicated curses, elaborate and destructive spells for which I searched all the volumes of Frazer, all the annals of the black-fellows and Bushmen! What countless widdershins I turned, what incenses I smoked, what Wattish hymns I repeated backwards (backwards, sideways, and vertically) to invoke ruin upon you! And as I crawled hungry about the fields, seeking roots to devour, iguanas to boil, did I not yell for joy whenever I lighted on the magical and sinister hellebore, an essential ingredient of witches' cauldrons? And then came your innocent letter and I wrote to Almeria and there learnt that the money was waiting for me at Ugíjar, at the house of an evil man. The ways of God are inscrutable; there is a moral in all this – 'how God answers our prayers, even when he is most deaf to them.' A nice little moral, and I took my Baal back into my bosom.

Did you suffer, tell me, from my curses? Did the ham choke in your throat, did the fleas and bugs rise in their armies against you? If they did, then I am sorry, I repent; if not, then I abjure all belief in magic, in spells, in widdershins, in incantations. Henceforth I will live a sceptic.

Now *cuñado mio*, to drop this jocular strain, how goes it with you? Is it well with Ahab? Write me a letter of four dimensions on the folly of professions and on the all-sufficingness of love. I myself go on very well and am in the pink of health and prosperity. I am turning author . . . and writing a book which is to make me rich. It will tell you among other things how to get from Órgiva to Cádiar even if you have piles. It will indicate motoring roads which the maps have not yet discovered, it will – but I will say no more, so as to whet your curiosity. I work very hard at this opus whenever I can, and I read a great deal.

Tout ça sert à m'amuser, even if it does nothing better. The country grows more and more lovely; its beauty seems to open out a little each day, like an unfolding flower. The nightingales are very plentiful; the cuckoos sing from the rocks; in my room there are great bowls of roses and branches of hawthorn; I drink tea, sit, write by the open window in the summer room, Lytton's room, and the noise of the waterfall comes in through the window. Since Lytton left there have been no bugs. I dare not, though, hint at the consequences of that statement. *No, no* – they came in through the window; it is well known how they crowd round poets from all sides. The summer room. Well, with such a fine house I thought I would be aristocratic. I have named the rooms: the green room; the blue bedroom; the sewing-room; the butler's pantry; and there is to be a Dormitorio de las Delicias and another de las Angustias (which translate as you please from the Latin or the Spanish) . . .

Time I stopped or Blair[1] will be paying double for my letter. But before I stop I should apologise for that gloomy, ill-looking fellow who presented himself to you at Yegen. He is a poor relation whom I generally keep at a distance, but at times he will take advantage of my infirmities to approach. Now I have driven him off to the mountains and rocks and caves, and you shall not see him any more. And now to God the Father – Yegen, and all her fountains and her hills, and all her goats and cattle, whom the priest all blessed last St Mark's, and all her old men and women, and all her virgins (which are here as common as gooseberries at Christmas) and all her maturing peach-fed hams, all send their blessings and their loves, on you and yours, for ever and ever.

I too send my little loves to you all. Such a nice letter as I got from C. I will answer when the spirit moves me, not before, for I keep for her letters my *summa inspiratio*.

G.B.

In the autumn of 1920, having come down from Oxford, Ralph started work at Leonard and Virginia Woolf's Hogarth Press. The job was ill-paid, but he welcomed it as a step nearer marrying Carrington. She still resisted his proposals, but agreed to live with him in London until Christmas to see how they got on together. They moved into 41 Gordon Square, taking over a flat previously occupied by James and Alix Strachey,[2] who had just left for Vienna, and went down to Tidmarsh together for week-ends.

YEGEN, 5 OCTOBER 1920

Dear Ralph,

I was glad to get your letter, and then yesterday to get C.'s. It is nice to think that you have such good work. I am sure that you are one of those people who, to be happy, have to feel that they are useful – and good printers are useful, aren't they? Also I am glad that you and C. are starting housekeeping in Gordon Square. I hope it may lead to a permanent arrangement. It is easy to ridicule marriage, but it is convenient. I have a great admiration for married people, especially when they have children. I am sure that marriage between sensible people is a

1. Gerald's brother.
2. Lytton's younger brother and sister-in-law (*née* Sargent-Florence). Both were practising psychoanalysts.

virtuous state. I say this although I am always somewhat afraid of married people. They live too much in their own world; two is a very formidable organization. Now thank me for my good advice!

Fact is I am writing awful nonsense. I am only writing a letter after having exhausted everything else – eating, drinking, drug-taking (quinine), reading. And reading and reading and reading. Till I can no longer take it in. It is in the middle of the night, or the early morning. I am in bed with a little fever (*vraie blessure d'embusqué*). I call it my trench fever. It reminds me of those trenches which alas! I shall never see again . . . It is midnight or early morning and very silent. In my ears there is the buzzing of quinine. It is not very poetical that at such a mysterious hour there should be no other noise than that, and yet it is rather a charming one. I shall spend the rest of the night listening to it. You know, a little fever makes one happy. The vulgarity of hopes and activities vanishes and only the past is left . . .

What is Virginia Woolf like? I have a very great admiration for her work.

Do you know anything of when Joyce's *Ulysses* will be brought out? It is very indecent – perhaps you will be asked to publish it?[3]

This is the last country to come to for Spanish literature. If one is to believe the booksellers, there is none. But I don't believe them. Quite recently I hunted through all the shops in Granada for several of the classics, among others Calderon. Not only had they no copies in stock but they had never heard of him and could give me no information about how I might get them. Even the History of Literature used in the University is by an Englishman – that semi-ass [James] Fitzmaurice-Kelly[4] . . .

I am trying through David Nutt[5] of London to get in touch with a Madrid bookseller and will let you know the result, but you could probably get books more safely through D. Nutt himself. Good-bye – and don't lament to me about your 'wasted life'. Books are not everything and you are something better than a bookworm – though of course it is good to read. And now what a pleasant life you lead, meeting agreeable people. But don't think I envy you society just at present, for who with a little fever and a ringing in his ears can feel lonely?

G.B.

3. *Ulysses* was indeed offered to the Woolfs; but the Hogarth Press was too small for the undertaking, and the risk of prosecution too great.
4. Professor of Spanish at King's College, London and the author of *History of Spanish Literature*, published in 1898 and translated into Spanish in 1901.
5. David Nutt, bookseller, was at 212 Shaftesbury Avenue, WC2.

Dear Ralph,

You and C. overwhelm me with letters, each more flattering than the last. Not that you have anything to flatter me about, as you haven't either of you seen a word of my writing. To disillusion you, and not to appear too boorish, I am sending some. I am very glad you are at the Hogarth Press. We shall then keep the same interests, and we are old allies. It is a great field for your energy, and you have made me feel enthusiastic.

What good things there must be to publish! You are right, the reviewers are mostly fools or parrots. I suppose that when one is a reviewer one degenerates very rapidly. It's a prostitute's life. The Gorky[6] was very, very good. It is a great deal to have published only that, and it was very beautifully produced . . . Has not Gorky done other good work? And have Tolstoy's later Diaries, etc. been published? And can't you squeeze something out of Dostoyevsky? We cannot know enough about the Russians. There are really all sorts of good things to publish, only it's not easy to get hold of them. For one thing there is Folklore. Folk tales have hardly ever been published as they might be. For one thing they are often 'expurgated;' for another they are published for scientific uses, in crude translations and with many different variants. And Folk tales *can* be the most admirable literature, as you know. Grimm is fit to stand beside the Bible . . . And wouldn't Joyce publish with you? He must be tired of the Egoist people.[7] Don't you think he is a writer of genius? One of the very few.

As for me, I should like to help you, but I don't see how I can do it. How can you ask me to publish anything? I have nothing that I can publish, nothing that will do. And you are only to publish good things. It is very nice to be asked, yes – I mean that – but I cannot, really. Not from modesty, but from a sense of the small value of what I have done so far, its incompleteness, its lack of solidity, its immaturity, and from a hope that in time I shall produce something more satisfactory – produce *a book*. But you have my promise that you shall have the offer of anything I have to publish. In three years, when I come back from the East[8], I

6. *Reminiscences of Leo Nicolayevich Tolstoi*, translated by Leonard Woolf and Samuel Koteliansky, published by the Hogarth Press in May 1920.
7. *The Egoist*, owned by Harriet Shaw Weaver, had with great difficulty (owing to printers' liability for prosecution under the laws of obscene libel) published Joyce's *Portrait of the Artist as a Young Man*.
8. Gerald had never quite given up his boyhood ambition to travel to the East on foot and still kept toying with the idea and even making plans, but these came to nothing.

expect to have a volume of verse and then it is likely that I shall settle down to write something properly thought-out in prose. It is just because I have a high sense of what I might do and of what is worth doing that I will not publish inferior and occasional work . . . I have no doubt that you will perfectly agree with me when you see the examples I am sending. They are *not* good. They are experimental. I am feeling my way along certain more or less definite lines; when I have more to say and know the form in which it must be said, *perhaps* there will emerge something good. I know perfectly well that my work shows 'promise', and I hate the word; for I know that most promise is unfulfilled. Only acts are holy. In art, only the complete work.

At present I am studying, and read so little modern literature and write so much to C. that I have no impulses to creative writing. But I may try and write some little tales this winter and I want you to help me by getting some books for me, preferably second-hand. I will send you my hieroglyph on Cooks for them, but I cannot spend more than 15/–. I want a book on *modern* spiritualism. I want it to give full and graphic details of séances, so that I can imagine to myself just what they look like . . . I have some very interesting private information on the Next World, which I might communicate to this world in that form . . .

MacSwiney[9] has just died. 'True unto death', the newspapers say; even the *Irish Times* and the *Pall Mall* say that. But what I say is that it is horrible and shameful that one poor beef-eating man should be sacrificed to public opinion. Why should this poor beast be forced to give his life drop by drop for some idiotic principle? Two months he has been in prison, and all over the world they have been counting the days and waiting impatiently for him to die. Out here even, in England, and especially in Ireland. They have now got a real martyr – that's all they wanted. What do they care for this poor little starving man for whom they made eating impossible? They only see the hero, the martyr, the Christ. But he was just a man, a Lord Mayor, one of the corporation, and they killed him, those Irish shopkeepers, because they wanted a sacrifice. And now they insult him with their martyr's crowns. 'True unto death.' But was that his fault?

I agree with you – what did we fight for in that war? But did you ever

9. Terence Joseph MacSwiney, Lord Mayor of Cork, was one of many Sinn Fein detainees who had gone on hunger strike in the hope of obtaining their release. He died in Brixton prison after seventy-five days.

think we were fighting for any principles or ideals? I didn't. I was fighting because it seemed natural to me to do so, because I was in that position, because it was fun, because I couldn't do anything else. I wouldn't walk across the road for any government's principles. And now look what they are doing in Europe, the brutes, the fools! And yet they're just like everyone else; they're just hungry, rapacious, fornicating, thinking only of their own ends. They're bloody and they're dishonest too – that seems worst of all – and it is painful to see those things done in the limelight on such an excessive scale . . . And whether you and I are better than they who do these things, just because we feel shocked by them, is doubtful. If 'better' has any meaning not altogether esoterical, I suppose we are better. But not much, and that only by the grace of God, because we are young men of easy incomes who like to indulge in our righteous emotions . . .

I feel angry when I read about Ireland.[1] The stupidest government in the world is governing the most hysterical people in the world. It is a pitiful sight, as when one sees some small terrified animal or child turn in desperation upon some big blundering beast that is teasing it. It is all about nothing. They would have got Home Rule, whatever that's worth, if they'd kept quiet; but reason doesn't count in these things. There are only two solutions – that the Irish should be given their independence or that they should be exterminated. In my mind the former is too impracticable and (since some end to the struggle is obviously to be desired) I thought of writing a leaflet recommending the second. I would, if I thought I could publish it. I should advise the Government to kill every man, woman and child that lived in Ireland, but (this I would insist on) none living in other countries. It would, in this humanitarian age, be a thing of too great brutality if they killed them by force – i.e. if they shot them. And the Irish might shoot back. I should advise the starving of them. I would give the method of carrying this out in some detail. Destruction of seed, of stores, etc. In about four months' time half the population would be dead of starvation, and by rounding up the remainder into the most barren districts, under pretence perhaps of feeding them in some systematic manner, they would all be got rid of. It would be best to leave Ulster out of the scheme, as the men of that county could be depended upon to do the blockading and driving and even (if the unfortunate necessity were to arise) the shooting of the population of

1. Gerald was closely connected with Ireland. His maternal grandparents were Irish and his father had served in an Irish regiment.

the South, without pay and from motives of pure patriotism. After that the Ulstermen could be easily disposed of in a variety of ways; anyone would be glad to cut their throats when it was pointed out in the Press how brutally they had starved their fellow-countrymen. Indignation would be aroused (it would be quite easy to arrange that in such a humanitarian country) and judgement would be executed upon Ulster until there remained no more human beings in Ireland than there are snakes . . .

This narrative is broken – don't read it. When I got a little further I began it at the beginning and wrote. God, how I wrote. Ten double sheets of paper, 40 pages. My hand now tired, I can hardly write. I finished it. It is good. I began to write to C. at 2 p.m., then began your letter, and towards dark had recommenced my 'letter to the Press.' I finished it and opened the shutters; the sun was up, people were in the streets . . .

Now it is nine o'clock. It is Sunday, Maria says. Sunday comes every two days here, but in Spain that doesn't matter. Soon I shall see my breakfast: bread and milk and coffee. You see I am mad, and also breathless. A breathless madman. Geraldo *el loco perdido*. The wise, mad, breathless man of Yegen. But I will confess a secret. I am hope-lessly, hopelessly excited, and though my hand aches I can't stop writing and can't help it all being rubbish. Oh, what a beautiful, beautiful morning it is, and the doves are cooing, but I am too excited to do more than say, 'What a beautiful morning,' and then look down at the paper. This letter – I call it 'a little project' or something of that sort (oh, my wrist!) – I will copy out tomorrow and will send you . . .

Here I pause. I am sane. What next? Why, we have to discuss Gibbon, and, just to show you my powers this jolly morning, I will begin . . . We have to discuss his style, only his style, which you compare to the greatest, but make it a sort of Caviar and you the only General to taste it. (Yes, that malapropism is quite deliberate and I shan't let you think me ignorant, because there, I'm not) . . . Moreover it would be simpler if we discuss only *The Decline and Fall*, for the autobiography is written in a different, and I think better, style. Let us proceed. If you examine the style of the *Decline*, or even if you don't examine it, you will find an extraordinarily common use of that grammatical figure called, I think, antithesis. I quote at random:

'It was fortunate for the repose, or at least for the reputation . . .'

'The learned and polite, however much they might *deride the miracles*, would have *esteemed the virtues* of the new sect . . .'

'The Christians *obeyed the dictates* and *solicited the liberty* of conscience . . .'

This figure of speech occupies a quarter of the room on each page. Then there's an unusual abundance of adjectives and adverbs of a rather abstract nature, used without any precise signification but with the effect of padding the sentence and so maintaining the required horsehair-sofa rhythm. (Not serious, that epithet, but that's how I see it.) Now these mannerisms are used with such frequency that there is scarcely a sentence that doesn't contain a more or less perfect example of one of them. Their effect is ironic, and we therefore observe a film of gentle irony distributed pretty evenly over the whole six volumes . . . You must have thought it strange to see the subjects most insusceptible to irony, such as the manner of fighting of the Huns, the helmets of the Gauls or the torturing of (so-called) innocent persons, treated in almost precisely the same tone as the enthusiasms and hypocrisies of the Christians. The reason for this is, I think, that the mannerisms I have described give a certain rhythm that cannot be obtained without them. These mannerisms are therefore a necessary part of the structure of Gibbon's prose and, as they inevitably carry with them a sense of irony, ironical Gibbon has got to be on almost every occasion, or else sacrifice some of the dignity of his delivery. Now I will not be so pedantic as to affirm that even the frequent repetition of the same mannerism is incompatible with prose of the first excellence, but I must and shall maintain that a tyranny of the rhythms over the subject-matter such as I have described to you as prevailing in Gibbon is a fatal bar to merit in his style. A style that is hardened to that extent, that is so inflexible that it cannot express the varying emotions of the author, is simply not a prose style. (Though I will not deny that it may be the most useful style for certain purposes.)

Style is something alive; it winds about and curls like a snake; it leaps up and up with a sort of opening and enlarging of the meaning, or else it trails behind, apparently forgotten, like a dragging umbrella or a tag of bindweed. It is alive, vivid, unexpected, and cannot be hidebound. Style in an author is like the face of a mime, but Gibbon's style is like a mask. If we compare prose style to handwriting, then the good styles are those that have 'character,' and Gibbon's style is a sort of copy-book style with witty flourishes but which is not above the successful imitation of any cultivated person. There is something closer than analogy in this simile . . .

When you say that the 'reverberating rhythms of Gibbon's prose are suitable for the reverberating rhythms of history,' or some such thing, it seems to mē the same as though you said that the vibration of the atoms in a pendulum is in harmony with its regular swing. No, perhaps that is not it – I retract that. But all the same you are at that old, and I am sure often repeated, heresy that the artist, in order to give the sensation of dullness and so on, ought to be dull and so on himself; or that raw sensations ought in any circumstances to be reproduced untransmuted. (This, in painting, is the false idea that one has to *imitate* nature.) . . .

Style depends so closely on the thought that any lack of merit in Gibbon's style must be traced to something in his thought. Now Gibbon was not extremely intelligent. He had not got that vital sense of the presence of the things he was describing. It is nothing whatever to do with the case that Thucydides wrote of the age he lived in, of events he had often participated in. That should have made it more difficult for him. The speeches, which are inimitable, are mainly of his own invention. You know Greek and I don't, but how could the Athenian envoys have addressed the assembly of Melos in the terms in which they did? Of course they didn't – none of Thucydides's characters is drawn in detail. It is a different sort of drama that he is constructing for us – let us say a drama of ideas. Thucydides is more civilised than Gibbon or than Thomas Hardy or W. B. Yeats, and much, much more intelligent than Gibbon. The fact that Gibbon was not a man of ideas and also not a man with any sense for the life, for the real presence of what he is describing, but only the conductor of a very superior literary cinematograph, is of direct consequence for his style.

From reading Gibbon one does not really understand that period, the most interesting period, I think, in all history. Gibbon himself says that he thought very little of Plato's philosophy; he thought the dialogues good as literature but not otherwise. That is a very bad beginning for the historian of a period that was moved more than almost any other period by ideas of which the main current was Neoplatonism. The great Christian scholars who contested with the almost as great philosophers in the 4th and 5th centuries were not pious buffoons, but more intelligent men than Gibbon himself was. We are shown the picture of a fantastic creed with its extraordinary dogmas overthrowing a mild, reasonable, learned but somewhat relaxed culture, until everything ended in general collapse. Those are, I believe, not the facts. What was the secret of the decay of Roman civilisation? How is it that in the Augustan age, and for some centuries afterwards, many of the richest, most prosperous and apparently most happy noblemen would suddenly for no apparent reason commit suicide? Then there were those religions of Attis, Mithras and others, with mystical rites which went far beyond Christianity in their barbarism and savagery. Some of the wisest of the emperors were enthusiasts in those religions. I forget how Gibbon goes into these matters, as it is four or five years since I read him last; but I know that he is so absorbed in his pasteboard, washbottle Deism that he cannot make any intelligent analysis of the position . . .

I've had my say. It has been my misfortune to have only attacked Gibbon, yet he is well worthy of defence. He remains one of the few great historians . . . His wit, his great slabs of fun, his long smirk, the great rolling sentences, all that one rightly enjoys. And the whole scheme is so marvellously coloured, so romantic, strange – yes, I love old Gibbon and shall soon read him once again.

I have overwritten myself and bored you. I have been writing now since 3 p.m. yesterday. It is now 11 a.m.; that is 20 hours. Impossible, but it is! I have not really stopped for meals. I took a walk for an hour, that is all. Forgive this awful letter. I will stop and get on to something else. Poor old Gibbon, he must be sick of me. I will send you that thing on Ireland in a day or two; you might ask Lytton if it would be amusing to publish it in some journal, or as a pamphlet even . . .

Are you preparing to come out to Yegen in the spring, you and your little mate who won't be married? Yes, do. Lytton shall come some time when it is summer. Goodbye.

G.B.

41 GORDON SQUARE, 31 DECEMBER 1920

Dear Gerald,

Unless he is very careful, a man will fill the letters he does write with explanations about those he doesn't and take a sort of credit for being plausible. I shall write exactly as if I had received your letter last night.

About the Irish question, everyone has good words for your solution, including Lytton and Virginia Woolf. We tried to induce Allen & Unwin to publish it, but what they call 'pamphlets' are the average publisher's bugbear, as they are extremely hard to get into circulation . . . Another impediment to its launching is the letter form, which is an essential as it now stands; it is too long for any magazine and it cannot be broken into two instalments. In fact with diabolical ingenuity you have hit on the one size, shape, tone and appearance of a volume which is hardly capable of formation. And again, you are superficially so like Swift, at any rate to begin with, that it is difficult to resist pretending you are some relative of his. I shall see Leonard [Woolf] again next week and we will not abandon it to a drawer, you can be assured.

Now if you were to continue in that vein and write some more letters to the public on other prominent topics, we could form a small volume and treat them as a purely literary, non-political product, which at present, in the ferment of general feeling, is not possible. My own view of it is that you are most successful and interesting when you are most yourself, because at first you seem rather hampered by the memory of Swift, so that it rather hangs. Of course it is best where it is most exaggerated and fantastic. I liked the prose piece about the Mortuary. If I may speak my mind, I think you ought to keep a watchful eye on the *general* cohesion; occasionally you make your reader into a steeple-chaser. But don't stop writing, at all costs, and don't stop sending what you wrote to your friends . . .

I had lunch with your great-aunt[2] and H[ope]-J[ohnstone] some time ago. She is a queer old derelict, but I rather like her. She has written me a letter since, but I shall not get involved too closely with her as H.-J. warns me she is liable to adhere. I think you are firmly stationed in her will, but she will certainly live for ever.

I am in an extraordinary position myself just now – financially very bad. My father, who has long been melancholic, has turned suicidal and now only thinks of death. I don't want him to die if he can be made happy enough to want to go on living, but if he really cannot bear existence it is only a shameful regard for society that would set about thwarting his choice. I have just spent four dreary days with him down in Devonshire. His one object is to live with my mother, and she, as is well known, has no intention of living with him. She is at present in Italy . . . and will not return before April. I have written to her to say that I believe the man *will* take his life soon unless she gives him some real hope of living with her again, but she has that female perversity which will never face probabilities and is perpetually amazed when they come about, so that I hardly expect she will do anything beyond telling me not to be deceived by father's passing depression. If she does not say anything to him to encourage him, I feel sure he may commit suicide at any time, which is a disturbing conclusion. I have offered to share our flat with him if he likes, but he is extremely sensible and knows perfectly well that he would not enjoy looking on at other people working and being happy. It

---

2. Baroness Adeline von Roeder ('Aunt Tiz') who, shortly after Gerald settled in Yegen, gave him an allowance of £50 a year and also made him her heir.

is very difficult to know what can be done. Meanwhile part of his melancholia is financial depression; he thinks he has very little money, and so my allowance lapses without even being mentioned by either of us. How I revolt against pecuniary uncertainty, not knowing whether one has enough to live on or not! It tinges my whole life with mournful anticipations.

Lytton is working hard at Victoria[3] and hopes to have her finished in a month or six weeks. She ought to be published early in May. Our book on Tchekov[4] only requires a little more translation to complete. We can't decide quite what length to make it. Constance Garnett apparently only translated about a quarter of the total letters and Koteliansky[5] wants to bring out the complete series in several volumes; but unless we are assured of a certain sale, say by private subscription, we dare not risk a failure.

The English winter is bad for the spirits. I am all woe-begone and the slightest event suffices to deject me. I started reading the letters I wrote my mother during the War. What an exciting life that was; there was always something terrific impending even at the dullest times. If only people were not killed I should love soldiering; but the element of risk is perhaps the greatest pleasure of all, and that would be absent. A righteous cause is all one wants, but there aren't any left. Perhaps the Moors might be rescued from the French.

My love to you. Your

Ralph

YEGEN, 20 JANUARY 1921

Dear Ralph,

. . . Thanks to your zeal the Irish paper seems to have had a narrow escape from being published. I am thankful it was not; I am too ashamed of it, or at least of a large part of it, to wish it to be seen by anyone. I thought of sending you a line before Christmas to tell you not to do anything with it, but then I said to myself, 'Of course he'll just read it and shove it quietly away somewhere; he'll see it's no good, that it's just one of my usual stunts.' So I did not write . . .

---

3. *Queen Victoria*, published by Chatto & Windus in April 1921.
4. *The Note-Books of Anton Tchekov, Together with Reminiscences of Tchekov* by Maxim Gorky, translated by Leonard Woolf and Samuel Koteliansky, published in the summer of 1921.
5. Samuel Solomonovitch Koteliansky was a Ukrainian Jew who had come to England in 1910. He was a close friend of Katherine Mansfield, and the Woolfs probably met him through her.

I agree entirely with your criticism of it. The resemblance to Swift does not matter so long as the invention is kept up, but when that fails – then, by God, it's terrible. I think I could rewrite a third of it and bring what is bad up to the level of the better parts, and if you send me back the MS. I will try to do so. But one thing makes me hesitate, for it seems to have a fault I cannot remedy and which scarcely makes it worth rewriting. There is a lack of any real insight into the Irish situation; the whole irony of it is too superficially grounded, too crude. England's 'crime against Ireland' is something other, and more difficult to get at, than mere ill-treating, mulcting, killing, etc. Once we used to kill the Irish wholesale; then we gave that up to rob and exploit them; and now what is it? We try to control them for our mutual advantage. I see the Irish point of view when I try to imagine that I am Ireland, and my father England, and that I am ten times more in his power than I have ever been in real life. Ireland is then a case of the Oedipus complex; Ireland has got into a very wicked and unfilial hysteria, and the father will not give way because he has principles. But I didn't bring that out, did I? – only laid it on thick with the exploiting and the killing.

That makes me feel that what I wrote is too much in the air; the blow does not reach any object . . . However, send it back to me and I'll try and rewrite it. I have a number of other ideas of a similar nature, but unpolitical; if I could realize them, a little volume might be got up. But I have so many things that I want to work at, so much to say and such difficulty in saying it, that I can't look on these writings as more than a very small sideshow.

I am sorry about your father . . . What stupid, gloomy things family troubles are, and how people suffer under them! I am always being astonished at this, and at the things people go on suffering for, and at the little power they have to free themselves. Yet how nice it must be to have a father who is more or less in sympathy with one! I suppose I was especially designed by God as a trial to parents – a sort of monkey-puzzle that they can't jump about on as they jump on their other children, a sort of young Attila whose whole devastations are comprised in one small family.

But I too have my point of view. I have had to watch myself necessarily and inevitably caring less and less for people who do care for me, and have had to watch myself practising all manner of lies and deceits as my only defence against increasing persecution. What is more brutal or more dishonest than the method of moral persuasion, coupled on the one hand with kindness and on the other with threats, that parents so often apply to their children? I know that they are neither brutal nor dishonest; indeed I think the honest, kind-hearted people of the world do more dirty actions than all the wicked put together. At present the situation is quite helpless; they are always asking whether I wear clean shirts, or else telling me I lead an unmanly life, or am losing caste, or else saying that I am so touchy that they won't say much – but don't I think I'm selfish?

It was fate and the malignant arrangement of things that made a lot of good-natured, home-loving, gutless people meet in the war and kill each other, and it is fate and the malignant arrangement of things, or else just a sort of toss-penny chance, a stray meeting of gametes in some unfortunate ovary, that is responsible for long warfare between parents and a son. It will not be over till we are all dead. If I had to die tomorrow I should at least be glad of this – that I should be putting an end to a piece of stupid chatter. And say, isn't it stupid that the valuable minutes of human lives should be wasted in such futilities? This waste of time – holy, incorruptible time – oppresses me and always has oppressed me like a nightmare. I'm always wasting it. I could write a sermon on its waste.

I hope your money affairs will improve. I should like to be able to say, 'My dear fellow, you can always count on me for a thousand.' But my poverty is notorious. I agree, this uncertainty is bad. You, with a house in town and C. to look after, are more involved than I am and must find it worse. I should be happy with £100 a year if I had it for certain. At present I am all right, but before long I must leave here and must go to the East. My aunt's will is like a knife over my head – I mean the loss of it – as I am incapable of ever making a penny except at the most humble trade. What will she say to the East? And yet I shall go there if I lose every penny by doing so. And then I am supposed to be writing something. What could I ever write that she should see? You are wise not to go and see her; yet, if you do for any reason, put in a good word for my literary ability and hold out no hopes of any completed work from me before I am thirty. Tell her I am one of those that blossom late . . .

This life, you know, is an exile. I never feel lonely, yet I need good company and conversation more perhaps than I know of. And women . . . Am I to spend the prime of my life like a monk in his cell? Will nobody come out here to see me? My house is so much better now than it has ever been. Do people only *talk* of going and living in Spain? Am I the only misguided, forlorn, miserable person to put this boast into practice?

My aunt is prepared to finance me a voyage to England. I must go in

May and June to see the long grass and the buttercups and I think I ought
not to do so this June, but had better keep on with my reading of which I
have a definite plan. Next winter I shall certainly pass on the roads,
making my way by photographing people – I want to learn that trade –
and then I shall come to England . . . Goodbye. Write and say how you
are and when I shall see you.

G.B.

Carrington finally yielded to Ralph's repeated proposals. They were married on 20
May 1921 and spent their honeymoon in Venice.

YEGEN, I JUNE 1921

Dear Ralph,

If anyone is to be congratulated upon engaging on such a perilous
enterprise as matrimony, I think you're the man. And though I'm loth to
say a good word for you I can't help adding that D.C. is scarcely less
lucky. *Fortunati sunt qui* – well, never mind that; the sum of the matter is
that you have my best wishes, congratulations, blessings, and when you
return to your Bloomsbury mansion you will find one of the choicest
fruits of Yegen[6] hanging from the rafters – one of the gooseberries that
ripen on these trees.

Well, I can't write, I have got a fever; but I suppose we'll meet in July
and clasp each other's honest palm. Is Lytton in Venice with you?[7] And
go, if you can, to Ravenna, a very beautiful town full of memories of
Gibbon. I don't think anyone could get the full feeling for *The Decline
and Fall* unless he had seen Ravenna in winter-time.

Goodbye. Good luck.

G.B.

As can be seen from his reference to meeting Ralph in July, Gerald decided to visit
England that year after all. He arrived in London on 13 June 1921 and, having spent
a few days there with his great-aunt, went on to his parents' house in the Cotswolds.
Early in July he went over to Tidmarsh for the night, and a few days later, while
Ralph was in London, joined Carrington on a picnic during which they kissed
passionately. When he saw her again at Tidmarsh two weeks later he knew he was in
love, and she seemed to reciprocate his feelings. They met again several times in
private, but did no more than kiss; and since Ralph might not have understood the
innocence of their relationship, they decided to tell him nothing about it.

In August Gerald joined Ralph and Carrington and Lytton at Watendlath Farm, in

6. i.e. a peach-fed ham.
7. He was, having joined Ralph and Carrington for the last week of their honeymoon.

the Lake District, which they had taken for a month's holiday. Here, while Ralph went off fishing every day, Gerald and Carrington would give themselves up to an orgy of kissing; but nothing more occurred and their relationship was still chaste when Gerald returned to Spain early in September.

On his way he spent a few days with the Dobrées, who lived at Larrau, a village in the Pyrenees. Bonamy Dobrée – 'a nimble second-rate man,' according to Virginia Woolf – was a writer and literary scholar. His wife Valentine, née Brooke-Pechell, was a painter and a great friend of Carrington's, and Gerald unwisely confided in her when she and Bonamy came to stay at Yegen at the end of January 1922. She had invited Lytton, Ralph and Carrington to visit her at Larrau in the spring and now asked Gerald to join them there, promising to take Ralph off his hands so that he could have some time alone with Carrington. Gerald agreed.

He set off from Yegen on 5 April and reached Larrau five days later. The atmosphere there was tense. Ralph had taken such a violent dislike to Valentine that when she suggested driving her guests over to Pau for the day he refused to join the party. On the way back the car broke down and they had to spend the night in a hotel. Gerald's room was immediately above Carrington's and he heard her calling, 'Cuckoo!' to show she was expecting him. Yet, though he longed to join her, fear of impotence held him back. Early in the morning he went down to her room to explain this to her, and was sitting on the edge of her bed when the door opened and Valentine came in.

Ralph was in a bad mood when they got back to Larrau, but then a very curious thing happened. He and Valentine, who till then had been like cat and dog together, suddenly developed a violent crush on each other; and by the following month, when all of them were back in England, it was clear to everyone that they were having an affair. This led to a change in Gerald's way of thinking and dispelled his sexual inhibitions. He spent most of the month of May at Tidmarsh and, whenever Ralph went up to London to see Valentine, he and Carrington made the most of it. But this situation came to an abrupt end when, for some reason, Valentine told Ralph that his wife and his best friend were having an affair, that everyone knew it except him, and that Gerald's presence at Larrau earlier in the year had been the result of a plot.

After a stormy confrontation with Ralph in London, and a final meeting with Carrington at Tidmarsh, Gerald once more went back to Spain.

TIDMARSH, 10 JUNE 1922

Gerald,

I said I would write to you, so I do. I must tell you that I don't blame you really, as you behaved just as anyone in love is always tempted to behave – that is, ruthlessly, except to the person you love. I'm sorry too that she [Carrington] wouldn't go away with you, but that is purely selfish as I'm certain, as certain as I am of anything now, she would have made me and you even more unhappy if she had. I have not yet come to a decision as to what I shall eventually do. I am tormented by the most horrible dilemma and confusion of feeling. In my real character I am utterly different from you and her – I feel, when I do feel, with such overwhelming intensity that my feelings are master of my behaviour. As a friend I cannot love her, because we both put no trust in each other; as a lover, not a husband, she is so tainted to me that all my love has been changed to loathing. And yet she has been three quarters of my life to me for many years, and I can't operate on myself for the removal of such a vital portion without intolerable pain.

Then there is Lytton, of whom I may possibly have spoken to you at times cynically; yet I do love him, for his real character, not for being a great man. He and I have welded our lives too, and that link would have to be broken too were I to leave her. I am trying to see a way out so that I don't have to leave her. If I can't I shall go, but at present I am doing my best to stay . . .

There is one thing that I must say to you and that is that on practical matters you mustn't let this make any difference to you. If you are at any time in need of money you must write and tell me. If you have scruples, which I can tell you are absurd, you must consider it an advance out of what your aunt may leave you or me as executor. Or, if you prefer it, Lytton wants me to say that he will do it, not I. At any rate don't let that add to your unhappiness. If you're as wretched as I am, I'm heartily sorry for you.

Ralph

YEGEN, 20 JULY 1922

Dear Ralph,

. . . I have been the cause to you of a great deal of unhappiness; I imagined that for the present, at any rate, you might not wish to hear from me or about me . . . If you will write to me I shall be very glad; I am certainly anxious to hear what you have to say. I have also something to say to you, but not yet, not until some time has passed, and even then only if you wish to hear from me. I am entirely in the dark as to your feelings, your wishes, your intentions; but you need not suppose that I am not anxious to be informed about them – the opposite is the case. You need not suppose either that I have unfriendly feelings towards yourself. There is no reason why I should feel differently towards you from what I have always felt, and I do not feel differently. But as to what my feelings are or as to what I think, I am not going to say a word until I can see some use in doing so. If your attitude is one of indifference or irony, then I have nothing to say; and at the present moment I know as little about you as you do about me.

G.B.

Dear Gerald,

. . . I will now be quite open with you about my relations with you. I am naturally of a confiding disposition to people I like and even to strangers, and one of the greatest shocks to me has been the revelation that one can never be off the *qui vive* in dealing with men and women. One cannot be confiding with impunity, because no one is utterly unselfish, and therefore in selfish moments people are often betrayed into exploiting the experience they have gained from others in unselfish moments. We all of us take advantage of our friends' little weaknesses when dealing with them and we rarely make an exact moral calculation, whether we have found out those weaknesses for ourselves or had them told us by the friends in question. This may not seem to you very *à propos*, but I was for a time so filled with mistrust that I mistrusted myself and my own behaviour more than any other person or thing. I still believe that no relations are far better than insincere relations with people, and with you I was tempted at first to adopt the first rather than risk the second. It is terrible, though, for me to live timidly – I cannot wait to calculate my words or balance the thoughts that I want to express. I cannot be afraid of you and so I cannot dislike you. And it is out of my lack of fear of you that now I am tempted to give you my mental states in the last two months, because they may interest you and in a way concern you.

I first was seized with the most violent frenzy of rage against you and D.C. I couldn't think or talk of anything else, and every thought and word gave me more physical torture that I could not avoid, as I did not want anything but to be tortured to death, or to someone's death. At that moment I was such a victim of tyrannous imagination that I am hardly able now to understand my feelings then . . . I wanted to drive you both out of my life, to force D.C. to go away with you, and to get clear from my continual mental hammering by eliminating you and memories of you both. As D.C. wouldn't go with you, I then thought of leaving her myself and establishing myself somewhere abroad, with a future and no past. But already my intense bitterness against her was passing, and when I came to the crux of abandoning all my Tidmarsh life and going, I felt that the combination of motives for staying was really more to me than the rage for flight; so I stayed and from that point it was clear to me what would happen to me.

My faculty for assimilating everything I encounter in life is not apparently diminished with age. I don't suppose I have 'nerves,' as many others have, or I may have my sensitiveness subordinate to my vitality, so that when there is a tussle my vitality triumphs and my sensitiveness is blunted. I have become reconciled to what has occurred more quickly than D.C. I lost all rancour against you more than a month ago, and my revolt against D.C. has gradually evaporated. I am now as attached to her as I was 18 months ago. It is a different person that I remember being tormented in June. A tame ending.

I can see that it may be much more difficult for you, and still more so for D.C., to swallow and digest these revelations of human character. We all thought ourselves considerably finer characters than we are. But my disillusion being about others more than myself, my *amour propre* was least wounded. I have lost my inert trust in my friends, but I have replaced it with a vigilant trust. I am quite sure I could trust you as long as you were in my company, but I should be sorry to stake anything on you in H.-J.'s or Valentine's company. But I am not adopting a lofty station saying this; I should be sorry for you to trust me in the company of any woman I was in love with. I should certainly not be unwaveringly loyal to anyone in such circumstances, and I should probably try to justify everything I did to myself by elaborate sophistry. It is not the sophistry which matters at all – you may call it 'moral judgements' if you believe in such a thing as morality – it is that life is largely a choice, and nearly always one choice excludes another, perhaps a previous, choice; and that should be recognized, not flattered by rationalizations. Very likely you have a moral code, in which case you will say that some choices are too terrible or too inhuman or too brutal. They are terrible, inhuman or brutal very often, but if one feels forced to make them, all their unpleasant qualities yield to the force that makes the choice. Christianity is a failure because it is not life; it is a Sunday school, only fit to function one day a week. Unchecked egotism is also a failure, because it isolates the performer to such an extent that it is imprisonment in a living cage rather than life. There is a mean, and that mean differs for the individual – either extreme is bad for any individual, I believe.

I now intend to go on living at Tidmarsh with D.C. 'as if nothing had happened.' Of course a great deal has happened really, but what I mean is I intend to stress the actual life we lead from day to day rather than the life we led six months ago. I shall fix my eyes on the present and the future to get satisfying emotions. I should quite like to write to you from time to time, even to see you. I know quite well we have a great deal in common, though either of us would tear the other's character to ribbons in his head in ten minutes if he wanted to. We approach our lives from different angles, but we do want both to have lives, and that places us in a very small category indeed, where one is always pleased to meet anyone of the same mind.

As for D.C., I cannot tell what her feelings for you have been or are, nor can you, or she. We three hold three several opinions about that. I shall not be so bold as to hazard an opinion as to what they are now – their complexity would be too baffling. It is possible that it is only when she can act that she has what I call feelings – that is, something she can value in her own head. Until something happens she is hardly conscious. It is difficult to speak to you about the future, because I am now very cautious and there have been so many mysteries – so many people get such exultation out of a mystery – that I think all ground hollow where I tread. I no longer anticipate meeting firm ground as I walk about; I am prepared at any moment for the nasty surprise. I have placed no ban on your corresponding with each other, but I have placed no blessing either – neither of you can expect that. You are both free agents and you must please yourselves. I shall certainly be cynical about you both if you do write, but chiefly about D.C.

Barbara[8] writes to you giving you the news, possibly the gossip. Don't let's have any more mysteries in that direction. If there is to be another campaign, let it be in the open. If there is anything you want to gain, I should distrust all your allies as much as your enemies. Counter-mines are often more successful than mines. But don't think you must throw dust in my eyes, or think of any of these real, vital matters in a purely formal, literary, conventional way – there is no code, no rules, under which one can conduct one's life. You made a mistake in thinking of me as the conventional rival before – not always, but when other people treated me so. That is not the way to live, to make assumptions because they simplify situations – that is the way our parents live. Every situation is individual and requires first-hand examination and an individual solution. Your situation was individual, but the chief reason why the solution is unpleasant to everyone is that you hadn't the nerve to face it in any but a conventional way, so now we have a conventional solution that leaves everyone unhappy.

If you dislike this style of writing, you needn't reply; it's easier for me to write like this than for you to answer it. I take a mean advantage – perhaps maliciously.

Your friend Ralph

8. Barbara Bagenal, *née* Hiles, Carrington's close friend and fellow-student at the Slade. She had worked briefly for the Woolfs as a typesetter.

YEGEN, 11 OCTOBER 1922

Dear Ralph,

I was glad to get your letter. I have a great deal to say on everything that has happened, which I hope you will not mind hearing. We have been friends for so many years and in such an intimate way, and I owe so much to you, that I cannot bear to leave things as they are and keep unsaid my version of what has happened. I hoped to have answered your letter at length long ago, but I have been away and then I have been distracted by the death of my landlord and endless complications about this house. This letter is only to tell you that I will write again soon.

I may as well answer now one point in your letter – your accusation of my flirting with Barbara, plotting – about what? I don't know. The facts are these: she wrote me a friendly letter telling me how you all were. I answered her, thanking her and asking for news about you, D.C. and Valentine. I assured her that I only wished to know because I could not bear to be suddenly cut off from all information about you; surely that is a very natural motive.

I do not know what kind of 'plotting' you suspected me of. If I had wished to do Valentine any damage I could (I imagine) easily have done so, and this fear was, I suppose, the motive of her letter to me just before I left England, asking to see me. But I am not revengeful and she can count on my silence. You might have had the sense to see that if I wished to 'plot' with anyone against you, I should not choose a person who is much more your friend than my own. I will answer all that you say about plots when I next write . . .

Please believe that my friendship for you has not changed in any way; if I have written more coldly it has been in deference to your feelings and to the situation generally. And thank you for having been so ready to forgive – little deserving of forgiveness as I must have been in your eyes. I will write soon.

                                                                    Gerald

TIDMARSH, 23 OCTOBER 1922

Dear Gerald,

D.C. has shown me your letter and hers to you. She did so to avoid misunderstandings, not because I wanted to see them. The fear of new misunderstandings makes everything so public that it is like indecent exposure. It is very safe, but a bit bleak for everyone. It may also be salutary, but it stirs up a great many feelings that are too tender for raw weather. I feel rather inclined to chip in and say some things to you about yourself – in fact that's why I started this letter – but as most of them would spring from your letter to a third party, I see now that you might feel it in bad taste; and in this sort of situation – in which, by the way, I'm quite at sea and have to work out every step of my behaviour by close reasoning – everyone's feelings are so delicate that one cannot afford the breaches of manners that pass unnoticed in happier times . . .

. . . The curse of life for human beings is the competitive mania that never really relaxes, however reasonable we think ourselves, and, like the Devil in the nursery, is always ready to slip in, at unguarded moments, to tempt us. It sounds unpleasant, old-fashioned and religious, but I think it is only just. The free play of individuality is a competition in which each individual asserts himself as much as he can, and the prize is self-satisfaction. I no longer believe in the liberty of the individual as the highest good. There are not enough desirable things in the world to go round – some people have to go short. I don't mean to be one of those people and, if I'm frank, I'm going to fight for my seat in these musical chairs. I recognize life as a competition, but there are rules to it and I'm not going to break them unless I find that others are breaking them.

Now this conception of mine is not accepted, I believe. There is a different conception, a far more agreeable one, which I used to believe in before. That is that life needn't be a competition for sensible people – that it is only stupidity that makes people compete, because the real things of value are infinitely divisible and everyone may share them without depriving anyone else. People compete for things that have only a fictitious value. Sublimate the mind and you avoid competition. There is everything to be said for this view; it is stimulating, sociable, progressive, delightful; but it relies entirely upon the facts of life to bear it out. It can only be true if it is probably true, not possibly true. It is already possible – lives can be spent in picture galleries, libraries, the higher mathematics, concert halls, debating societies, in all the aesthetic enjoyments; but are they? And if they are not, once you go down the National Gallery steps you have to find truth in a competitive world. Aesthetics, *at present*, are the only field where there is socialism. And I've never yet seen or heard of an aesthete *pur et simple* – they don't exist and I, speaking for myself, would be bored to death by them if they did. There is great fun in this competition, but great danger, and one is always ready to run risks for really desirable things – it is because risks are risks that we are all in the present mess. The only escape from risks that I am aware of is by the mechanism of deliberate choice. If one abandons a desire for another desire, one lessens the risks, though one loses the pleasures. My own enthusiasm for the exercise of choice is largely moral, because I believe in keeping the rules of competitive life as far as possible and not interfering until one is interfered with. When my view is accepted, or when I'm converted by fresh arguments to another view, then it will be easier to come to a settlement; because while I hold one view, you another, and D.C. a third, there is enough suspicion and misunderstanding generated to wreck any restoration.

I'm opposed to too much reliance on the healing effects of time. Time is short, much too short, and there are better uses to put it to than the tedious process of natural healing. Surely one's reason is an antiseptic and there is no possible objection to using it. If the only point you can see in the next year is the softening of our mutual aggravations, I think that ridiculous. My mind is perfectly restored to its balance. What are your feelings for me, what for D.C., what value are you prepared to give your own judgement of your own feelings, what are your aims with me, with D.C, how certain are you of your aims? These are a few of the pertinent questions that are a great deal more to the point than the mere lapse of time! The only reason for time to elapse before something is done between us is because you or D.C. require the lapse of time to settle your own minds. I am not going to alter from my present attitude unless for something a good deal more sensible than the fact that I'm 28 instead of 27. It is too insulting that my suspicions must be lulled. I have renounced my suspicions, but I retain my judgement. I should like to know quite why you and D.C. are determined to be unhappy indefinitely; it strikes me as absurd – unless your feelings on both sides are dimmer than you care to admit. I confess I lose patience.

R.P.

YEGEN, 31 OCTOBER 1922

Dear Ralph,

The arrival yesterday of D.C.'s answer to my letter of last August has crystallized my thoughts and made me more certain of what I want to say to you.

I do not know if these letters between us are to be looked upon as attempts to find some ground on which our past friendship might be renewed; whether this is the case or not, the thing that is of the greatest importance to me, and my principal reason for writing this letter, is that you should understand better how I have behaved towards you in the past – what things I have done and what I have not done. It is only when this has been decided on that we can try to discover whether there exists any firm basis on which your confidence in me could be restored; for without this confidence it is useless to talk of friendship between us . . .

You will, I think, be more ready to believe my account if you understand better what my character is, what my feelings for D.C. have been, what my hopes and desires have been, what they are now, and so on. You and I are very different characters and perhaps we have both got into the habit of exaggerating the difference and supposing each other stupider, or rather less 'understanding', than he is. If you could put yourself not only in my place but in my character, you would see that my account of my behaviour is more plausible than it appears. You, I know, are not going to be satisfied with the assurance that I am the sort of person who loves his friend too much to betray him, and you are right to distrust such assurances. Your own experience of 'love affairs' is probably that they are accompanied by violent feelings of jealousy and lust, and that the combative instincts are greatly increased.

None of this is true in my case. My feelings are quite different. Though I felt myself irresistibly drawn towards greater intimacy with D.C., my affection for you at the same time rapidly increased and I associated you together in a way it is difficult to explain. So far from ever feeling that you were my rival, or being tempted to plot against your happiness, I associated my interests with the maintenance of your marriage and the Tidmarsh ménage. I will not put this down to any altruism on my part, although my affection both for D.C. and for you (and affection is, if anything is, altruistic) demanded this; it is sufficiently explained by the importance your joint friendship had for me in the life which I have designed for myself. I have never desired for myself the life of tranquillity and security and solid happiness which most men aim at. I shall never settle down, marry, sit in a library in England and write books. This is not because I do not appreciate the pleasures of such a life; it is rather because I do not believe myself suited to live in that way; I have not got what is called a lucky palm; the more solid benefits of life do not stick to me, and I am content to live on the outskirts of civilization, in a rather vague and shadowy region, and call myself – whether rightly or wrongly – a poet. Even if both you and Lytton were removed, even if I could supply your place, there would be no room in such a career for a woman like D.C.

You and she, however, have filled an important place in my life, more important than I could ever fill in hers or yours, and our annual meetings and my correspondence with D.C. have been a kind of nourishment that I cannot easily dispense with. When the immediate regrets and nostalgias which this disaster has occasioned have subsided, there will still remain for me a permanent loss, something which could almost be weighed and calculated, by which I shall continue the poorer. You must consider yourself what sense there could be in supposed treacheries.

My efforts were always bent towards establishing my position as permanently as I could with both of you; it seemed to me the necessary condition imposed on anyone who was attached to D.C. to accept both you and Tidmarsh; your friendship also was prized by me – not a little – and so was Lytton's, and the contact with civilization that Tidmarsh stands for.

My first idea for consolidating this position occurred to me in London, immediately after the sudden change in my feelings for D.C. that I have told you of. It was the justification I made to myself for going to the Lakes instead of returning to Spain. I thought that my character and the circumstances of my life would allow me to have a relationship with D.C. of the same nature as that of Dante and Beatrice, the troubadours and their ladies, or Shelley with Emilia Viviani[9] and Jane Williams,[1] and that you would approve of such a relation. When I reached Watendlath it suddenly seemed absurd and unreal, and I did not even mention it to D.C. After that I dallied with the idea of confessing to you; this also was not genuine, for I realized that this would mean an end to my relations with both of you, which I had no intention of risking.

My next and last idea may have been a 'justification' of my conduct or it may have been based on a genuine insight into the facts – I am not competent to decide. It was that when more time had passed I should be able to confess everything to you and so stabilize my position; for I knew that some time you would have to know. I thought that as you got accustomed to our triple alliance you would have less reason to fear me and consequently to feel jealous of me; I also thought that a gradual revelation might be a good thing, by which you would already, when the time came, have guessed half of what I had told you, and this was the motive for my telling you that my feelings for D.C. were not platonic and so on – at Larrau. Another hope was that, as I had noticed a change in

9. Shelley's impassioned but vague and fanciful attachment to this young contessina produced the transcendental love-poem 'Epipsychidion'.
1. The wife of Shelley's friend, Edward Elliker Williams, and the subject of 'With a Guitar' and other exquisite lyrics.

you during the past year, you might at the end of another year be less rigidly attached to D.C. – less 'domesticated', as I would have put it. The plot that you should have an intrigue with V. sprang partly from this idea; I did not suppose it could make you less fond of D.C., but I thought you would be gayer, freer and, according to my ideas, more civilized. I had hopes of leading my own feelings for D.C. into a safer and quieter channel; for the Dante-Beatrice idea, which seems in many respects to suit my own character and D.C.'s as well, never left me.

It has always been the rarity of the occasions when I could be with D.C., and the knowledge that in a day or two I was going to leave for 12 months, that have kept my nerves on edge and reduced me to states in which I could hardly control myself. I felt sure that if I could feel that time was not running short, I should be quieter and happier and would be able to live my ordinary life of reading and writing. My stay at Tidmarsh, I felt, would be such an opportunity; but actually it turned out quite different, and that dreadful beating in the head and chest which exhausts one so much and makes ordinary life impossible was worse than ever. One of the reasons, no doubt, was that I was deprived the long walks alone with you, which had meant so much to me at Watendlath and Larrau. It is quite true that on such occasions, when the weather was fine and you were in a good mood, I was quite as happy as I could have been with D.C.; you were in some degree substitutes for each other and, if to you I talked about her, when I was with her I talked very often about you.

I believe that if you make an effort to recall Watendlath and Larrau you will recognise the truth of what I say. What I wish to persuade you of is that my crime consisted only in being too attached to D.C. and in concealing this from you. Whether this is immoral or not I do not care; most people would say so, but for me it was just inevitable and natural to my character. Had you been in my position you would, I think, have come and told me to look out for myself or else gone away. But then your feelings would have been different from what mine were – they would have been more violent and dangerous. For you, being in love means an enlargement of your whole character; you are at once better and worse than you generally are, and your moods and passions find immediate expression in your acts. With me the kind of congestion I always suffer from is intensified; my moods, my excitement rarely find expression; they are turned inwards upon myself and produce either a secret delight or a secret agony. I am more incapable than at any other time of showing intelligence, of talking sensibly, of behaving well in society; I feel that my

eyes are bandaged, my arms bound, and that I will gladly do anything
that other people tell me to do; it is as though I were mesmerized, and I
feel that most of my selfish interests are purged away and that I desire
nothing.

These feelings are of course not my only ones – it is not often that I feel
as extremely as this. At Watendlath and Larrau I often felt detached
from what was going on round me – detached and yet very close to it. I
felt I was living in a dream and had no desires of any kind, because I was
already so happy. This happiness of the imagination is the greatest that I
know of, and it is for me the special feature of my relations with D.C. Its
greatest manifestation came when you were present also, especially
when you sang songs. One occasion – it was the last day I spent at
Watendlath; we had lunch by a stream and you sang about the frogs –
was perhaps the happiest in my life. To you, who find your happiness in
more real and solid things, this may appear strange and fanciful; but it is
of such unsubstantial elements that my life consists.

You wonder what I say about you to Valentine and H.-J.? What have I
said to you about him? Things that I am ashamed of, I know, but not
things that he would not allow for or forgive me. I have told H.-J. nearly
everything that has happened; but, since Watendlath, I have said
nothing about you that you could resent; before that I had dissected your
character to him, as I am sure you have mine. H.-J. has not been a
conspirator with me – he has throughout disapproved of my conduct,
both to you and to myself. My worst things were said to Valentine, but
how much worse has she not told you? I always insisted to her on my
friendship with you, my peculiar feelings for D.C., her attachment to
you. We discussed whether your marriage would be permanent or not –
but I am not going to retail all this. My memory is vague, but I have an
unpleasant feeling that my cursed love of babble, made up of envy,
silliness, vanity and all the petty vices, choosing a moment when I had
not seen you or D.C. for 8 months, ran away with my good sense . . .

I can see that the fact that Valentine and through her Bon[amy] knew
of this made it seem much worse, and this makes me feel very ashamed
for not having managed to conceal my feelings for D.C. from strangers.
But even allowing this, I believe that if the revelation had been made to
you by, say, MacIver[2] instead of Valentine, your mind would not have
been confused by stories of plots and dark treacheries; and instead of
those stupid and horrible moods that dominated us all, we should have

---

2. Alan MacIver, a young friend of Ralph's and Carrington's, was a witness at their wedding.

discussed the matter round a table like sensible people and should have found ourselves at once in the position that we are in now – our friendship broken and your confidence shattered, but still sane and able to grapple with the situation. And very soon you would have found yourself in a position that sooner or later I believe you will reach – your knowledge of my character and modes of behaviour improved and your confidence restored . . .

I have nothing more to say except to tell you what decision I have come to about the future. I am not going to have any communication with D.C., at any rate until the spring. When I do write you will know, for I shall write openly. But I am not making any promises – I do not believe in promises – I am simply telling you my present determination, which might possibly, though it is very unlikely, be changed. My reasons for this decision are firstly, that D.C. wishes it – which I find quite a sufficient reason – and secondly, that I think that even if you say you do not mind my writing I still should not write at present. If I resume a correspondence with D.C. I should like there to be a certain gap to separate it from last June. I could not write regularly with pleasure at present. And there is another reason – that you do not wish me to write; you say that you allow but do not bless such a correspondence, that you would be ironical about it. Of course I should write to D.C. without asking you, if I wanted to, but I *do not want* any relations I might have with her to be a cause of friction between her and you or to make you feel hostility towards me. She would not consent to write to me under such conditions, but nor should I want to; you and I have been very intimate friends and I still have for you the same feelings that I have always had; I cannot and will not, if I can help it, be an object of even suppressed jealousy and irony in you . . .

I am not returning to England next year – I hope to live in Italy and Germany, wherever it is cheap, and write. There will be time, therefore, for something new to spring up before I see you or D.C. again. If at any time you have any suspicions of 'plots', etc. engineered by me (such as you speak of in connection with Barbara) I expect you to write and ask me about it. Whatever our relations are to be in the future, there must be nothing doubtful or suspicious about them. Whenever I write to D.C. again I will write openly, and she will tell you she has received the letter and decide for herself if she will show it to you or not. My principal reason for writing this time through H.-J. was that she insisted on my not writing to her. I thought there might be some promise between her and you and I wished to leave her free to accept or refuse the letter.

It is useless for me to sign myself your friend; good feelings and pious hopes do not make for friendship – but only confidence. We are no longer friends in any ordinary sense; if it is possible for us to be friends again as before, it is for you to say so. But please do not let us make any mistakes about that or set up some ill-defined and half-hearted relation. If we cannot be to one another what we have been before, let us agree to have no pretence about it. Rather than see myself only half trusted by you, I would prefer to have only a distant and formal acquaintance.

Gerald

YEGEN, 9 NOVEMBER 1922

Dear Ralph,

I have torn up the first 2 sheets of this letter; they were in answer to the more theoretical parts of yours and do not appear to me worth enclosing. That is why there is a lacuna. I have such a headache I can't write.

Please say everything to me you want to and don't consider my feelings. Letters are hopeless – I can say nothing I want to. My own, when I re-read them, make me sick. And I have not the energy to write them over again.

To come to the point – if you want to be more competitive yourself, please be so. I should be very far from blaming you. If you wish to keep me at arm's length, you must do so and not have a bad conscience about it. If you think I am dangerous to your happiness, you would be a fool not to protect yourself against me. You have all the weapons in your own hands and can make your will law. I shall not oppose you openly or secretly, for one reason because I am not a person who struggles or competes with others.

My belief is that a certain egoism makes for honesty and sincerity in one's actions. I distrust feats of generosity unless they are backed up by self-interest. If you make friends with me it will be because your desire to please D.C. and the pleasure you get from our friendship outweigh, in your eyes, any danger you anticipate from me. My own belief is that you have not the slightest reason to fear me, that I could not possibly hurt you if I tried, that I should never try. By answering your questions I shall try and supply you with some facts to base your judgement on.

My feelings for you are what they have always been. I should very much desire a restoration of our friendship even though I were not to see D.C. again. I have *never* had any feelings of jealousy, envy or malice for you. I wish not to deceive you again. My feelings for D.C. are difficult to define. They have never been constant; but on the whole they seem to me to resemble hers for me, but to be stronger – at moments much stronger. They depend – not for their strength but for their 'tone' – on various circumstances: where we are, if you are there also, if my stay is to be long or short, etc. I have always believed they were fairly elastic and that in favourable circumstances they would conform to what the circumstances require. But I may be wrong.

If we met again as friends it would be my aim to keep everything as open as possible. How far I was able to do this would depend largely on your feelings for me. If you and I could establish more intimate relations than before, the experiment would be a success. If our relations were cold and suspicious, I should certainly go away. If I could restore my former relations with you, I should consider I had got all that I wanted. I should not deceive you again . . . I don't ask you to believe this; I only believe it myself because I think that things would really turn out like that. My relations with D.C. would be such as you would not disapprove of . . . It is only if our friendship is to be thoroughly restored that I want to meet you and D.C. again. It is only if that happens, and if I can relate all my feelings and thoughts to you without restraint, that you can feel unsuspicious and I happy.

I know that it is not in your power any more than it is in mine, even if you desire it, to restore our friendship. Above all I do not want any insincere relation; that could only be a source of irritation and suspicion to both of us. The events of last June must never be repeated or even threatened. I think that you, I and D.C. are united strongly in one desire – that the stupid and sordid events of the last 4 months must never recur. It is for this reason that I insisted in my last letter that it is useless for us to renew any kind of friendship unless you believe that I never plotted against you or treated you as a 'rival'. Let us for God's sake try and be reasonable and examine coldly whether there really is room for a genuine and intimate friendship between us. Promises, guarantees, publicity, limelight – none of these is of any use; they drive one's thoughts and actions deeper out of sight and prepare the way for every kind of delusion.

If we could meet (you and I only) and discuss the matter, we should soon discover what is possible . . . There is little chance of our meeting before 1924. Will not some provisional arrangement and attitude carry us along till then? I agree with you that the factor of time is not very important; really everything depends on the result of our next meeting. I have written to D.C. this morning, but only on the question we are discussing. It seemed to me pedantic not to write if there was a sensible reason for writing. She will show you the letter which, all the more because I wrote it for her only, will give you a clearer idea of how things stand. But, though I have written this letter for a particular purpose, I do not want to correspond with her until next spring; and clearly she thinks the same as I do. It is simply that I don't want to write until all this tedious discussion is finished.

G.B.

TIDMARSH, 27 NOVEMBER 1922

My dear Gerald,

. . . I have had spasms of sense and one or two talks about you with D.C., but nothing very much emerged. After just re-reading your letter, it strikes me as a much clearer statement of your position than I can hope to give you of mine. If we were the only 3 human survivors on this planet, I shouldn't have the least hesitation in proposing that we all three lived together for the rest of our lives. It is the existence of other people that complicates our relations. We are all three sufficiently egotistical not to identify ourselves with anyone else, so that when in company with others we take our own line and our *amour propre* insists on differentiating it from that of anyone else. What I drive at is that in the case of a final choice our bonds of affection give way to our egotism . . .

There would be no opportunity of displaying our latent egotism if it were not for these other people. I might find it intolerable to go on living at Tidmarsh and want to live in Mexico. You might suggest it, Noel Carrington might suggest it, at any rate there might be an overwhelming personal motive to go there. Should I allow myself to be retained by D.C. or Lytton? No, I say – and mean. D.C. would either have to go with me or take her own line. Lytton would have to do the same. It would be one of the egotistical impositions that face other people with dilemmas – one's own decision is taken. Now I don't like these egotistical impositions from other people. I object to being horned upon a dilemma because someone I'm fond of chooses to put me there. And instinctively one places one's affections where one feels least likelihood of such impositions. You and D.C. imposed like that on me once and it is obvious to everyone, particularly myself, that my relations with D.C. are permanently weakened thereby. I retaliated with my own imposition, and that again weakened the connection.

We have now struck a compromise and have abandoned our impositions on both sides, and the bonds are stronger . . . My relation with D.C. has reached the stage that it can only continue by a mutual compromise. It may look strong, but it has all these old patches which would open if any new crisis came. As I wish our relation to continue and see the possible dangers, I have voluntarily abandoned making any impositions myself and even, to satisfy D.C., eliminated the possibility of an imposition in the quarter where it is most likely to occur. As I have treated myself like that, I don't feel inclined to treat you and D.C. any better.

D.C. was not satisfied with my promising not to impose on her; she wanted me to leave all possible temptations to impose. Being of a jealous turn of mind, I feel a strong inclination to treat her in the same way. But my reason tells me that, though she may be unreasonably jealous, that is no reason why I should be. Her jealousy was unreasonable to my mind because, though superficially the dangers she was afraid of were alarming, yet I relied myself on my knowledge of my own character to avert them. And my character has not yet deceived me, however it may anyone else . . .

I ramble on, but I don't conceal from you that I'm not easy in my mind . . . I haven't the least objection to your writing to each other as often as you like, in whatever way you like, or to your seeing each other; but I find it out of my power to abandon myself blindly. I shall certainly be observant of you and her, not in a jealous or in a suspicious way, but just watchfully, because D.C. cannot be trusted to be observant herself – and I believe she would be sorrier even than I if she glided mysteriously into a position that makes me abandon the compromise between us. Only she is very much bolder where she herself is concerned – naturally. It is hard to become quite unselfconscious in writing to you all at once, but I shall continue to send you letters on different subjects.

R.

YEGEN, 10 DECEMBER 1922

Dear Ralph,

I was glad to get your letter this morning. As time passes, one's view of the situation, and especially of the future, changes. I feel quite differently now from what I did six weeks ago, when these letters between us began. Everything appears a little easier, flatter and less lurid than it did then.

What is the position now? We are, I imagine, on friendly if somewhat uncertain terms; we are anxious to renew our relations if that appears safe, feasible, and so on; we are unable to decide about all that at once – so one puts off the whole question indefinitely . . . With regard to our negotiations, I would like you to understand two things. One is that I am not just trying to patch up some kind of new relation between us. I naturally, like most people, turn towards where I see happiness lies; but I have no convictions about the future, no determination about it, only the desire to explore its possibilities. I have no conviction that when I meet you and D.C. everything will be easy and pleasant, and it does not seem to be so much you that are running risks by our meeting as I myself.

Secondly, I am not just trying to resume my friendship with D.C. by making up to you. I value your friendship for its own sake, and my way of living makes your friendship of more value to me probably than you imagine. I have always counted on our going away to some amusing country together when [Aunt] Tiz dies, and I still hope this may be the case. Even if the triple relationship is not resumed, our private friendship might find a life of its own, at any rate at certain moments. We have a great deal in common both in our tastes and in our past history; it is scarcely possible that we should in the future be strangers.

I agree with pretty well everything you say in your letter; I agree especially with what you say about egoism. To be a decent human being, a certain core of egoism is required; one's character, spirit, intelligence all lie in that. When one's essential interests are at stake, especially if they are opposed by less essential interests of other people, it appears to me right to follow them – wrong not to. Anything is better than to live in a false position; Bonamy is an example of what happens to one if one neglects this. I think that both you and I are fairly healthy in this respect. You and I show our egoism in different ways, that's all – you, by fighting and cutting your way through things; I, by retiring into myself and refusing any entanglement. If I were married and lived among people, as you do, no doubt my policy would require modification.

As regards what you say of my conduct in the future, I cannot guarantee it until I know more of the conditions. I haven't much belief in prodigies of the will, self-control, etc. If I realize that with my nature I behave in certain ways under certain conditions, I can often foretell those ways. But I believe, what you seem doubtful about, that the future cannot possibly be like the past. Everything has changed; time will show more clearly than it can be seen at present. It is useless to discuss this in detail; I believe, however, that everything has changed – your 'watchfulness,' D.C.'s clearer understanding of where her interests and principal affections lie, and my own character which is very sensitive to its environment. I am very impressionable to people I like, and your knowledge would make me in future extremely circumspect and very alive to the slightest hint of danger. For isn't any falling back into the past as dangerous for me as for you? Firstly, because it would at once lead to a second and even more complete bust-up. And, for quite other reasons, I don't think I could ever be led into deceiving you again . . .

I shall write to you and I hope you'll write to me when you feel like it. As regards my writing to D.C., you say you don't mind at all. If that is so, perhaps there is really no point in my not doing so; but I will leave you to decide that with D.C. . . . You said one other thing, which perhaps concerns me very indirectly but which I don't agree with. You said the connection between yourself and D.C. was weaker than it used to be and was based on compromise. Now often an outsider can see things more clearly than the person concerned. It is perfectly clear to me, first, that D.C.'s part of your connection is stronger than it has ever been, and secondly, that the double connection is and always has been a very strong one – first, because you are all attached to each other; second, because you have all formed habits that you will not willingly break.

Your Mexico is like my South America or Central Asia. I am always planning to go to these countries, yet clearly I shall never go unless some new event makes my present life no longer endurable. Nor will you leave D.C., or she you, unless outside events compel you to. Probably almost all marriages contain these elements of dispute and compromise; if one is married one sees little else at times; one's whole life appears very unstable looked at from within; but to outsiders it is as solid as a rock. Last June it appeared to you possible that you would not return to D.C. Yet certainly I, and probably other observers, never thought of doubting that you would return. I wrote not long ago to H.-J. saying it was extremely probable that I would sail for Buenos Aires when I got my Christmas money. My health had been bad, I had been unable to write or study; I felt certain I would sail. Now my health is recovered, I am writing, I shall not sail. He never even troubled to answer my letter.

And you are less likely to leave Tidmarsh than I the literary life, because the conditions that make my life possible are always more precarious. It is pleasant to imagine one is a free agent, that one can start at any moment for America or for the East. Perhaps neither you nor I could consent to live as we do if we had to give up this belief that some day we should go somewhere or live a more heroic life. And it is not only, of course, habit that restrains us – powerful as habit is. Commonsense tells us that assured happiness is better than a very dubious heroism. Things are probably, after a few months' excitement, as tame in Mexico and the Pamirs as in Tidmarsh and Yegen; for tameness and monotony are part of the material of life itself. Do you remember how the greatest war of history nearly killed us with its boredom? Those wet days at Sailly, mending roads, talking to stupid peasant girls, going to bad cinemas. One remembers the days at Amiens, the raids, the battles, the treks, and forgets the hideous monotony that linked them together . . .

I feel so light-hearted tonight that I can with difficulty imagine that everything in life is not easy and simple and agreeable, that we are not all here to be jolly and amuse ourselves. Yet there are principles and compromises and contracts and choices, difficulties of every kind, some of which can be dissolved by commonsense and others which cannot. But it is often hard for me to remember all this, and my character is perhaps not a very solid or serious one. Yes, all these difficulties are so many mysteries to me; I put on a grave face when I am confronted by them, but I have no real belief in them and at the first moment I forget them . . . Goodbye.

Gerald

TIDMARSH, 22 DECEMBER 1922

My dear Gerald,

I haven't got your letter here, but I recollect it was very pleasant to read. As our respective positions, which are at the best very fluid, have now been declared, re-declared, confirmed and receipted, I think we can now begin to correspond again like gentlemen, the choice products of Radley and Westminster culture.

The breach with the Woolfs, long anticipated, has at last been achieved – by whom I can't say, but not consciously or deliberately by me. The temperament of Leonard, the sensibility of Virginia and my own pig-headedness now admit the impossibility of a coalition. I didn't comprehend them and they didn't comprehend me, two years ago, or we should never have embarked on partnership. Virginia, almost at the last moment, suggested that I should set up a Tidmarsh Press here and work in connection with them, I doing the printing, they doing the publishing. But when it came to defining the relations between the two presses, there was a conflict of opinion as to finance and control. The upshot was that Leonard felt it would be better to part amicably and suggested my setting up a Tidmarsh Press of my own. This idea had occurred to me previously, but I had subordinated it to the continuance of my partnership in the Hogarth.

All this will seem a mere business haggle to you, but the point, from my view, is this: that I'm now considering buying a press and setting it up here and printing and publishing on my own . . . To do this I want to have some inkling of whether there will be anything for me to print and publish in the world besides unending series of Carrington's wood-cuts. I think I may get some things from Lytton, but probably chiefly indecent items for private circulation. Have you written anything you would be ready for me to print and publish for you?

What I should like to do is to print here for about eight months of the year and travel for the other four. That would be extremely amusing for me, and it seems to me that it might quite easily suit a few odd people in the world who would like to have things published in a queer sort of way like that. As my expenses of living here are very low I could run almost any risk in the publishing line, as there would be no office expenses. I should like to hear your opinion on it.

Lytton, I know, would like to have a press of his own like that for his extravaganzas, but by himself he could hardly keep me supplied and I shouldn't like to lie idle one year in two. It may seem rather a desperate venture, but no more desperate than a descent into the obscenities of British business which otherwise will have to be my fate. After all, with a press at one's command one can commit a thousand amusing indiscretions. I am so intent on settling this knotty question that I have hardly a thought to spare for anything else. The boredom of public and private lives in England is well-nigh unbearable. And yet, after all, 'A man who lives today will often be alive tomorrow.' (Spanish proverb) Yours,

R.

GRANADA, 2 JANUARY 1923

Dear Ralph,

Your letter was forwarded to me here, where I am staying as the guest of various English people. Upon the project of setting up a press of your own, I am of course quite incompetent to advise you. I should have thought it would be very difficult to make money in that way; but if you do not risk much by it, it is an amusing experiment; and every year which maintains the Tidmarsh establishment unimpaired is a year gained, 365 days of happiness snatched from the malignant fates.

It is very difficult for me to say what I could contribute. It might be nothing; it might be a good deal. Nothing if I were to go to South America. My plans are quite ripe for going there; I should raise the money by selling the house to some English people, with power of repurchase. For £25 I ought to be able to ride from Montevideo to Quito – which would take me a couple of years – and there I might find congenial employment. This is, however, an extreme course of action which I hope to be able to avoid at present; I reserve it for when *emmerdements* of all kinds, due to Tiz and my parents and the impossibility of ever travelling, accumulate so as to make my life in Yegen troublesome and unproductive. Supposing, therefore, that I remain in Europe – I ought then to be able to provide you with something. My plans for writing are fairly settled. In the few days I have been able to write this autumn, I have made rapid progress; the two things I am working at *ought* to be ready by the summer. But I can prophesy nothing, promise nothing. I am a person you cannot depend on. I have very little stimulus to write from outside. I write when I do write because I have to, just as hens lay eggs. It gives me pleasure at the time, but afterwards no satisfaction of any sort.

Apart from this, my life during the last two months does not promise well for the future. With occasional bursts of energy, I have lived on the whole like an opium-eater. When one has no energy for work, one dreams; a habit is soon formed which it is hard to break, and day after day is spent in long rambling dreams about the future. I lie in bed some days till very late, listening to the cocks crowing and allowing a succession of images to pass through my head. The sun is setting perhaps when I get up. I have breakfast and read Horace. I then go for a walk; the stars are already shining clear. When I come in I eat a little *puchero*,[3] and in an armchair by my fire I read Montaigne or a textbook of physiology or perhaps a huge commentated edition of Euclid. When I am tired I get out the map, and that is an inducement to spend another hour in dreaming; a whole complicated life in South America, crossing the Gran Chaco, riding into La Paz, comes up before me. Then perhaps I go to bed at midnight, after an 8-hour day.

Some days that is my life; on other days I work desperately 8 or 12 hours, translating Tacitus, reading embryology. If I could always work like this I should incidentally write more regularly; but this state of lethargy, when to get up in the morning, to eat food, to talk, to write are all difficult and unpleasant, appears to be my regular state and as long as these moods prevail it is useless to expect anything of me. But I will do what I can and, if I make only a very little progress in what I am writing, I think the result would be of use to you.

At present I am staying with some people called Temple. They have built a large and comfortable house on a hill beside the Generalife; there are real Moorish pillars, beautiful carpets, beautiful woodwork and

3. Stew.

large rambling rooms. In the bedrooms there are fireplaces built in alcoves half way up the wall, a most excellent idea. Mr [Charles Lindsay] Temple is a very charming man; he spent years surveying the interior of Brazil and afterwards became Governor of Nigeria. On his own subjects he is interesting and intelligent, not on others. The moral attitude ingrained in some form in the character of all Englishmen seems to make intelligence on general subjects almost impossible. Mrs Temple is herself a bit of an explorer. Before she ever met her husband, she had eaten her anchovy sandwich somewhere east of Lake Chad. Her father, who is also staying in the house, is a Scottish baronet[4] – rather a *grand seigneur*, one of Gladstone's young men.

One meets interesting people at the house – a French engineer, a Belgian financier, a Spanish socialist, and so on. I have always liked the better sort of businessman and now I see that they are some of the most interesting and intelligent people one could find. They are more intelligent and more genuine than most literary or arty people, no doubt because the subjects they deal with are clear and indubitable. Conversation on literature nearly always becomes a dispute between tastes; nothing can be learnt from it and no doubt that is the reason why the level of intelligence among literary people is so very low. But in the higher branches of business there is, strange to say, a demand for intelligence of a fairly general sort, applied perhaps to rather dull subjects but not specialized as it must surely be in Science. When I have some money I shall travel ceaselessly to satisfy my curiosity about the world, and I shall try to move sometimes in business circles, never among artists or literary people. I hope this year to read a few books on banking and on the economic structure of the world generally, and also on technical subjects such as mining, cotton-growing, etc. There lies a whole side of life of which our cultured people know nothing.

Has it ever occurred to you that the chief characteristic of English literature (poetry apart) is its boredom? That it is most of it written by people like Bonamy and Augustine Birrell[5] and [David] Bunny Garnett,[6] over firesides, to the purring of cats and the mild flavour of port, and sustained by gentle reminiscences of far-off classics? To be 'literary' it

4. Sir Reginald Macleod of Macleod.
5. A politician and man of letters, Birrell was Chief Secretary for Ireland in Asquith's Cabinet, from which he resigned after the Easter Week Rebellion in Dublin in 1916.
6. The prize-winning novelist, son of Edward and Constance Garnett, the distinguished translator from the Russian. He was then running a bookshop in Bloomsbury with Augustine Birrell's elder son Francis.

seems almost essential that one should have water in one's veins and blotting-paper in one's head. Your knowledge of the world made you suspect (I remember) that there was a kind of conspiracy among writers to support one another; I quite agree with you. Apart from poetry and poetical prose it seems to me that our literature could be reduced to twenty books; of these only three or four would be of general interest; outside the twenty not one but could with profit be burned. This would be the opinion of foreigners, who do not admit we have more than two or three prose books worth reading. I agree with them; what is more, I doubt if among the authors of even these good books we have one person of genius.

It is easy to see why the Bonamys of each generation, who write our histories of literature, smack their lips over Addison, Fielding and Landor. This is how they would write themselves if they were a little more able. The kind of ability required to write like these authors does not impress me very greatly. Even Jane Austen – I would submit to any death rather than cast a stone at our great idol; but if I could find a place sufficiently lonely, sufficiently secret, I might whisper under vows which you would never dare to break that after all she had the mind and the outlook of a governess.

That is why I dare not proclaim aloud what I think of Bunny Garnett's book.[7] My private impression was that the story was stupid and the style castrated; the latter made me sick; for all my moral feelings, nearly atrophied where individuals are concerned, are vigorous towards ideas and books. But that if he were a bit more slick he would be nearly as good as Addison, I don't doubt; and whether *Lady into Fox* or *Vailima Letters*[8] is the better book, I couldn't say. To me they are both just emetics and I can't distinguish the different qualities of things that produce on me one identical result. It may seem a little ungracious to say this of a book that you sent me; but, to make up, I was very pleased with the Dostoyevsky[9] and I thought Virginia's book[1] was really successful. It is much better than the others. Isn't she one of the lights of this age? What does Lytton say? I should write to her, but I haven't the energy.

I have found a new friend and ally in Robin John.[2] He is not a

7. *Lady into Fox*, published in 1922 by Chatto & Windus.
8. By Robert Louis Stevenson, published in 1895.
9. *Stavrogin's Confession*, translated by S. S. Koteliansky and Virginia Woolf, published in October 1922.
1. *Jacob's Room*, published in the same month.
2. The third son of the painter Augustus John and his wife Ida, *née* Nettleship. He was staying with Gerald for a few months to recover his health and to learn Spanish.

shopkeeper or a hair-dresser's assistant or an *embusqué* or a cretin, and these deficiencies make him an original character. He is perhaps the first person I have met who has the same sentiments on life in general that I have. I think if one could combine Shelley and Madame du Deffand one would get an idea of what I mean . . .

I am writing this in a café. In these houses, with their armchairs and their writing-pads, I can neither write nor read. I even sleep badly; I dream I am stifled. I am sick of this place, of these people, of their houses, furniture, especially of their meals. When I was here before, in old and dirty clothes, and fed on buns and coffee when I wanted, and went where I wanted and could walk down the main street without the terror of being recognized and shaking hands and being made to say something, then I was happier. For two days it is amusing to chatter and grin, and then a longing for silence comes over me and, above all, for anonymity and obscurity. I came here for reasons of high diplomacy. The moment I am able, I shall fly back to Yegen . . .

If you travel for 4 months, you must come out here. Oh God, to have a little money! With £150 or £200 a year the world would lie open to one. With only £60 one has to live in one's rabbit hole.

G.B.

YEGEN, 27 MARCH 1923

Dear Ralph,

. . . After three practically rainless months, we are having fearful downpours. Day after day, thick mist, driving rain, blackness. Tomorrow I start for Órgiva and Granada to meet the Woolfs.[3] The river will be too unpleasant; a combination of motor-bus and mule must bring them another way. For Virginia I have oilskins and an umbrella as big as Robinson Crusoe's; for Leonard, a canvas tent to wrap round him as he sits on his mule.

I will be very careful to act discreetly whilst V. and L. are here; but you must remember that if they feel malicious about you when they return to England, they can quite easily make use of things I may have said to them. About the events of last summer I shall not say a word; I have no wish to discuss them with anyone and, with people who know all the actors, less than with any others. But they are sure to discuss you and D.C. and Lytton, and so on, and probably no good resolutions will

3. Leonard and Virginia had arranged to spend two nights with the Temples in Granada before moving on with Gerald to Yegen, where they stayed from 5 to 13 April.

prevent my indiscretion on general subjects of this sort. In fact I feel that if one cannot speak as one pleases but has to constantly, among friends, exercise a kind of restraint, it is better to be a complete hermit and know nobody. But you, I know, agree with me in this; and you also know, I think, how entirely friendly my feelings are towards you – not less than they ever were – and that I shall not say anything worse about you than I have always been ready to say in the past, or you, I hope, say about me . . .

The great event is my parents' visit in May.[4] It *must* bring me some money: not now but, say, next winter. I hope yours are coming round also. I am enlisting a band of old ladies, etc., in Granada to sing my praises when my parents come out. And they will learn that Mrs Wood[5] feeds me on butter and gives me 5/– to take my friends out to tea – that ought to humiliate them. For, you know, if I don't get a little money by next Xmas I am done for. My income is £60 a year; with every economy I cannot live on under £80. And to waste my whole youth, alone, at Yegen, is more than I can bear. Next spring has got to mean Italy – or America.

The rain falls and falls; I have a bad cold coming on. Tomorrow I have that 8 hours' journey, the mud, the swollen river. I am looking forward to it, however; a journey is always an excitement. And at Granada no miserable *posada*, dirty bed, cheap oily food, but the magnificent luxury of the Temples' house. For Mr T. wishes to meet Leonard who wrote, it seems, an admirable book on Africa;[6] and we meet there . . .

I understand your feelings about working with Leonard; it was not an arrangement likely to last – is their business sufficiently flourishing to find room for two capable and energetic men? And those awful office hours! . . . Well, write if you are able. Love to all.

Gerald

TIDMARSH, 29 MAY 1923

Dear Gerald,

I don't feel at all easy about writing to you, because I vacillate between wanting to preach my good gospel to you and a disinclination to obtrude

---

4. They stayed for a week and were so impressed by the order and civilization Gerald had introduced into his remote mountain home that his father offered him an allowance of £100 a year on condition that he returned every twelve months to see them in England. So his days of real poverty were over.
5. The senior member of the foreign colony of Granada, she was born in 1840 and lived on to 1935 with all her faculties unimpaired.
6. *Empire and Commerce in Africa*, published in 1920 by Allen & Unwin.

myself at all. The shock of viewing Tidmarsh with a keen African eye[7] was very great. It is tame, without a doubt, hopelessly domestic, provincial, unimportant, smug and ridiculous. There is a cringing subservience all round – the flowers, the furniture, the tame birds and the wild birds, all very respectful and very well trained, but crushing, with the whole weight of England, Home and Beauty behind them. For a few hours one's intelligence is insulted by one's previous intelligence, one's present thoughts are insulted by one's past, which is resurrected on every wall and stares one into shame. Then it passes slowly, first the comfort, then the quiet, the lulling lack of outside stimulus, then a touch of old habit, and finally the key to the group, the order, the arrangement recommends itself unobtrusively. At least things are in their place. I don't know which is the better state of mind, the revulsion or the acceptance, but the clash is bitter and lowering . . .

It seems that you found Virginia's bosom warm and were melted. But it hasn't fused very well into your relationship with D.C. I don't include myself, because I am more detached than she is from your real day-to-day life. I seem to have told you one thing quite wrong, though I never meant to. The one *authenticated* case of Virginia's discretion in regard to confidences was about me and D.C. – she never told a soul, which was amazing of her, and I have never thanked her enough. At any rate what indiscretion she indulges in is nothing to yours, because you invariably start off a sincere conversation by telling all you've been told about your *vis-à-vis*. I rather guessed you would when I talked about Leonard and Virginia to you. Not that I mind if you passed it on accurately, because my opinion of them both doesn't alter and I don't mind them knowing it; only my affection for them varies with their affection for me, and people's affection varies often for unknown reasons which are impossible to explain to the other person. Just now their affection for me, what there was of it, has retreated out of sight. It may revive, as it has before, and it may not. If only Virginia was as devoid of feminine weakness as she is of most of her sexual attributes, she would make an ideal connection. I expect a great deal of good may have come to you by striking up an intimacy with her; but from my point of view it seems a pity she should dislike me more than before, that you should stop writing to D.C., and that we have to find out what's happening to you from such

7. Ralph had just come back with Carrington and Lytton from a two months' holiday in Algeria and Tunisia.

previously improbable sources as Barbara [Bagenal], [E.M.] Forster[8] and Leonard.

We are told that you are marrying E.[9] D.C. is in favour of it, and I am strongly against it; but our partisanship is academic. It is fatal to friendship perhaps to write too many letters. You may have been lonely and needed them, but I don't think you can be so any more. Are we (you and I, that is) to go on writing? It's no good to either of us if it's going to be a half-hearted affair on your side, and that's what I think it will be if you marry E. . . . I can't be intimate with anyone who is only sympathetic at moments and is antipathetic in the background. If, as a result of your visitors' visit, you now think of me with a touch of exclusiveness, as being outside the inner ring – it's hard to get clear, but it's the complacency of condescension that is associated in so many of our relationships and that has never been mine with you – then we had better pause until you feel differently, if that should happen. I have become touchy, you may think. I don't intend to be touchy, but I am quite decided about many things now. I'm not entering for any more competitions. If the 1st prize is to be in your confidence, and the consolation prize to supply a topic to a conversation, I shall not enter the lists. I don't want this crude *exposé* to be laughed away because it may seem highly exaggerated, if there is a substratum of truth. The data I work on are 1. In the only letter received at Tidmarsh since the visit of the Woolfs to Yegen 2 months ago you said the conversation had turned on last summer and Virginia would tell us all about it. 2. Virginia, when asked, said you had been rather mad and talked a lot and then turned the subject. 3. Leonard is told that you are about to marry an American. 4. Forster confirmed this, saying he had had a long letter from you recently. I like to imagine you were joking with Leonard and Forster, and that Virginia was just tired and not eager to talk, and that you will eventually remember our existence. If my desires are justified I shall have to submit to your howls of derision and execration. If my fears, then I shan't expect to hear much more of you except from Virginia and Barbara. This is a growly letter, but I feel rather enraged with this English world. I nearly

8. Forster had himself proposed coming out to Yegen earlier that year, but Gerald had discouraged him, not because he disliked him as a man but because he could not bear his novels which he thought woolly and sentimental.

9. Virginia had told Carrington that Gerald had written to Leonard saying he was 'engaged' to an American girl he had met in Granada. In fact he had only had a mild flirtation with her. When he made some physical advances to her one evening in the Alhambra Gardens, he was repulsed.

made up my mind to come out to you with Barbara, and then I turned against you with a snarl. Explain yourself . . .

Ralph

TIDMARSH, 17 JULY 1923

My dear Gerald,

. . . I have had a week's carouse in London. At least no woman captivated me and I feel much better for it. We had very great heat for a short time and I never stopped sweating day or night. I work in the garden and among the hens and contemplate learning book-binding in September. I don't feel the oppression of idleness as much as I used. I'm very glad to have cut adrift from the Woolfs. They never allowed me to assert myself, and for me self-assertion is essential; otherwise the point, the interest, the gist of every activity vanishes. Here I can assert myself or not, as I like, and the latent power is even pleasanter than the display itself.

Do you like Herbert Read's poems[1] that the Hogarth published? I much prefer him to [T.S.] Eliot. I don't like *The Waste Land* at all and, unless Eliot has a nervous breakdown or a sudden shock, I think it improbable that I shall ever like any poetry he may write. Garnett was awarded a prize of £100[2] for *Lady into Fox*, which even Mr [H.G.] Wells can scarce forbear to cheer. I am still dubious about it for all that. Why do you dislike it so much? I can read it and at the conclusion feel neither exhilarated, depressed, angry or bored; it has the effect of a workaday session in the W.C. – toneless and immediately forgotten . . .

I'm tired of this letter and want my lunch. I wish you would write to me or D.C. Curse Virginia. She says nice things about her friends in a way that makes them look like posturing ants. I'm sure she's cast the glamourie over you. Curse her again. She will have her monopolies just to spite everyone else. And what of Saxon[3]? Do you too think him such a great man that you emulate his silences? – *Les Silences du Capitaine Brenan*, composed with the author's usual mastery of his subject. If you would only come home and drink two or three bottles of our newly imported claret, you wouldn't see quite how numerous are our defects.

I rather want to go in for trade and sell Morocco slippers from a

1. *Mutations of the Phoenix*, published in May 1923.
2. The Hawthornden.
3. Saxon Sydney-Turner. A brilliant but extremely taciturn member of old Bloomsbury, he spent his whole career in the Treasury.

pedlar's go-cart in the West End. I have a vicious craving for dealing in leathers. There is something superb in the smell and the texture and the toughness of leather, and the differences between each skin. It is the best substance to have dealings with, infinitely superior to wood, metal, silk or linen. Will you cross to Africa with me if I start? Love from yours,

Ralph

CORDOBA, 4 OCTOBER 1923

My dear Ralph,

I have been here three days and am going on this evening to Seville. Cordoba is an interesting town, but not what I am looking for. Movement, streams of beautiful women, rivers of scent, dance-halls, a garden to sit in in the evening and cafés decorated with gilt mirrors are what I ask for; and, if possible, the sea. It is the great beauty of the mosque, so unexpectedly superior to the brothel water-closet style of the Alhambra, that has detained me; for the streets, the white houses, the immense bridge, the yellow stagnant water covered with newspapers, and the dusty landscape – these, though beautiful, it is enough to see once only and they will thus be more clearly remembered.

The principal brothel is next to the Military Governor's HQ – very convenient. There are 20 or 30 girls; some of them are beautiful; and the whole company sit in armchairs round a large patio with palms in it, talking and smoking and drinking *coñac* and soda-water. Most of the men know one another – they are among the principal people in Cordoba: the head of the telegraphs, the colonel of the local infantry, a hotel-keeper, various landowners, and so on. The more beautiful girls seem to be engaged, for though the official price is 15 pesetas some men give 100 or more to a girl they like. Most of the visitors went, like myself, to have a drink and look at the girls, resisting the temptation to be lured into those little bedrooms where the pink quilts and red shades of the electric light promised pictures perhaps none the less real for being so tawdry. The marked friendliness of all the men visitors, their air of being at home or in a club, seemed to me very unusual; there was none of that furtiveness which I remember to have seen in German houses; they made room for me and drew me into the general conversation, whilst the women, in loose dresses, with their pasty bodies, thick voices and exaggerated gestures, sat on one's lap, then got up, danced, moved about, and (as in musical chairs) collapsed upon some other gentleman. But happiness that is too easily obtained is suspicious; to treat human beings as automatons, or rather to expect of automatons what only human beings can give, is too difficult for pleasure. Whores don't excite me and the amusement I get in watching them is purely ironic.

Spanish whores are more vigorous and more honest than those of, for instance, Amiens. They are never sentimental, they make no pretence to respectability, but use the most direct language and are continuously gay in a rather hard and brilliant manner which I approve of but find difficult to reply to. The extraordinary ease with which they pull up their clothes, open their legs, show their breasts, takes away from me the slightest curiosity or interest I might have felt in their doing this; yet if they resisted one's attacks, it would be from hypocrisy or from a modesty (in any old hand) forced and out of place; and that would repel one even more than their *insouciance*. With no hope of their being alluring, they may however show a certain energy, a ferocity almost, that as a spectacle is beautiful – in the manner of certain episodes in the Russian ballet.

One hope I always have, though I know it to be an illusion: that some evening, suddenly emerging behind Madame in the purple dress and with eyes like agates, there will come forward between the lights and the shuffling dancers . . . a girl of whom Madame will say, 'This is a new arrival.' As when, in some dull and tedious company, the voice of a nightingale floats in from the garden and is heard by just one person alone attuned to it, so for me and me only would this new arrival have any peculiar meaning. And just as once, 1900 years ago, Simon Magus found in a brothel in Tyre a woman who was Sophia, Eternal Wisdom (a golden spark fallen from the outer heaven, one of the aeons, into the shapeless abyss, who in one of innumerable incarnations had been Helen of Troy and was now a Phoenician harlot) whom he led away into Samaria for the salvation and redemption of humanity, so one might come upon this mythical creature, virgin and harlot, endowed like the houris with a perpetually renewed virginity . . .

This is what comes of being unable to read. My eyes this week are so bad that I cannot read anything. I am forced therefore to write though I have nothing at all to say . . .

I look forward immensely to seeing you in December, either both Partridges or the male bird alone. And I am very grateful to you for being ready to come so far to see me. If you are not too proud, tell me how you think of coming and I shall send some useful information for the journey.

Adios. My address is Poste Restante, Seville indefinitely.

Geraldo

P.S. My eyes are cured. I have so much to tell you, I am burning with impatience to see you.

My dear Gerald,

As far as I can see, we shall wait to spend Christmas with you . . .

There is any quantity of news, but I am incapable of doing it all justice on paper. Book-binding seems definitely to be my career. It is pleasant, and possibly profitable, and there is no Leonard at the helm. A great effort was made by my mother to make me considerably poorer by my father's death, in order to drive me into a 'gentlemanly profession'. It was a drawn struggle – I remain about as well off as before, but my prospects are far brighter. I have a vested interest under the will which will bring me in about £500 a year when my mother dies, so that is something to look forward to. It's splendid how charitable our parents make us! I positively gloat over the old lady, she has behaved so disagreeably.

There is a house,[4] quoth he. Such a house! A dream house under the downs near Hungerford, a refuge for old age. We gibber about it all day long. And yet it costs £3,000, they tell us, and we can never find more than £2,000. We bully the agents by every post; if we lose it, I doubt if you will see us at all; life will be unendurable . . .

November. I now feel more communicative; your letter gives me so much pleasure. Your Latin studies appear to have left you with a lust for the ablative absolute; I had a momentary inability to distinguish where the sentences began and the ablatives retired. Have you a genius, or is it a fancy? Your letters please me so much that I can't distinguish how much is affection for you and how much an unwilling tribute to the great writer. You command all my admiration, which is more than our other great genius Mr [D.H.] Lawrence does. But how can I possibly give you any pleasure in return? I have no talent for writing anything but love letters, and what could you do with *them*? But I shall see you and talk to you very soon, and then, if I'm as indiscreet as I generally am, you may hear some stories to amuse you . . .

I keep seeing new people, a younger generation than Bloomsbury. There is a Marjorie Joad,[5] who has taken up my duties at Hogarth;

4. Tidmarsh was proving too damp for Lytton's health and for some time he had been looking round for a new house. Carrington came across one that obviously pleased them all. It was called Ham Spray, and Lytton and Ralph eventually bought it for £2,300.

5. *Née* Thomson. She was then living with, and had taken the name, of Professor Cyril Joad, a civil servant in the Ministry of Labour who was later to become a popular member of the BBC 'Brains Trust', but she left him a few months later. Ralph had had a brief affair with her. Then she married Frances Marshall's youngest brother, Thomas.

Frances Marshall,[6] who sits in Birrell and Garnett's shop; various Cambridge young men with good looks and posts at the *Nation*; rising talent, dancers and party-goers; the 1917 Club,[7] new faces, with a hope of new minds. I shall raise a new campaign shortly – 'back to virginity' will be its aim. Ah! could we only recover that, the world would re-open for us. I want to have every experience again, *for the first time*. I rather envy the people who have never been to Spain. Yet I don't, with the other half of me. I wish I could furbish up my emotions without wiping out my memories. I don't believe you have the same difficulties; yours is a more elastic nature. But I find it harder than ever to talk about psychology in a comprehensible way. I hate the vocabulary so much. 'Emotion' does not convey emotion, nor 're-action' reaction. They are Anglo-Saxon ideas that have to be expressed in Latin and Greek words. I want desperately to talk to you about the workings of the consciousness, and yet the words exasperate me so much that I cannot bear to write them.

I am more or less in love with five different people at the moment, so it's hopeless to try writing to you in this mood – it makes me almost think I'm in love with *you*. Ugh! Ugh! you grunt. But I'm fond of you and feel demonstrative. Yours,

Ralph

GRANADA, 3 DECEMBER 1923

Dear Ralph,

If you are not here by Christmas I will never forgive you. I have spent £8 on groceries: bottles of wine, of liqueurs, tins of pâté, kegs of butter, cheeses, almond paste, all kinds of sweets. There will, I hope, be a turkey – and why not geese, ducks, partridges, thrushes, larks, humming-birds? As for fruits, expect grapes, oranges, apples, melons, quinces, lemons, persimmons, pistachios, olives, sweet potatoes, chestnuts, honey in the comb and honey in jars, jams of many classes. Do you like Green Chartreuse, Curaçao, Crème de Menthe, Manzanilla, Jerez, Marsala? Will you smoke hashish in the pipe I bought in Morocco and read the *Mille et Une Nuits* in my embroidered *djellabah*, in a room that smells of attar of roses and orange flowers? If you bring out a gun, you may shoot

6. A beautiful and highly intelligent young woman who had read philosophy at Cambridge. Ralph fell for her at once and soon she was responding to his affection, though she would not permit his advances to proceed too far.
7. A left-wing club with premises at 4 Gerrard Street, Soho, it had the merit, said Virginia Woolf, 'of gathering my particular set to a bunch about 4.30 on a week day.' Its membership was a mixture of the political and the literary and artistic.

partridges, rabbits, vultures – but in that, I fear, I will not join you. And in the evenings my minstrel will sing to you *coplas* and play on his guitar . . .

I will not allow you to go away under 6 weeks, which 6 weeks will cost you nothing. If you arrive at Órgiva and do not find me, on no account forget to ask at the Posada de los Pescadores for some oilskins, umbrellas, thermos flasks, etc. which I will send to await you, and bring them along on your mule even if they are not needed . . . I go to Yegen tomorrow. When you see the food prepared for you, you will think me the best friend you ever had.

Gerald

Ralph and Carrington reached Yegen on Christmas Eve and stayed with Gerald for a fortnight. The visit, of which all three of them expected so much, was entirely successful in so far as it eradicated once and for ever the bitterness that had divided them. Now that Ralph was involved with Frances, his attitude to Gerald had softened; he was no longer jealous of him and had no objection to any relation he might have with Carrington. But Gerald himself was uncertain of his own feelings for her; nor was she sure of hers for him. He was as fond of her as ever, but no longer in love with her; and she, though deeply attached to him, was reluctant to go further for fear of losing Ralph altogether. The situation was still unresolved when the time came for the visitors to leave. Gerald accompanied them as far as Granada and spent several days with them there.

MADRID, 10 JANUARY 1924

Dear Gerald,

Blessed are the pure in heart, for they believe in the efficiency of Spanish railways. At midday the great *bulto*,[8] the Ark of God, had *not* arrived – *et voilà pour lui*. I have now got an appointment for 10 a.m. tomorrow with two degraded roughs outside the goods depot, when I shall either get the *bulto* or something of equal value, or nothing at all but a towering rage. If the *bulto* continues to lie *perdu*, I shall just go away and leave the ticket with an agency to collect it in the course of the year and forward it at infinite expense to England. Not that I am in the least put out – yet – but I shall be tomorrow. The scene at Baeza would not have tolerated the added *bulto*. By singular address we got ourselves and objects into the tail of the express at the last moment. Two little lepers assisted at the gallop and were paid 70 centavos for their speed.

I hear today that my lady[9] goes to Paris on Saturday and I hope to see

8. A crate, packed with china and other purchases.
9. i.e. Frances, who had arranged to join Ralph and Carrington on their way back to England.

her on Sunday. The emotion I had on reading this ecstatic news was complete indifference. I felt frozen and rather terrified, if anything. On reading it for the third time a sort of pleasure seems to be creeping over me, or is it just nerves? I can't decide. A charming letter – and long too – what a shock! . . .

I hear Bunny [Garnett] has written to you saying he is coming to Yegen with his Central African wife.[1] What'll you do? I shall say nothing at all to anybody except that you are *absolutely undependable*, so I shall be right whatever you do. If you see him, don't mention me and Frances in the same breath; but do, in different breaths, so that we can hear what Bunny has to say.

I was very happy staying with you – in my quiet way. I'm very fond of you by yourself, and fond of you and Carrington together; it didn't agitate me at all to see your affection for each other. It is important always to be able to discuss these things without feeling the sensations of 'indecent exposure', and it is most important to discuss things *before* anyone is unhappy – because the moment the element of unhappiness intrudes itself, it makes discussion more emotional than intelligent and it is the inability to keep one's emotions down while one thinks that makes for suppressions and secrecy and worse unhappiness. But this must be treated as S.O.S. Regulations – I'm more convinced of the probability of our all three having a happy relation than I was before I saw you. And just tell me if ever anything I do distresses you directly or indirectly. I really love you; from a strictly detached consideration of myself, you are as sympathetic as I ever can expect to find anyone of your sex. I think this is all I have to say on that subject for the time being . . . Yours,

Ralph

YEGEN, 11 JANUARY 1924

My dear Ralph,

I have most unwisely put all my news in D.C.'s letter, and so what shall I say to you? . . . Unfortunately, too, I feel uncommonly blockish tonight; I can invent nothing. Now God knows why I began this letter. Of course I might keep to those subjects, almost my favourite ones, which we hold peculiarly in common because no one else will discuss them. I will exchange some Remarks on the Pleasures of Inhaling Certain Sorts of Sweat against an Essay on the Physiology of Water-taps. But not

---

1. An uncomplimentary reference to Frances's older sister Rachel (Ray), whom Garnett had married two years earlier.

tonight, for I have just come from reading Virgil. And you, fresh from Paris and from your lady, will ask for higher topics . . .

But my desert breeds no food for letters. Some rumours from the village – Felipe found the keeper lying on the floor on top of his wife. In his own house, too, among his own vermin – think of that! The keeper had unslung his gun and laid it down beside him. Felipe, the lost innocent of idiots, snatches it up in a fine pretence of rage and fires it at him. Misses. His ten infants rush out and overpower him. Victoriana gets up and wipes her thigh with her skirt. 'You bloody idiot,' she says, 'you fucking old egg, always interfering!' Felipe abandons his home. The wife of the keeper, young, beautiful and vigorous, comes in with the crowd. 'Aren't you ashamed of yourself, demeaning yourself with that syphilitic old hag?' And Victoriana is, quite true, the most hideous, dirty, stinking old reptile you could imagine – mother of ten starving brats. But she has, the villagers say, this fatal body that makes her to men what valerian is to cats. Though when I saw her loose pregnant stomach and, through her gaping blouse, two yellow dangling udders, I feel myself to be a kind of cat in whose pharmacopoeia valerian has been put among the poisons.

Well, the night moves on. I sit here alone, scratching myself. You know, I miss you a lot. Will you laugh at me if I tell you how much I like you, how very charming I think you? Or if I say I have never known anyone so kind and so generous as you are? If I say what I feel, you will laugh; but if I do not say it, you will never know. I will not forget how you came into my room that night at Granada because you thought I was unhappy. There is only you to act as perfectly as that. If I have made you unhappy, it was not intentionally. I had meant to talk to you about my feelings for D.C., but no good occasion turned up. So I will say a little in this letter . . . One cannot define and classify feelings with any accuracy, but I should tell you that I am more devoted to D.C. than probably I gave you the impression of being the first day we talked of this. I am probably more firmly attached to her than I have ever been, but, I can assure you, in a different manner. To be with people I care for even slightly is always a little agitating for me who am accustomed to solitude, but during your visit I went through nothing stronger than this. And now you are gone I am a little bored and lonely – that is true – but nothing to the zone of darkness and despair I went through after Watendlath and after our rupture, before I could return to normal life. You will appreciate the crucial importance of this difference . . .

You have known for years that D.C. could not find in you all the sympathy she required, and your remarks on her interest in young

Cambridge men simply confirm this. You yourself tried to find in her nearly everything and when, as was natural, you had failed – after putting the blame for your failure on her – you began to distribute your affections and so to lead a fuller and more sensible life. That at least is my view of the situation. You will think I am leading up to a sermon on free love, but this is not so; for I see that about some things there are peculiar difficulties, and in our matter they are not to the point. My contention is that there is room for a friendship between D.C. and myself, not a rather casual one but intimate, which will not injure you nor touch your particular claims. On the contrary, since you and I are already of our own accord attached to one another, it ought, if we are sensible and tactful, to increase the happiness of all of us, since more mutual affection can only lead to more happiness.

Lytton's relation with D.C. was only resented by you so long as you expected of her what was in any case impossible – complete surrender. Now it is an advantage to you. One can only take from a person what corresponds to something that is already in oneself, and it is as a rule only rather elementary characters who are mutually all-suffering. You and I are so different from one another that we must always occupy in D.C.'s mind very separate partitions, and once one sees this it seems to me that any idea of choice or competition becomes meaningless. You have already – and I shall never cease to be grateful to you – consented to the renewal of our friendship. It is a new relation and I should like to develop it along particular and rather literary lines, the limits being always what will give you pain or cause you any feelings of jealousy. Now what do you say?

I have one more thing to speak of. This last week you have said to me or to D.C., 'If Gerald went off with you . . . if I went off with Frances,' or something of that sort. Now I must tell you once again that so far as I am concerned no such thing is either possible or desirable. All my instincts are opposed to anything violent, and I do not believe that you and D.C. could separate without giving great pain to two or three people. If, in the depths of my heart, there were anything that would be glad of such an event, you would perhaps be justified in suspecting that my selfish instincts would in some form or other creep through my unselfish ones – my desire to see neither D.C., nor you, nor Lytton injured. But in a fairly free friendship I get all I want from D.C., and she, I believe, all she wants from me. A more intimate relationship with her I would regard with great misgivings. I talk lightly of marriage but, if it ever came to the point, you would see what a horror I have of it and how much I prize my liberty. I should not have thought it worth while saying this if you had not sometimes, half jokingly, spoken of a possible separation. Everything is possible, but at the same time this seems to me a thing above all to be avoided . . .

Well, it's late, past midnight, and I have run out of material. I think now I must eat something. Why, what insensitiveness! The chair opposite is hardly cold from the pressure of your body, and I feel very cheerful. I have written myself into a good mood, and you perhaps out of one.

Your visit brought nothing but happiness to Robinson Crusoe,[2] and if he has recovered from the sadness of your departure it is because he never stops thinking of you. I hope you are enjoying yourself with Frances; write me a long letter. If it is not rude, give her my love. I once saw her through a window and was told she was a great beauty; but great beauties at forty yards are indistinguishable to me from monsters, so that I can't say that I saw *his oculis*. (That's Latin for you!) This last inch of paper must contain my love to Lytton and a message to D.C. that my letter to her goes off tomorrow. And then my love to you.

Gerald

TIDMARSH, 21 JANUARY 1924

You there, you Yegener, it's you I'm writing to, partly because there's a railway strike, perhaps slightly because I've had a letter from you, but chiefly – no, I think entirely – because I'm thoroughly irritated, exasperated and almost senseless from the hard knocks at my brain delivered by the cold.

The china now – or, rather, what was once the china – is littering the library. About half the plates are broken, but none of the jugs. The great earthenware mandarin's hat received the coup de grace appropriately enough from the vigilant French at the Gâre d'Austerlitz (if they will call stations after battles you can hardly expect them to move your luggage intact). The carpets are dirty but entire; the iron contraption was fortunately made of iron, or it would have gone hard with it; your Irish pack-saddlery is best suited no doubt to Ireland, but it served.

Every meal today by electric light, and the garden flooded – that's England for you all over. D.C. lies in bed suffering from the effects of a remedy for sea-sickness. It goes better than sea-sickness, it almost

---

2. Gerald's own nickname for himself.

remedies life itself, the panacea for existence, a horrid lingering death, but effective, oh yes.

I went to Paris, as you know, and there I found a lady whom I thought I knew quite well; but I know singularly little now about her except that her hands have those nice blue veins running down them, that she likes pictures which I don't as well as those I do, that her face is a beautiful mask, and that the pupils of her eyes dilate strangely when she's thinking about something else – moreover (mark the correct use of the word) she has a nerve of iron; she walks into shops and out of them without 'the intention to buy'. We saw the Louvre from cover to cover, or from the p.c.'s of the Gioconda to the uttermost Corot . . .

As for Bunny, I hope you meet him in Almeria at your dentist's, take him up to the highest peaks of the Nevada, show him all the kingdoms of the Abencerrages (perhaps) and talk to him of Love, remembering the capital (you indicate it in pronunciation by a slight upward thrust of the chin, at the same time dropping the eyelids a millimetre). 'Bunny on Love' is the next thing I want to hear from you.

Shall I talk to you about D.C.? Or shan't I? I will see tomorrow.

Tomorrow has come and gone, and several moons more, and now I hear that Bunny has eluded my enquiries and that you never said a word to him from morning to night. How could you fail me so? . . . If I started to correct this letter I should say that the lady I met in Paris is, on the contrary, much better known to me now; but as the Parisian purge took several days to act, how was I to know that four days ago? Her charm and her sympathetic character are even more pronounced than I originally thought, and if only I could account for what she sees in Bunny I should feel I knew her intimately. But what's the lady to you? – a mere name rather rashly attached to a fleshy object seen without your glasses through a thick pane of glass.

But let's come to Carrington, to D.C., to the Great Gorgon with the heart-rending hair – the Gorgonzola, may we say? I do not dispute the attraction you have for each other, nor am I now made unhappy by it, because I am more reconciled to my own relation with her than I was. I do not perpetually watch jealously for signs of people making headway with her where I cannot. I used expressions suggesting that I might go away with Frances, or you with D.C., mainly from recklessness, because I like to play with the idea of being free, however much I'm really bound. Also, I believe, slightly because I wanted to see what effect such suggestions might have on D.C. I'm not satisfied that she is incapable of being jealous about Frances. When she gets ill or tired she very often makes unpleasant remarks about her and raises difficulties to my seeing her. She regrets them later, but her lack of jealousy is largely intellectual; she feels it is the keystone of her own liberties not to be jealous of mine. Where you will probably disagree with me is in my next statement. I believe D.C. to be actuated strongly by a desire to control and dominate – she won't let Lytton go, or me, at any price. If she feels sure of me, as she tries to make herself by pointing out to me the defects in my lady-loves, she doesn't take so much trouble about me and is readier to do things I dislike. If I say out loud, 'If I go off with Frances, or if G. goes off with you,' she senses that I am not tied hand and foot to her and is careful what she does so as not to hurt me. I think it legitimate, because it has been proved that she only believes what she wants to believe, unless it is constantly being pointed out to her that it is untrue. She is capable of thinking that the very fact that I can take her to you, leave you for long hours together and still feel quite happy, a valid reason for expecting further indulgences. Unfortunately one can never really sound her feelings. How much my position with her is due to our mutual positions with Lytton, I shall never know. All I know is that her affection for the two of us will influence her where her affection for me alone will not. To come to a more delicate question – her sexual desires are not great, mine are; she is unable to satisfy mine entirely, but in the ordinary course I ought to be able to satisfy hers. If, however, she were to find that she wanted sexual satisfaction apart from me, I should have some very paradoxical feelings – (i) inferiority feelings, that, half-sexed as she is and fully sexed as I am, I am unable to satisfy her; (ii) rage, that she should try to satisfy others when she refuses to satisfy me; (iii) revolt, that I should have to put up with a fraction of her already limited sexual feelings; (iv) jealousy, that I should have to share anything so small and yet so precious to me; (v) despair at losing the department in her where I have a monopoly, when she has monopolized so many of mine. The upshot would be certain – I should leave her for F. like a shot, and to remind her of that seems to me quite a prudent thing although it is rather a roundabout way of doing it in public. It is practically certain to my mind that the day I no longer care for D.C. sexually, the day when she is free to make her own sexual choices – that is, without worrying over me – will be followed within a few days by my departure to a fresh sexual object. I believe the sequence to be inevitable, but I do not feel sure whether these two events are absolutely desirable.

How stern and solemn this has become! I love you.

                                                                    Ralph

Dear Ralph,

Your coughs and colds and floods and electric light are too horrifying; shall I tell you how at Yegen the sun shines in the clear air and the almond trees are in blossom? But to confess the truth, it is a little cold and after breakfast I had to move down off the roof . . .

Bunny's visit was completely dull. He talked about you a good deal, but said only what one would expect him to say. A conversation he once had with you on how to seduce women had interested him; but afterwards he had thought, 'Are not these successive affairs a little dull and sordid?' The animal! As though he himself were not a kind of automaton at them! Then I told him that you were not an intellectual but a force of nature. Like the waves on the beach, you invigorated – I forget what it was now: some nonsense. He told me he thought 'Doric'[3] extremely intelligent. I disagreed and changed the subject, because it does not amuse me to discuss either you or her with other people. I could not have obtained revelations without myself talking intimately. But he was kind, friendly, amiable; if these qualities were enough to make people attractive, he would be extremely so. I made no headway with Ray; I thought she was probably rather a silly creature. I could see she didn't like me.

We discussed *Lady into Fox*, but only got so far as the punctuation, on whose correctness I bestowed praise. But, see my subtlety! I praised Defoe enormously; he was, I said, with Hardy our only novelist. Now Bunny is so much the reflection of Defoe that he might well take what I said as a compliment to himself. He was very bitter against Virginia[4] and I showed him, in the enthusiasm of a bottle of sherry, my two sonnets to her. He criticised them very sensibly, praising one or two lines and saying others were 'too appalling'. This frankness pleased me . . .

Your account of your relations with D.C., and so on, was very clear and frank. I confess that there are things about you that puzzle me. I cannot, for example, see how you can give this importance to 'copulation', 'satisfaction', and so on. And yet surely all men are alike in their sensations; I find it very pleasant, just as you do, but I do not make so many things hinge upon it. Perhaps if I were married I would alter in this respect. To tell you the truth, I am as ready to hate these things as I am to like them. I have never yet been able to control my sexual life properly,

3. i.e. Carrington.
4. Probably because she had not been enthusiastic about *Lady into Fox*.

and this is a constant motive for despair with me. If I were married to a woman who liked copulation, I should probably do this two or three times a week. But I should be miserable, because I should find regular work impossible.

Artists, scientists, and so on, must live fairly chastely. If one does not have to spend part of one's day alone in the endeavour to concentrate one's mind, if one does not feel the necessity of having one's mind sensitive to aesthetic impression, one does not notice the insidious and fatal effects of it. As I have little self-control in this myself, I pray never to be married to a woman who was not naturally much chaster than I am. It is habit that I dread in these things. In my mind there are always so many obstacles to going to bed for the first time that it is only after a certain passage of time that a woman can appear to me sexually exciting . . . At least that has so far been my experience. These sudden movements of lechery which you described to me, when you have to get up and walk about, I scarcely understand. To sum up, I do not think that physically I am cold; indeed I wish I were; but my mental processes are more independent of my physical cravings than yours are. The function of the latter is sometimes to create a pleasure that I approve of, but more often to impair the proper working of the former.

Well, is this not dreary? Let us stop. I am tired of analyses. But you are wrong in thinking that I do not wish to hear about F[rances] M[arshall]. I am very interested . . . Love.

Gerald.

PART TWO   1924–1934

After five years of self-imposed exile Gerald decided to go back to England, where his great-aunt was very anxious to have him. He left Yegen at the end of March and reached London early in April. Carrington was at Victoria Station to meet him.

He was greeted by a letter from his father threatening to cut off his allowance unless he got down to some serious work. But what work? All he had ever wanted to be was a poet, but he could hardly expect to earn his living by poetry. He would therefore have to embark on some other form of literature and, since he had not had enough experience of the world to write a novel, he contemplated a biography. But of whom? St Theresa seemed to be as good a subject as any, so he decided to try his hand at her. Having managed to convince his father of the seriousness of his intentions, he joined the London Library, got a ticket for the British Museum Reading Room, and moved into a cheap bed-sitter in nearby Millman Street.

25 JUNE 1924

Dear Ralph,

. . . I enjoyed seeing you very much. Will you come again? And I should like my room to be of use to you and Frances. Please tell me when you want it, and *never* be afraid that I have reactions afterwards. When you are in a friendly mood you are so much more sympathetic to me than anyone else, and you help me to be reasonable.

The worst horror of all agitations is that they deprive one of one's power of making judgements. Everything melts and swims and becomes uncertain. Truth has disappeared and everything fluctuates from one extreme to the other. You are far the most sympathetic person I know, and the best. I too often forget this and treat you casually; but you should know that beneath this I do attach a very high value to your friendship.

Gerald

Gerald's 'agitations' – since his return to England he had been suffering from insomnia and nervous depression – were due to Carrington. In spite of himself he was in love with her again. But her feelings towards him were ambivalent. They wrote to each other almost every day, but Ralph still insisted on his right to read their letters, so that Gerald was never able to express what he really felt. From time to time she came up to London and spent the night with him, and now and then he went down to Tidmarsh for the weekend. But this was not enough for him and when, in the early summer, the move into Ham Spray began, she was kept very busy and had even less time to spare.

At the beginning of August he went down to Kent to spend the summer holidays with the Anreps[5] at their beach cottage, Warren End, on Romney Marsh. They needed a tutor for their children, Anastasia and Igor; and Carrington, who was a friend of theirs, had suggested him. On 8 September Carrington arrived at Warren End on a long-promised visit. It was not a success. She spent the first night with Gerald and he made love to her again and again; but all next day they quarrelled and she left early next morning. A few days later she wrote to him and they made it up.

HAM SPRAY, n.d.

My dearest Gerald,

You very nicely let me sleep in your room long, long ago, which was extremely useful to me at the time; only I found that all your instructions were askew. The keys opened the door quite easily; the bolts and bars you had installed are quite useless except when you're in the flat, and then they're superfluous.

We have just had 3 weeks of Barbarism[6] and even now it remains at our door, in a farm at Shalbourne barely 2 miles away. Fortunately they are uphill miles . . . Now we have Alec Penrose[7] and Philip Ritchie[8] and tomorrow we have Ray Strachey,[9] on Saturday Richard Braithwaite[1], next week Dadie[2], and so on. Will you please come and stay either here or at the inn at Ham as soon as you can. Morgan [E. M. Forster] came for a weekend. I go on liking him but he is terribly difficult to get on with. His sense of humour is so insistent, and his inflection of voice so undeviating, that conversation never seems to improve or deteriorate with him. It is fixed from the start, and a conversation that has no possibility of doing anything venturesome has no attraction for me. But Morgan I like – his friendliness and his kindliness make it impossible to dislike him, and yet it isn't very thrilling . . .

What a poor opinion you have of me, but what of the opinion I have of you? – hmm! 'He's Irish,' says Morgan. 'Very,' say I. 'But nice.' '*De temps en temps.*' I hope you're enjoying yourself. Yours,

Ralph

5. Boris Anrep, a Russian, was beginning to be known as the leading mosaic artist in Europe. His wife Helen, *née* Maitland, had been the mistress of the painter Henry Lamb and was about to leave Boris for the painter and art critic Roger Fry.
6. i.e. Barbara Bagenal.
7. Eldest of the four sons of the painter James Doyle Penrose and Elizabeth Josephine, daughter of Lord Peckover, a Quaker banker.
8. The Hon. Philip Charles Thomson Ritchie, eldest son of Lord Ritchie of Dundee, was a new love of Lytton's.
9. *Née* Costelloe, second wife of Lytton's brother Oliver.
1. Richard Bevan Braithwaite, moral philosopher, Scholar of King's College, Cambridge, an Apostle, and a member of Maynard Keynes's inner circle.
2. George Humphrey Wolferstan Rylands, Scholar of Eton, later Fellow, Dean and Bursar at King's.

Gerald did not return to London until 8 October, when he moved into a studio at 18 Fitzroy Street which he rented from Roger Fry for 15 shillings a week. Carrington had promised to dine there with him and make love, but refused to spend the night because, she said, the studio was dirty, noisy, and smelt of cats. They quarrelled again, and again were reconciled. But not for long. Quarrels and reconciliations continued throughout the autumn, increasing in violence very time. They therefore agreed to stop seeing or writing to each other until the New Year.

They met again by chance at the Anreps' house in Hampstead and decided to renew their relations. These improved so much that early in May she suggested finding lodgings for him in Shalbourne (probably in the same farmhouse where Barbara Bagenal had stayed). This would make it possible for them to see each other more easily and more often. He agreed with enthusiasm. But no sooner had this new phase begun than the scenes and quarrels started up again. By mid-summer it was all over.

27 JULY 1925

My dear Ralph,

If you come up this week could you bring with you my books and clothes from Shalbourne, leave them at Paddington and post me the ticket to Fitzroy St. I am going to Gloucestershire³ in a week, then abroad, and would like to collect my things before starting.

You will have heard that I have broken definitely with Carrington; everything had in fact of its own accord come to an end and there was nothing more to be done than to recognise it. Such – not very different from an affair with Marjorie Joad – is the course of these life-long friendships. But perhaps the less I say about it at present, the better.

You will not mind if I avoid seeing you for some time.

Gerald

Gerald had been working steadily for a year at his biography of St Theresa when, one September afternoon, as he sat on the top of a bus on the way to have tea with his great-aunt, he had a strange experience. He found himself occupying the mind of a person who was very different from himself and feeling that person's thoughts and words pour through him. He got off at Victoria Station, bought an exercise book and a pencil, sat down on a bench and began to write. He wrote for several hours, and many hours more during the next few days, before he realized that he was writing a novel in diary form about a man called Tom Fisher who was spending the summer in precisely that cottage on the Kentish coast where he had stayed the previous year with the Anreps.

3. To stay with his parents. But he didn't go abroad until the following spring.

Dear Ralph,

I lie here on my couch, I can't move, I can't read, I can't think. My head turns; I can do nothing better than write you a letter. I have climbed on to so many buses, seen so many people, talked so incessantly, that now I feel as though I were going to have pneumonia . . . I hope soon to go back to Theresa and Mr Fisher. This brings me to the motive of my letter. Helen told me that you or C. imagined that some of this book was taken out of our relations during the last few years. That is not the case. Incidents, characters, even feelings, all are purely invented and are on a different level to ordinary experience. Boris also fears that it is an account of himself, with almost less truth. The fact is that, being a very sordid, horrible, disgusting, cruel, stupid story, everyone will quite naturally see in it his own biography. It gives me great pleasure to write, everything being told in a light, amusing and fantastic manner; but the difficulty of some of the scenes is so great that I doubt if I can do them.[4] At least, since I came to London, depression and headaches and insomnia have made me doubtful if I shall ever write a line again. Oh, I am tired. I wish myself back by the sea or, if the rain would stop, in the country. One's senses are starved in London. People exhaust one . . . When I think of this last year, of the pain I suffered and still do suffer, of the rapidity, the ease, the cynicism with which people remove the affection they have given, I am frightened. It seems better to live without attachments than to risk these catastrophes. And yet the arguments will neither prevent one from falling in love nor assist it.

Why did you ever come out to Spain 3 years ago? For I cannot think that any other woman would have wound in the affection she had given so rapidly and completely as C. . . . But I write on a subject I am determined I will not write on or speak of except to one person. Unfortunately it occupies my thoughts incessantly – is it possible, I ask myself, is it conceivable? . . . How absolutely, how entirely, during the 3 months' correspondence that followed your visit to Yegen, C. led me to love her and believe in her affection for me. All mirage, all mistake, all flattery! Or nearly all. Or else women can step into a sort of affection like

4. In fact he found himself unable for the time being to continue with such a difficult task. So he put it away, though for many years he kept a notebook of Tom Fisher's peculiar thoughts and images which would come into his head at odd moments. In the summer of 1950 he took it up again, then stopped a second time, and it was not until 1956 that he made up his mind to go through with it. He finished it in 1960, and in 1961 it was published by Hamish Hamilton under the title of *A Holiday by the Sea*.

actors into their parts. I do not know. I understand less and less and grow, it seems to me, more uncomprehending, more embittered. I think that now I only wish to live in order to write; and I mean, by write, *brand* on to the paper some of the horrors of life, show how the natural happiness of being alive is torn and poisoned by the cruelty, the uncertainty, the stupidity of human relations. I have a theme to fill a hundred books and, when I am well and have no headaches, characters and situations crowd into my head. After all one cannot exaggerate the irony of life . . . I am only happy now when I can write; in that I seem to redress the balance against me, to repay some of the damage I have received . . .

Gerald

10 DECEMBER 1925

Dear Ralph,
    . . . I have done nothing but visit and chatter for two days and have amassed some gossip . . . My most amusing is of a party which Sebastian[5] gave at Nottingham to his fellow professors; they got very drunk and began to show a kind of gauche amorousness. His is apparently the centre of a small but enthusiastic circle; lank-haired lady professors sit at his feet and awkward red-faced young men drink in, rather in gulps, the new doctrine. All Nottingham is shocked by the spectacle of him and his servant . . .

I had tea yesterday with Virginia. She was at first in her most provoking mood, took everything I said in its most stupid sense, and paid a great deal of attention to quite trivial things when Sanger[6] said them. As soon as he had gone she changed and became altogether charming. 'I hear, Gerald, that Roger Fry is madly in love with Helen Anrep and that you've been in it from the very beginning . . .' But I am tired and cannot write any more conversations for your benefit.

We had a conversation at the Café Royal last night about happiness. I was held up as an example of a happy character and did not contradict it. What do people mean? In company I am neither happy nor unhappy but, at my best, animated. Alone, whenever I have any feeling about my

5. W. J. H. (Sebastian) Sprott, Lecturer in Psychology at Nottingham University, was one of a new generation of Apostles gathered round the distinguished Cambridge economist Maynard Keynes.
6. Charles Percy Sanger, Chancery barrister, friend and contemporary of Bertrand Russell and R. C. Trevelyan at Trinity College, Cambridge.

private life, I am melancholy. But this melancholy I hardly ever carry into my relations with other people, because it is incommunicable, it is for the time suspended. For the last 4 months I have kept a very detailed diary of my own feelings. I find on reading it over that not one of the entries made in London is happy; some are very miserable and embittered . . . It is, in my experience, human relations that more than anything else give this character of unhappiness to life; if one were the only person in the world one would be dull but happy. Yet whilst I see this perfectly clearly, a great deal of my energy is spent in forming new friendships. The one that fills me just now with the greatest hope and expectation is that with Lettice Kirkpatrick,[7] whom I met at a party but, because she attracted me very much by her air of gaiety and affection, most carefully avoided. I have everybody's taste in young women. I like vitality, youth, a little character, a little beauty, and as much human feeling as possible. The oddities leave me cold and I dread anything neurotic. Do you see how conventional I am becoming? The conventions are nearly always the line of least resistance, and that is all that I am any longer fit for.

But I am too sleepy to write any longer. You were so charming last time I saw you – and the time before so superior and grumpy – that I thought I would treat you to some of my store of gossip. But though I have written three pages I see I have said nothing of any interest and that it is all very muddle-headed. Goodnight.

Gerald

In the autumn of 1925 Ralph and Frances had gone to the south of Spain together. When they returned to England she knew she was in love with him. So the eventuality which Carrington had always dreaded – the break-up of the Ham Spray ménage – had arrived. She was saved from having to face it by the generosity of Frances, who suggested a compromise. She and Ralph were to rent a flat in London, but would go down often to Ham Spray. So in May 1926 they settled into the rooms at 41 Gordon Square where Ralph had lived previously with Carrington. He told Gerald that he now regarded himself as married to Frances and that his feelings for Carrington, though still very strong, were more like those of a brother. Gerald's own feelings for her still oscillated between love and hate. He had decided to live for a few months in the south of France and before leaving England he arranged a meeting with her – the first since their breach in the previous summer – at which they agreed to resume their old correspondence.

7. The handsome daughter of an engineer who built the largest dockyard on the Thames. Later she married a much older man, a doctor, and left him.

PARIS 3 JUNE 1926

Dear Ralph,

I am incorrigible, hopeless, irremediable in my management of money. I complicate my own life beyond endurance and now give, I fear, irritation and inconvenience to my friends. I will tell you the new story of my difficulties. I went to the Louvre[8] immediately on getting your money and bought you 4 tablecloths and 8 napkins for 180 francs, which is what one would pay for them in England. I was intending to leave that night for Toulon, though I had not grasped that what with my hotel bill and railway fare I had only *just* enough for the journey. But your commission brought me this adventure.

I left the book I was reading in the shop and when in a bad hour I returned to fetch it I found a young and very pretty English girl trying to make herself understood. I interpreted; this led to long explanations; the long explanations to taking tea together. Her situation in Paris seemed to me mysterious and I asked her to dine with me. We dined. She was unfortunately committed to going on a charabanc tour round Montmartre with some American friends, but she agreed to meet me when this was finished at midnight. I missed her through an accident and when I got to her hotel behind the Madeleine I found her in bed. We had a conversation through the door. This was disappointing as she had appeared to take an extraordinary interest in me, had seized my hand in the taxi and let me embrace her . . . and, though telling me quite frankly in an odd way of hers that she was resolved 'to keep something for her husband when she married', had yet given me to understand that, on condition of my observing this, she *might* spend the night with me.

Then who was she? Why alone in Paris? She was very secretive about herself.

I came home, however, resolved to leave the next day for Toulon; to my surprise, on counting my money, I found I should not have enough by some fifty francs. This put me in a great state of despondency, remorse for my imbecility, fears as to the complete hopelessness of my character, with the effect that this must have upon my writing. I wired therefore to you, telephoned to Elaine asking her to come to the Closerie des Lilas, and began this letter. She came; I explained my situation; we had lunch together at a cheap restaurant, she offering to pay her share. The hotel-keeper had moved me into the room occupied by you and

8. The department store, not the picture gallery.

Frances;[9] I took her there after lunch 'to hear the gramophone'. She would not take off her clothes, but we embraced in a rather perfunctory way upon the bed. She seemed very shy and timid and at the same time, in little bursts, audacious and passionate.

Her history is as follows. She is the daughter of a rich tradesman who has married again and settled near the Crystal Palace. She does not get on with her stepmother and is allowed to live where she pleases under colour of 'studying languages'. She has travelled about Europe, usually with American friends, and is engaged to marry a Czechoslovak. Her character is not very interesting – her chief interest is in motor-cars, and she was once in love with a man who designed motor engines. Her age, 21. You see what this amounts to – but add to this that she is very, very pretty, vivacious, passionate. It seemed to me impossible that she should not have had various love affairs. We went out for a walk and returned to my room after tea. She became extraordinarily affectionate and allowed me to take off most of her clothes. I was able to give her a certain amount of pleasure; she then broke out into a kind of ecstasy. She had never known that before, had never thought so much pleasure was possible . . .

She seems actually to be in love with me. We hold hands continually, look into each other's eyes, and everywhere – in restaurants, in the street – she kisses me. Then this is the happiness so greatly longed for, fallen upon my head like a thunder shower! And yet so little built am I for the Nirvana-states of love that I am delighted at the thought of setting off today without fail. She, it seems, will follow me later to Toulon en route for Czechoslovakia. I look forward to a few nights with this lovely and passionate creature, but by day my taste for some sensible occupation will assert itself and she will begin to bore me . . . If one is ever right in being flattered by the devotion of young women, I should feel flattered by this; for (for the first time in my life) I feel that what has happened to this young woman could not have been brought about by any other newcomer.

Your money has just come. Thank you a thousand thousand times; you are a perfect friend and I hope that some time you will find yourself in even greater difficulties so that I may step in to assist you! In any case you'll have the money back almost immediately. I hope the cloths will be satisfactory. They are, I am sure, just what one gets at

9. Ralph and Frances had stayed at the same hotel, the Pas de Calais, on their way back from their holiday in Spain.

Harrods, but there were no better ones available. My love to you and Frances.

Gerald

TOULON, 4 JUNE 1926

Mon très cher ami,

I left the arms of my beautiful Elaine – is not this how I ought to begin? – to step into a 3rd-class railway carriage and rattle through the night in company of 5 Armenians of the poorest class. One had leprosy and groaned till I felt obliged to give him my pillow, after which I conceived a perfect detestation for his yellow spotty face; another talked to me of boy-scouts and football in almost unintelligible French; and the women tucked their feet under their skirts and scratched themselves. At Avignon two schoolmistresses and 11 children got in and I preferred to leave and stand up in the corridor, where there was the usual smell as though four or five people had eaten a dinner of fish and then been sick. The schoolmistresses were perfect. One was very thick and podgy and with poodle eyes; she never looked at me but took every opportunity she could to rub herself against me as though I were a post for removing flies. The other was very cheerful and talkative and was perpetually taking parcels off the rack and putting them back on it and arranging in what order the children should get out of the carriage when, at the end of two hours, they should reach their destination . . . And when this order had at last been arranged, and the children catechised, she began all over again on a new concatenation by which the eldest got out last. I could bear her voice no longer; I abandoned my luggage and moved into another carriage.

By this terrible journey on a wooden seat I saved 7/–, which at any moment in Paris I was ready to throw away on a trifle. For what reason? I will confess a secret. Railway journeys are one of the occasions when I like to fall back into a life of poverty for a moment and become simply an anonymous unit indistinguishable from a million others. From these experiences I draw a feeling of the greater *reality* of my own life. And then to wake up in some stuffy den and see beyond the panes of glass the stars paling and the dawn altering the fields gives me sometimes by its contrast a secret ecstasy. I cannot express the sense of ease and freedom and happiness I feel in being alone where no one can ask me questions or expect me to unroll thoughts or feelings or opinions on any subject. A change of habit often throws a new light on one's own character. I realize now for the first time what a quantity of effort and trouble conversation costs me; when I am alone and relieved of this drain my life at once becomes richer and more varied. I begin to think and to feel from the moment when I cease to chatter. Yet every evening, towards 6 or 7, a vague melancholy creeps over the landscape. A few days ago my over-estimation of the happiness of love affairs was the cause of it; now it is the loss of Elaine, whose charm has moved me more than I thought possible.

I spent yesterday afternoon with her in a room which I took off the Rue de Montmartre. Her extreme youth, the loveliness of her body, her gaiety and especially that appetite for love affairs – such as young swallows have for the air when, scarcely fledged, they dive off the house-top into it and at once know all the plunges, all the passes – reminded me of the young women whom Casanova lay with in four-poster beds, by candle-light, with supper laid on a table by their side. The young women I have generally had to do with have had little of this responsiveness, little sense too for the geography of the male body – rather they seem to lie there in expectation that they are going to be massaged very agreeably. Elaine was the exact reverse.

In conversation, in bed, the secret which I felt she was keeping from me came out. When she was 17 she became infatuated with a married man of 35. He was violent-tempered, jealous, brutal, masculine – exactly what all girls of 17 ask for. She felt no pleasure at all and a month later saw she was going to have a child. She had an operation, which upset her health and nerves very greatly. Since then she has felt such a repulsion and fear of physical love affairs that she has always backed out at the last moment, but she 'felt confidence in me' and that is why I was able to reap this harvest of gratitude and pleasure. I seem indeed to have upset her plans in several directions; she has decided not to go to Czechoslovakia to her fiancé as she thinks he would be too cold a husband for her; she will return instead to London. She proposes that we should live together this autumn in Paris – 'for me the only point in marriage is that I may have a car of my own, which I can't afford at present.' But, alas, perfect as she is by night, by day she would bore me desperately. She cares only for cars and for tennis; nothing else interests her. I could not endure it over a week. If she had only the curiosity and adaptability of Anne Moore,[1] she would do; for nothing would suit me better this winter than to have a mistress. As a writer I fear the isolation from human beings which this strolling life directly leads to.

1. A working-class girl whom Gerald had picked up in London. It intrigued him that she had the same name as the wife of the poet John Donne.

Saturday. Toulon is a very charming town, with narrow streets, good cafés and crowded plane trees. I pay every compliment to Frankie [Francis Birrell]'s good taste, tell him, and civilized manners in recommending me this town, for no other place on the coast is humanly habitable. From 10 in the morning to 8 at night there blows a violent hurricane; when the mountains prevent its blowing from the north it comes over the sea with redoubled violence. When, late at night, the air being still, one walks out into the country, everything – pine-trees, rocks, ant-heaps – are deep in dust. As for *walking* out of Toulon, one cannot do it; railway tracks, blank walls and advertisements for BYRRH utterly frustrate it. But in five minutes one can cross the harbour and find oneself at once in the wilds, looking, that is, at scrubby little trees and dirty little stones, whilst behind one a sheer mountain rises, all rock and schist, out of a sea which smells of dye-works and is the colour of a chromolithograph.

I saw Cassis on the way here – some wretched little trees and precipitous rocks and dust and urine, with an abominable architecture. How much longer shall we continue to bow the knee to these barbarous painters who sacrifice all the amenities of life for an unchanging light and two or three yellow lumps on the horizon?

Perhaps I am jaundiced this morning – wherever I go, a taste of fish. Have I caught the Armenian's leprosy? I suspend my final judgement of this country, therefore, until next week and end this letter. My love to you and Frances – but tell me, don't you get tired of this mutual love? I have had in 2 days enough holding hands and gazing into eyes to last me 3 weeks – and then, consider, there was all the charm of the novelty! How you go on year after year is most surprising and, I think, very creditable. Some day I'll ask you to explain it for my instruction.

Gerald

During all that summer and autumn Gerald kept working at his biography of St Theresa, but got more and more bored with it. Then he started a picaresque novel about a commercial traveller, but this too went badly. Ralph and Frances, who came out to visit him for a few days, urged him to drop both these tasks and embark on something easier. He had recently come upon a pamphlet by the Spanish satirist Francisco Gómez de Quevedo y Villegas (1580–1645), which Swift later made use of in his famous spoof prophesy of the death of the astrologer John Partridge. This piece must have been at the back of his mind when one evening he started writing, without any previous plan or intention and almost as though the words were dictated to him. He went on till four in the morning and took it up again next day. By nightfall he found he had all but completed a short volume, to which he gave the finishing touches during the following three weeks.

TOULON, n.d.

Dear Ralph,

I think I must be one of those persons to whom the parable of Balak and Balaam is applicable. When I set out to write a book in 3 weeks to make money, the voice of God speaks through me in tones so cynical and disagreeable that only the most hardened readers will listen to it. Heinemann will never take my book, nor will C[hatto] and W[indus];[2] though if someone else publishes it, it will serve to make my new picaresque novel[3] more sellable . . . I really hope to finish the Introduction (which is all that matters) before I leave Toulon . . . You shall have myself and the Almanack together in the early part of next week.

Gerald

Gerald was due to return to London in the middle of November and Carrington, with whom he had been corresponding regularly, agreed to meet him in Paris. She spent the night with him there; but when they reached Calais next day she insisted that they separate on the boat because in a sudden access of respectability she feared he might be taken for her lover. This did not augur well for the future of their relations.

When he got back to London he found that Roger Fry's studio in Fitzroy Street was no longer available, so he had to look for other quarters at once. Carrington showed a great interest in the flat he eventually found, on the top floor of 14 Great James Street, and helped him with the furnishing and decorating. But very soon they were quarrelling as violently as ever. Luckily he was by now less in love with her, and so was less affected by the scenes and reconciliations that succeeded one another for the next two years. Long before his final breach with her, in the autumn of 1928, he had become involved with several other girls, most of whom he picked up in the street.

Meanwhile his great-aunt's mind had started to go and she began to suffer from delusions. For her own safety, he and his father had her certified and committed to a small private asylum run by Catholic nuns. She settled in happily and he visited her several times; but after a few months she ceased to recognise him and, since there was now nothing else to keep him in England, he decided to go back to Spain.

YEGEN, 13 MAY 1929

My dear Ralph,

Imagine, if you can, someone that looks very like myself, but is not yet myself, sitting by a fire of brushwood and green ilex logs in the *granero*.[4] Outside the window the sun is shining, the birds are singing, the roses in the garden in flower, and the shadows floating over the Sierra de Gador. If you can imagine this or believe it possible you are luckier than I am for,

2. Chatto and Windus did in fact publish it, but not until 1934, under the title of *Dr Partridge's Almanack* and under the nom-de-plume of George Beaton.
3. But this novel was never published, nor even finished.
4. The granary, which Gerald used as a sitting-room.

though every second tiny messengers hammer at my eyes and ears telling me that it is so, I can do neither. Except that five cherry-trees have been planted in the plaza by order of the Dictator,[5] and that all the little girls have become *mozuelas*[6] and all the *mozuelas* are married and have several children, there is not the slightest alteration in Yegen . . .

I arrived on Friday after midnight. The beauty of the green trees and running water and starlit mountains astonished me – then of the house, which surpassed all my expectations. It had been whitewashed from end to end, it seemed so large and, like a greenhouse which gets its light from inside (from the natural phosphorescence of the walls) instead of from without, it was full of green shrubs and trailing plants and flowers. In the hall and *granero* were pots of arum lilies, and in all the chief rooms vases of lilies, roses and seringa.

The delight of Maria and Angela[7] was another thing that surprised me. Maria is just the same, but Angela has completely altered. She has become a lovely and *very* charming girl of seventeen, with the same gaiety and cynicism and love of peace and quiet that her father had. But just as he, the most intelligent man in Yegen, was an agnostic, so she, being quite uneducated, is, by just the same qualities, pious and goes to Mass every Sunday. For Maria and most of the noisy quarrelsome people who come to this house are all *condenados* and go to Mass at most once a year. For four years and more she has said her prayers every night before an image of San Geraldo, which with the aid of a papal missionary she obtained from some nuns in Granada, and the result is that she is in a chaste way a little in love with me. As we are alone in the house together most of the day – for Maria, more frantic and restless than ever, is perpetually washing clothes with a row of harpies, or planting melon seed, or milking goats, or on some errand – I find that very delightful. And I am confident that I shall never break the charm by making love to her . . . The old kitchen that you knew, they don't use much; they prefer the inner one with the baking oven which I made, whilst I live in the *granero*. The house is as silent as a tomb, as clean and fresh as this sheet of paper, and they seem to anticipate all my wants before I express them. As I have brought out about 80 records, including a number of Spanish ones and 'Ramona', which (after a 9 months' vendetta) I have taken to heart, we have concerts in the evenings. The

5. General Miguel Primo de Rivera, who had ruled Spain since 1923.
6. Young women.
7. Angela was the daughter of Gerald's maid Maria, fathered on her by his late landlord Don Fernando.

visitors have been an infliction; most of them would earn first prizes for boredom in any country. I have just, for instance, learned that the 'Indians of India' do not like the English, that my countrymen are dying of smallpox, and that America (the nation that will fight us in the next war) is building a canal at Panama. And I have had to give the interesting information that neither figs, nor grapes, nor pomegranates, nor oranges, nor even prickly pears or bananas, can be grown in England. It is the more simple ones that ask these questions; the *educated* know that they cannot do so on account of the dense black fog. Only one man is interesting to talk to – the shopkeeper. He has spent five years trading with Indians all the way from Ecuador to the Argentine and up again to Paraguay and Brazil, and liked it. They asked a lot of questions about you and Carrington, and were especially curious to know how many children you have had. 'None at all,' I said, but to save your honour I have had to climb down a bit and remember half a dozen that died in infancy. Maria and Angela send you and C. their love.

Perhaps you have already guessed from the flat style of this letter that I have the flu. That is to say I feel very tired by day and wake up several times in the night soaking wet with perspiration. The sun is hot, the air cold, and so one catches complaints unlike any that one suffers from in England. I feel the fragility of life more strongly here than anywhere else; one might develop pneumonia and die at any moment, and then one would be put, like a bundle of legal documents, into a drawer in that horrible columbarium.[8] All my Gothic blood rises against it. I chose long ago my grave on the summit of the little hill overlooking the village and tomorrow I am going to have another look at it. Unfortunately there is not the least chance that they will let me be buried there. How do you tell when you have a temperature? I put my hand or arm in my mouth and I know I have one if it tastes sour.

Do you know I have once more performed my old feat of reaching my destination penniless? I left London with over 1000 pesetas and arrived here with 1.25. I need no money in this village except for stamps, and within a day or two some is coming. In the ten days I spent in Almeria I wrote some 50 pages, about the best, I think, I have ever written (at any rate the most controlled, the most consistent) and much above the level of any other part of *Jack Robinson*.[9] They described the illness and death

8. Space is so limited in Spanish village cemeteries that many corpses are pigeon-holed in cavities in the walls.

9. The new book on which Gerald was working after abandoning his novel about the commercial traveller. It was published by Chatto & Windus in 1933.

of a character called Lily[1] and in the course of it I took my reader on one of those long walks (instituted by [James] Joyce, copied by Virginia and almost *de rigueur* in a modern novel) round the streets of my favourite city. My itinerary was not Virginia's, my hour was not day but night, my weather was not fair but foul, I was traversing not a civilized and refined but a barbarian and monstrous capital; yet I think the streets of London ought to rise up and bow to thank me, since I am sure no one has ever before offered them in words such passionate and heartfelt adulation as I have.

This morning a charming letter from Frances, which has made me feel very gay. I will answer it, tell her, in a day or two. Winny[2] is always doing things that astonish me; she has written me two very lively, very long letters – just when I thought she was completely tired of me ...

Whilst I am here I hope to divide myself a little more and let that part of me which judges and which writes retire a few paces up the slope of the hill behind, whatever you like to call it – the arena, Tom Tiddler's ground, the field hospital where one suffers one amputation after another, the putridorium. With regrets at ending on a morbid note when my feelings are so cheerful, and much love to you and Frances. Yours,

Gerald

YEGEN, 2 JULY 1929

My dear Ralph,

I am sorry to hear you and Frances cannot come out now; this is the finest time in the year for a visit. But I forget the attractions of London. I am not going to write you a letter, for I slept badly and my head is tired. Nor is there much to say. My life is uneventful. I eat a great many cherries and nectarines, read when I feel inclined, and make love very indolently to two sister shepherdesses – one of whom apparently likes me, the other even more apparently does not. In the evenings we dance and drink brandy. Then I go to bed on the roof, where I sleep till sunrise under a sky of extraordinary brilliance. A week ago I walked far above the snow-line to see the streams rushing out of caves of snow on to green meadows. I walked about 45 miles and climbed in all about 12,000 feet, but I was tired for two days after. So perhaps I shall have to renounce Mount Everest!

1. Based on a real person, Lily Holden or Connolly, a prostitute Gerald had picked up in Greek Street, Soho.
2. Winny Stafford, one of the Cockney girls Gerald had lived with in London.

I have had an offer of marriage. Doña Clara[3] told me it was the wish of her heart that I should enter their family; therefore, she said, if I would marry Angela, whose charm I had praised to her, she would give her as dowry her father's very large property at Yegen including a great stretch of mountain pasture and, on her death, the house and land near Granada. Since I have declined this offer, the poor girl, it seems, is to receive nothing.

Tomorrow I am off for three days to Almeria, to stew and boil and make myself sad at the sight of the fishermen's daughters bathing in the sea. The call of the pavement. It has taken me 35 years to find out that I belong to cities . . . But my omelette and my cheese curds are waiting for me. I finish.

Gerald

41 GORDON SQUARE, 22 JULY 1929

Dear Gerald,

You have surely heard that Tiz died on the 14th. I found a letter here when I got back this afternoon, to say that I and Mr Ernest Garnett[3a] must prove the will as you are in Spain. There is clearly no need for you to do anything. The will has to be obtained from Lloyds Bank and I will keep you informed of whatever happens, but there won't be any difficulty before they get probate. After that you'll have to decide whether you want your shares transferred to your name, or sold out and the money transferred to you. I don't know if you can draw any money direct before probate, but if you can't I'll arrange with the bank to continue paying at least whatever your allowance was into your account, if you'll tell me where it is and how you draw on it from Spain. Will you stay in Spain? I should, at any rate until we get probate, because you won't be able to control the money until then and there isn't anything for you to do about it. My father's probate took 4 or 5 months, I think, and his will was quite straightforward, so I expect this is the ordinary minimum time. The lawyer's letter was the first I heard of her death. I was going to write to you today anyhow, but this event has rather disorganized my thoughts.

I have been to Amsterdam and since that to Ham Spray, to

---

3. The widow of Gerald's landlord Don Fernando, who fathered Angela on Gerald's maid Maria.
3a. Ralph's co-executor; no relation to Bunny Garnett.

Charleston[4] (to stay with Raymond[5] and Frankie [Birrell]) and for the weekend to Owley.[6] Now we shall be here for some time, probably till September, when we were thinking of Yegen if our money would take us as far and our host were still there. Lytton, Carrington, Sebastian [Sprott] and I went to Holland for eight days. If I ever wished to cure myself of lust, I should go and look at the Dutch. They have all the repellent qualities – lack of vitality, lack of taste, lack of beauty and a nonconformist religion. They are also abominably tidy and dote on insipid cheese. At the cinemas no one under 18 is allowed to look at Greta Garbo. The national drink is gin. The national costumes are despicable. The national part of the body is the bottom, and the national joke is babies shitting. What an austere setting for Rembrandt to develop his technique and sensibilities! There are many beautiful houses, particularly the warehouses along the canals. But all that water carries the night sounds afar, and night is dreadful in Amsterdam with trams and trains and unceasing chiming from belfries. And superadded to everything, the expense – nothing is to be had for less than 1/8, an absurd sum but ruinous in no time.

Ham Spray was a great relief. The weather became dependable and pleasant, and we found a crop of mushrooms on the downs waiting to be picked. No visitors disturbed us. We bathed in the river and were joined by voluptuous ploughboys, one of whom, in a blue bathing dress, struck my fancy so strongly that I could quite imagine myself making improper suggestions to him. As it was, I examined his foot carefully when he cut it, and told him to tie it up.

At Charleston journalism was supreme. Frankie and Raymond simply revel in it – no book can be talked of, except for publication. They review everything, they have an attitude ready for any surprise, they are so astute that you can't possibly catch them out, they have written a play which is so amusing it can't fail to succeed; the BBC cannot do without them; everywhere they are indispensable and triumphant; there can be no doubt they have thoroughly 'arrived'. Lady Colefax[7] came to lunch oen day, being driven from London in a car just for the pleasure of seeing Charleston for the first time in her life. She was enthusiastic and we were all as kind as we could be to her. *I* thought her a charming woman and I

4. Vanessa Bell's house in Sussex, a Bloomsbury stronghold.
5. Raymond Mortimer, the literary critic.
6. A beautiful old house in Kent belonging to Frances's eldest sister Julia (Judy) Rendel and her family.
7. The famous London hostess, *née* Sibyl Halsey, celebrated for her indefatigable pursuit of 'interesting' people.

like Raymond v̄ery much and have the greatest affection for Frankie; but they buzz rather too much for a fogey like me, who am amazed if I can ever find anything to say in company.

Poppet and Vivien[7a] have saved a young man from drowning – quite a pretty young man to judge by his photograph in the papers. They dived into the river at Fordingbridge and fished him out and applied artificial respiration and kissed him so frantically that he returned from unconsciousness to find that he had an erection, but there was no photo of *that* . . . Have you heard that Valentine [Dobrée] is at last with child? She has returned to England and is said to be going in for children and farm life in the country. I wonder who the successful, the miraculous father can be. Some say a man from India did it in Egypt – one of the Magi perhaps, at any rate a wonder-worker from the East. That's a titbit of news in this dull summer. Love. Yours,

                                                                                       Ralph

                                                             YEGEN, I AUGUST 1929
Dear Ralph,
    I will send you a few words by return. I am very glad to hear you are coming out in September. Saxon [Sydney-Turner] thinks of coming too, with or without Barbara [Bagenal]. I really do not want B. and in any case, with you here, it would not be possible unless you let her sleep in your bed and eat out of your dish. Perhaps you would phone Saxon and make whatever arrangement suits you. *Anyone* can come in October, when I am not here. Even *mantequeros*[8] are now safe; Maria will look after them all . . .
    I shall certainly not return yet to England. My aunt's death simplifies my affairs but makes me very little better off. I cannot yet afford, unless I sell my book, to live in London. I can run to an occasional spree if I atone for it after; and I control the capital. I can ask Jane Norton[9] or Beryl de Zoete[1] to marry me, but where is my Daimler to come from, eh? Or even

---

7a. Elizabeth Ann (Poppet) and Vivien, then aged seventeen and fourteen respectively, were the daughters of Augustus John and Dorelia McNeill, his mistress and, after Ida's death, to all intents and purposes his second wife.
8. Mythical monsters, in which the simpler Spanish peasants still believed. On a visit to Gerald, Lytton's nephew Richard (Dick) was mistaken for one and barely escaped with his life.
9. Jane Elizabeth Norton, the Gibbon scholar and author of *A Bibliography of the Works of Edward Gibbon*, was then a partner in Bunny Garnett's bookshop. Her brother H. J. T. Norton, the rich Cambridge mathematician, had helped Lytton financially while he wrote *Queen Victoria*.
1. Linguist, translator and an authority on Balinese dancing, she was the consort of the distinguished orientalist Arthur Waley.

my *diner de luxe* to Mr Partridge at the Ivy? I shall still have to go on being agreeable to people if I want them to talk to me. Now when I am really rich I shall be as disagreeable as I please, and then – champagne and pâté. As a hedonist you ought to look forward to that, for you will come in for a rich endowment . . . With love to you both.

Gerald

There were no other visitors to Yegen in September after all. When Ralph and Frances arrived, they found Gerald deeply involved with a fifteen-year-old village girl called Juliana, whom he had seduced after taking her on as a maid. He became completely obsessed by her and made love to her several times a day. But these erotic performances had a devastating effect upon his intellectual and literary life and he found himself unable to get on with his book. In October, therefore, when his guests had left, he set off for Seville in the hope of concentrating on it there.

SEVILLE, 23 OCTOBER 1929

Dear Ralph,

I have been here five days, all the time in deep boredom and depression. How is that possible? I have just remembered that what made my happiness before was a girl who danced every night at the Kursaal. But now the Exhibition[2] is on, the tourists are here and all the charm of Seville has taken flight. The state I have been in has made me reflect very seriously on my condition and draw a number of quite contradictory conclusions from it. I ought to change my way of life and marry or form a liaison. If I do not within three years do this, I am in for a bad end. But what shall I do?

1. Marry someone like Esme[3] and live in Kent? But in order to meet even young women like Esme I must have friends who will introduce me to them. And none of my friends know any young women of any sort.

2. Marry a village girl in Yegen and take her to live in Kent.

3. Employ Mrs Temple's *entremetteuse* to find me a beautiful girl in Granada, either to marry or live with abroad or in Kent.

4. Form a regular liaison with Lily. Lily is the only person in the world for whom I have the feelings that are called love. But unless the wear and tear of life have altered her, I do not see the possibility of any relation lasting more than a month.

5. Marry in Spain, live in Spain, and give up literature.

For if I ruin my life, then let me ruin it in style, without perpetual

2. The Great Exhibition or World Fair had opened a few weeks before.
3. Esme Rudd had just married Richard (Dick) Strachey, eldest son of Lytton's brother Ralph.

complaints and grimaces – either willingly and gaily in the clear air and
climate of my village, or running through my fortune in three years with
Lily and blowing my brains out. At the day of judgement I shall put the
blame on Carrington. The situation is, however, a little premature. Give
me your advice if you have any to offer. I shall pay great attention to it.
And now I come to the primary object of my letter.

On 1 December I want to have £50 in my bank. Will Tiz's money be
through in time and, if not, can you get me an advance for me from her
bank or the lawyer? I shall have to spend some time in Granada on my
way back and I want to buy a number of things there for the house –
bedclothes, curtains, baths, etc. I must get it in better order. Then there is
the *entremetteuse* and Utopian experiments of that sort. The moment I
am back I want to get in the mason, as Bunny is coming out after
Christmas. The Black Witch[4] and her daughter will have cost me a pretty
penny by the time I have done with them. Why should I contribute, I
wonder, to the happiness of people who have no talent for it? . . .

To return to what I was saying, will you see what you can do about
this and in any case write me a line very soon. I shall stay at Seville till 8
November (date of arrival of telegraphic money order) and then I shall
go to Tangier . . . If Tangier is no use to me, then I'll take the boat to
Oran and go to Figuig; for if I go back to Yegen before I have written the
capital passages of *J[ack] R[obinson]* I see no hope of ever finishing it. I
shall have to consider hanging myself. For what's the use of being a
writer if I spend three years over such a wretched, drivelling little book?
And if I hang myself, there is this to be said: I shall automatically cease to
belong to the same species as J. C. Squire[5] and Mrs Enfield.[6] And I'll
leave every penny I have to prostitutes. And I shall be buried in some
secure place with ten tons of stone over me. Thus, if there is a resurrec-
tion of the dead, I shall be left out of it and be safe from further dealings
with those who, like Carrington, grow fat on what they suck from
others. Vampires haunt churchyards, they say, but they cannot drain as
much blood from me dead as they have already in five years from me
living. I shall do another thing. I shall have an inscription cut on my tomb

4. i.e. Gerald's maid Maria. She had suddenly claimed that Gerald's ex-landlord Don
Fernando, who had been her lover and the father of her daughter Angela, had left her his house
when he died and that Gerald was therefore her tenant. The situation became so intolerable
that Gerald had had to dismiss them both.
5. John Collings Squire, editor of the *London Mercury.*
6. Doris Edith, *née* Hussey, wife of the economist Ralph Roscoe Enfield and author of two slim
volumes of biography written in the style of Lytton Strachey.

enumerating all my faults and weaknesses, especially my egotism and my insensitiveness to others, and then one virtue – generosity. For I might have bought that revolver and shot Carrington, and I did not. If, for such technical offences as theft, society gives long periods of imprisonment, what does not that person deserve who lightly and deliberately, over a long period of time, poisons the life and sanity and happiness of others? If the relations between human beings are necessarily of the kind called moral, this raises an insoluble moral problem. For I cannot avoid seeing that in many respects she is a good character. For her one or two crimes, what indefatigable atonement! All of which goes to prove how careful one should be of people who are always doing good to others. They are the very ones, in a quiet place and moment, to cut one's throat.

I have now written myself into a mood of gaiety . . . Will you write me as I have asked you. To both you and Frances, my love. I don't need to tell you how much I am attached to you, for my life has been so wound up with yours that the connection is now organic and does not depend on whether we continue to please one another. Yours,

Gerald

41 GORDON SQUARE, 29 OCTOBER 1929

Dear Gerald,

I have written to ask the lawyer if the estate can advance you £50 by 1 December; but if it can't for any lawyer's reason, I will do so myself, as I have more than that sitting at my bank waiting to be invested and there is no hurry to invest money these days (but you probably don't follow the great Wall Street slump). So anyway you can count on it in your calculations . . .

It is ridiculous to offer you advice when you manage, by writing 2½ pages of anathema, to give yourself the only necessary advice, which was to abuse all women and drive a long nail into Carrington and feel better at once. Moreover you need no advice, because your doom is certainly sealed. Somewhere the daughter of an Irish earl or the sister of a London Group artist or the niece of a clergyman in the Isle of Wight is preparing herself, by the study of Milton and T. S. Eliot and the Lives of Shelley and Byron, for the decisive moment when she will put into your head that you are to do her credit in Bloomsbury and to save her from Mr Drinkwater by making her your lawful wife or, more likely, your still more lawful mistress. You can set your mind at rest. So many books about Byron come out every month, so many talks are given on the wireless raising the prestige of anyone who knows Virginia Woolf, that the number of aching females is steadily on the increase; and now that Dick Strachey and Henry Lamb and Tommy[7] are snatched, only you are left to assuage them. You have not five alternatives, not even a single alternative; the very fact that you dwell in a world of alternatives makes your destruction all too inevitable. As things are I shouldn't, if I were you, waste money by marrying a Spanish girl, because annulments by the Pope are so expensive. Marriage will not preserve you, it will only make you more luscious . . .

We got back to hear that James and Alix [Strachey] want to turn us out of our rooms before Easter, and the shock of this at once gave me diarrhoea. Why come back to England to be so rudely welcomed?

We spent last weekend with Boswell[8] and Mrs Boswell at Hilton and talked of aeroplanes, on which Bunny is dead set. There is an aerodrome within 2 miles of them now and they go up for flights and get extraordinary bird-like sensations when they look down on fields and trees, but you'll hear all about that in Bunny's next work for sure[9] . . . Tommy and Julia were at Ham Spray for a weekend with us, with Tommy finishing Lytton's head. This head, unlike the previous débacles, has been miraculously put together again, and the mould taken, and it will be visible in bronze some time this week . . . Helen [Anrep] had lunch with us and we had to give her all the news of 'the Poet'. Naturally she disliked the J[uliana] liaison and began to croak; but I will always maintain that if it's a choice to decide whether you're a crook or a gull, you're not a gull anyway, and if you're incorrigible, it is not in innocence that you are so.

I dislike English country, I find to my surprise; it is really very amateurish and water-colour after Spain, so flat-chested too and boneless at the same time. Where *is* the backbone of England, I ask you? It is an impossible country to fillet – only those great meaty slabs of earth, marked off into convenient joints for a butcher's eye to digest. And the meat so hairy, too – if only it were properly shaved now! Only under the breasts of the downs is there a vestige of comfort, and even the breasts are stretched and shapeless from too much child-bearing. As you say, you and I are like ingrowing toenails to each other; we may pare down

7. Stephen (Tommy) Tomlin, youngest son of Sir Thomas Tomlin, was a sculptor. Like Henry Lamb and Dick Strachey, he had just got married. His wife, Julia Strachey, was a niece of Lytton's, and a childhood friend of Frances; she wrote two outstanding novels: *Cheerful Weather for the Wedding* (Hogarth, 1932) and *The Man on the Pier* (Lehmann, 1951).
8. i.e. Bunny Garnett.
9. Ralph was right. See David Garnett: *A Rabbit in the Air* (Chatto & Windus, 1932).

the relation, but we shall carry our toenails with us to our graves. I have become devoted to mine in course of time. Yours,

Ralph

SEVILLE, 3 NOVEMBER 1929

My dear Ralph,

I was delighted to get your letter. I live in such a state of solitude that a little envelope with a stamp becomes an event of the greatest importance. And everything you said in your letter pleased me. I am now practically living in my book. I have my special corner in the café where four times a day I come with my despatch box under my arm, like a Chancellor of the Exchequer crossing from the Treasury to Downing Street. As yet I have not done very much – I have been tired, the fish at the hotel poisoned me, there are the inevitable accidents – but I realise that this is the place and atmosphere that I can best work in. Sooner or later I shall do all that I have to do.

I have come back to my former opinion that no town in Europe suits me as Seville does. Helen may talk as she pleases, but I can think of no deeper happiness than to live here almost like a workman with a girl of the working classes, come every day of my life to the café to write, and return to her in the evenings. For, in considering how to arrange my life, I have to take into account the great difficulty there is in combining an active social life with that required for literature. In any case a kind of gulf separates the two; it takes me *days* to move from the former to the state of mind required for the latter. And I have such a restless disposition, and throw myself so easily into what is going on round me, that to write I have to isolate myself. That is why, though I am always avid for any new experience, I believe I should think far more deeply than you imagine before committing myself to a cultured young woman. A short and stormy love affair, yes – but oh, not marriage . . .

. . . I have not answered your letter, have not said how sorry I am you have lost your rooms. What does Alix want them for, eh? I scent a fine mystery. And wherever shall you go to? Everything seems to indicate a house in Essex, a rock garden and a perambulator . . . I hope in any case you will leave Gordon Square, enter a new world, meet fascinating young women and then, bowing yourself out of their presence, leave them with me. I, in Seville, will do the same for you – there's my hand on it. Such an exchange will ensure a life-long friendship and a wreath of violets on your grave or on my grave after our deaths. And a motto: *In pandere semper fideles*. But that is dog-Latin, so I'll write no more, only thanking you again and again and again for your offered loan if the lawyers are recalcitrant.

Gerald

SEVILLE, 17 NOVEMBER 1929

Dear Ralph,

... I have been ill again and can read and can write and can do nothing. I am going back to Yegen tomorrow. My visit to Seville has been a complete fiasco, and five weeks of constant effort and almost continual solitude has added six indifferent pages to my book. If I could I would give up literature, but I know it would only be to begin again. Juliana writes, or rather dictates, me charming letters. I shall see if I cannot find some future for me in that direction. If you have an opinion on that, give it.

Gerald

41 GORDON SQUARE, 21 NOVEMBER 1929

My dear Gerald,

... As you didn't see yesterday's *Evening Standard*, I can only tell you that under a snappy title of WAR HERO REWARDED we read that Marianne von Roeder had left her nephew £7,700 'for his self-sacrifice on our behalf', and probate has been granted. I have been hearing from the lawyers that some £800 or £900 of stocks must be sold out to pay off the death duties, so I shouldn't count on more than £6,500 when all the charges and fees are done with. If you take £500 of that for immediate needs, the £6,000 left should give you £360 a year at 6 per cent.

I'm sorry Seville has been so poisonous to you and so infertile ... We have got our flat at the Nonesuch[9a] – have I already told you that? – and we move into it on New Year's Day ... I give up now. Yours,

Ralph

YEGEN, 7 JANUARY 1930

My dear Ralph,

... My life here proceeds calmly and lazily and, I imagine, happily, though I will leave the decision of that point to you hedonistic philosophers. White Mary[1] has turned out to be a treasure of hard work, tact

9a. The Nonesuch Press, founded and owned by Francis and Vera Meynell, was housed in a beautiful Queen Anne house at 16 Great James Street. Ralph and Frances had found quarters in part of it.

1. Gerald's new maid, another Maria, called White to distinguish her from her predecessor.

and capacity. With Juliana there are the usual ups and downs. I perform prodigies of nightly valour – though you no doubt will turn up your nose at them – and have never been in better health and strength in my life. We have jealousies, we have quarrels, we have reconciliations, and none of them affect our appetite or our good spirits. But I see that any attempt to prolong our relations after my return to England would be a mistake.

The village festival is just over. I took a most active part in it. On the second day I was having my usual late breakfast when the two rich young men of the village arrived, carrying several bottles of rum and a bag of cakes and followed by a number of others. The Rats[2] arrived; we began first to drink and then to dance. I danced – yes indeed, I danced – a thing that even you have never known me to do. The wind began to roar, snow and hail beat against the panes, and we continued drinking and dancing for twelve hours until midnight. This was the sequel to a dance which I gave the day before to the aristocracy. Tomorrow the mason comes in to make the room at the end of the passage habitable, and when he has gone perhaps I shall be able to collect myself a little.

This is all that I can think of to say, except that if Frances could possibly find time to send me copies of the photos of Juliana (in duplicate) I should be very much obliged to her. Your devoted

Gerald

Gerald had always wanted to visit the Sahara, so in February he started out for Almeria on the first stage of his journey.

ALMERIA, 23 FEBRUARY 1930

My dear Ralph,

. . . I am engaged on an Italian intrigue over Juliana. My friend Paco would evidently like to sleep with her and – who knows? – she perhaps would like it too. I saw signs of this before I left and now I hear that he has gone over to sleep in the house 'to protect the two women.' I have therefore done this: written him a letter suggesting he should try to seduce her, saying I am anxious to test her and that because I have no confidence in her I have ceased to care what she does. Paco has been in my confidence or semi-confidence throughout and his *discretion* is to be trusted. He is going on military service in 3 weeks. I took great pains with my letter and I think it will have put his *amour propre* into full motion,

2. Two sisters, Isabel and Ana, who, like the rest of their family, were called the Rats after their mother's *apodo*, or nickname.

for my appeal was both to his talent for friendship and to his Don Juanism. I therefore think he will tell me, but if he does not – and I have doubts – I will spring a scene on J., *say* he has told me, and force a confession. I should not get a full confession, but I ought to get a partial one which would allow me to infer the rest.

Why all this? Because only action, successful action, cures the mind of jealousy and also because I should like to put J. in a weaker position. Her attitude of a seduced and helpless maiden is an absurd one, for she is really a nymphomaniac. If she can be caught by Paco I shall make a sham confession of a love affair in Africa and we shall be in a much more sensible situation – that is, one more in accordance with the real facts. For lust is the only tie that unites me to J. and J. to me. I do not mean by that to diminish it; it is a strong one. So long as I am at Yegen I can control her conduct – I cannot and do not want to control it in my absence – but in these matters there is a certain sensual pleasure to be got from honesty. Let her have what young man she wants in my absence and confess it, but not dupe me. In the middle classes married women often come to love their husbands more from deceiving them: a reaction of their conscience, a feeling of pity, and so on. The lower classes do not think in this way; they despise them. I should make a serious mistake if I did not have a scene with J. in which my chief object must be to show her that I cannot be taken in by anything . . .

Tonight I sail for Melilla.

Gerald

16 GREAT JAMES ST, 25 FEBRUARY 1930

Dear Gerald,

There have been too many deaths of one sort and not nearly enough of the other. My mother, you know, is completely alive and even improving her iron constitution by sun baths at Mentone. But Charlie Sanger died soon after Frank Ramsey,[3] and Dora Sanger[4] did nothing but complain that he took so long doing it and even dared to ask for a little commiseration while *in extremis*. Lettice Ramsey[5], who has a huge heart without a trace of sensibility, sits like a leech on Frances, quietly appeasing her thirst for sympathy, while Frances hopes she's doing good but is certain she will soon go mad with any more of it . . .

We are very contented here. For one thing we have definitely sunk in

3. The brilliant King's College philosopher who died aged twenty-seven.
4. Anne Dorothea (Dora), *née* Pease.
5. Frank Ramsey's wife, *née* Baker.

the world, once across Southampton Row. If we had lingered on in that refined quarter, I might easily have become a successful man. Now there is no fear of such a thing. We are on the very brink of the slums, I'm glad to see, and shall soon be sucked into them . . .

When you leave Yegen for England, remember that Frances and I will probably have to retire abruptly to some foreign country and live on £100 a year; for when Greville[6] ends at Easter and my mother returns invigorated from Mentone, I see no future for us but that. *Monsieur Robinson, ayez pitié de M. et Mme. Vendredi.*

Ralph

BENI-OUNIF DE FIGUIG, 13 MARCH 1930

Dear Ralph,

What am I to say about the desert? I have seen everything – dunes, rivers, oases, sunsets, camels (the caravans from Timimoun arrive exhausted and drooping and camp at the door of the hotel); and having made various enquiries and formed various projects, I am returning tomorrow by motor-lorry to Oudjda and so Melilla and Almeria. I need scarcely tell you that I spend most of the day dreaming and planning to cross and recross the Sahara – no, that would not be enough, but to spend a year in the tents of the Touareg.

The French military out here are on a par with the Anglo-Indians, only more active and efficient. Same romantic feeling about the desert and the East (they all read a novel in which the desert appears as a woman who calls them *home* to it at the end of their lives) and the same total incomprehension of the Arabs. At the most they have some acquaintance with the oasis Arabs. Can you believe it, I have been unable to discover the name of the tribe of the nomads encamped at the edge of the village! (I can only suppose from the map that they are the Oulad Amour or Amouriat.) They are simply *'les nomades'* and because they are not dangerous no one takes any trouble about them. But they seem to me a degraded lot; their tents are low and dirty and they hang about the outskirts of the village in a very un-Bedouin fashion. The Touareg? *'Ce sont encore des Arabes'* – that is all they can tell you about them.

---

6. In 1928 Lytton Strachey had been commissioned to edit a complete edition of the *Greville Memoirs* (1814–1860). Ralph and Frances were to do all the groundwork by transcribing the original manuscript, bound in many quarto volumes which were kept in a safe in the British Museum. This arduous task, at which for a long time they toiled every day, sitting side by side at a table in the narrow gallery of the Documents Room overlooking the Magna Carta, was not to end as soon as Ralph feared.

However, I have discovered this: that I can travel cheaply by one of the weekly caravans from Timimoun (a journey to 2 to 3 weeks, according as to whether they cross the waterless Erg or follow the Zousfrana to pasture their camels) and that the French would put no difficulties in my way so long as I did not attempt to travel in the unsubdued parts of the Atlas. Though for the time being nothing is possible, I can see that I might do worse than spend three years travelling or with the Touareg in the Sahara . . .

The hotel here is comfortable and simple; it has been converted from a disused redoubt. The bathing in the river is rather spoilt by alligators, of which there are great numbers. But the mornings, the evenings and the nights are marvellously beautiful, the air is invigorating, and I either go for long walks across the stony desert plain or lie on my bed reading the *Odyssey*. There is an Arab brothel with four dusky beauties and a Senegalese proprietress, old, black, wizened like a monstrous frog, and here they dance to the deafening music of a trumpet and drum, and I sit drink tea, repeat my four words of Arabic and then, yes, then – unite my body to this burning continent in the figure of the brown-limbed, queenlike-gestured Fatmah. This letter is very slapdash for you hypocritical *raffinés*. I can't help it.

Gerald

16 GREAT JAMES ST, 26 MARCH 1930

Dear Gerald,

I had no idea you were returning from Africa so soon or I would have written to Yegen earlier. Your £500 was paid into your bank over a month ago; so you can draw on it any time and, I fear, for any purpose . . .

From what I read on the blank sheets in your letters, Juliana is going to prove a delicate negotiation. Has this long-promised bastard taken root at last or is it only your knowledge of Yegen character that leads you to suppose he will appear at the critical moment of your departure? I suggest if you are going to endow J. at all, do it by post from Almeria or take her into Almeria and give her the money there. Once you begin handing out pesetas in bulk in the village, you may get a lot of disagreeable claims which will delay you even though you don't have to settle them in the end . . .

We have had a French cook since I last wrote and now we don't seem to have one at all; all we get is breakfast and we fawn on our friends for the rest of our food. Our French lady was left a fortune, conveniently at a weekend, so left abruptly, taking with her the housekeeping money and a frying-pan and saying she hoped to be back soon . . . I shall go on writing to Yegen unless I hear to the contrary. Yours,

Ralph

YEGEN, 2 APRIL 1930

Dear Ralph,

Well, as you have at last written to me, perhaps I may write to you. I have a rather fantastic story to tell you. You will remember that when I began to suspect that Paco would try and succeed in sleeping with Juliana, I wrote to him encouraging him to do so 'to test her' . . . I have now to tell you of the admirable success of my stratagem.

On my arrival at Ugíjar, Paco met me with great expressions of friendship and told me that he had, without any resistance on her part, slept with her about a fortnight after my leaving the village, that without my letter he would never have dreamed, etc., etc., and he gave me all the details. We arrived at my house. Juliana appeared, looking embarrassed. We went to bed. And now I was in a position in which we all long some time or other to find ourselves, but which is very rarely granted. I was in a position to experiment, with perfect confidence in my results, upon the nature of deception. I was in the highest spirits at the thought of this and treating her very affectionately (all the more because she looked so seductive). I rallied her on her inconstancy, telling her I could see in her eye that she had slept with somebody, but that I forgave her freely because I had done the same, etc., etc. Her lover, I said, must be Ramon or Ezekiel (the Rat). She lied with magnificent brazenness, telling me she had scarcely spoken to them, *that if I doubted her I could ask Paco*. One lie led to another. How could I *possibly* imagine she could even look at anyone else?

To put this more shortly, she gave all kinds of small signs – false emphasis, embarrassment, lack of abandon – that something had happened; and these signs would certainly, had I known nothing, have made me suspicious. But not only were her lies plausible in themselves but they offered her an outlet from her embarrassment into a more abstract, more imaginative sphere where she felt quite at home. Thus, as soon as her lies began to gain a certain momentum, she became perfectly natural. Had I been able to make the experiment ten years ago, what a quantity of suffering I would have saved myself!

Well, I pretended to be convinced, for I wanted to see what she would do with the rope I gave her. She did not waste any time. Her independence, which had been growing before, took a leap forward. She disappeared the next afternoon and did not return till nightfall. When I said something, she became irritated and threatened not to sleep with me that night. And so on. It was clear that I had lost all hold over her. Well, I had a secret consultation with Paco. 'Tell her,' he said, 'that you know everything because in Almeria you consulted the Niño Dormido.' The Niño Dormido is a child of 10 or 12 who is put into a mesmeric sleep by its father and on awaking from its sleep answers questions. All the poorer classes believe in this form of divination and I saw at once what a good suggestion that was.

That night in bed Juliana began her usual questions. 'When are you going to give me a child?'

'In a moment,' I said, 'but first I must tell you a story. When I was in Almeria three days ago I went to consult the Niño Dormido.'

Silence.

'I went first of all to ask it whether our child would be a boy or a girl, but when I arrived there I thought of another question.'

'What question?'

'I thought I would ask it whether you had kissed anyone, or even slept with anyone, in my absence.'

'And what did it say?'

'This.' And I gave her a dramatic account of everything that had happened between her and Paco.

She turned very pale and when I had finished said: 'But the Niño often says things that are not true.'

'That is so,' I said, 'and at first I scarcely knew myself whether to believe it. But when I saw you I could tell at once by your manner that it was true. I am not so easily deceived as you imagine. I therefore decided to talk first to Paco. Yesterday afternoon I went out to the vineyard where he was working, told him I had consulted the Niño Dormido, told him I had spoken to you and that you had confessed. He then told me everything and, as he had done no more than any man would do in the same circumstances, I made it up with him. Now you have deceived me within three weeks of my leaving the house and told me a great many lies; but still, as I know you cannot live without men and that that is in part my fault, and as I too have slept with someone else, I am going to forgive you and make it up with you. In fact I will take the whole of the blame on myself. You know the proverb – "Whoever owns a beautiful house must keep the stable door locked."'

But Juliana had covered her face and was sobbing loudly and, for all I could say to comfort her, kept on sobbing and crying half the night. The first effect of this has been a great return of affection towards me and ascetic resolutions about everything else. But I was determined this affair must have a gay and happy ending and, after the comedy of a reconciliation with Paco, we all four – Maria, Juliana, Paco and I – celebrated the occasion by a picnic high up in the mountains, where we cooked a rabbit, drank a great deal of wine, milked goats and bathed or paddled under a waterfall.

The advantages of my position are obvious. Juliana has forfeited all rights (legal or otherwise) to marriage with me or to having a child. She cannot expect to deceive me again because I have only to write a letter to the Niño. I have not strained this too far, since I have told her that when I return to England I shall consider her free to sleep with whom she pleases. I have also ascertained that, in all probability, she has not slept with anyone besides Paco – no doubt for lack of opportunity. She is at the present moment altogether – that is to say, rather overwhelmingly – devoted to me. I on my part am more attached than ever to her. She has developed very rapidly. When I see her naked body, so fanatical for pleasure, already so expert in every form of enjoyment, lying on my bed like a Titian Venus, and think of all the stages of modesty and timidity through which, in her relations with me, she has passed to reach this, I can hardly believe that it is for me that this feast of love and beauty has been prepared.

There are of course many reasons why the life I have built round me here cannot continue. Juliana had a chance of being permanently established in my house, and she has lost it. I have not sufficient confidence in her, despite my affection, to give her another. And there are further considerations. I must put an end to these continual love affairs and accustom myself to a more independent life if I am to do any work and not ruin myself . . . When I come back to England at the end of the month I shall live quietly in the country.

The weather is charming just now, all the fruit trees in flower, all the fig trees and poplars springing into leaf. My household has never run more smoothly. I sit in my new sitting-room with its windows looking over the village; whilst I read Pastor's *History of the Popes*, Juliana irons or sews – for our relations are now perfectly undisguised. In the evening I go into the garden with her and Maria to water flowers or to see how the lettuces are coming up. At dusk Paco drops in for a glass of wine; in the evenings I teach Juliana to write. Your supposition that I shall have to pay out large sums of money is quite wrong; money has never entered into my relations with her and I don't think she can count above fifty pesetas. Unless in my absence she has been given a child, I do not anticipate any difficulties. She will go to Motril or Granada and marry and live happily, since to be happy six days in the week and to cry one is her nature . . .

Gerald

YEGEN, 12 APRIL 1930

My dear Ralph,

. . . There is not much to tell you. I live on honeymoon intimacy with Juliana. – embraces and tears. We have never loved one another so furiously, nor quarrelled so much. We now live together openly – that is, she sleeps in my room and gets up when I do. I am saved from a serious entanglement only by the knowledge that if I left her alone for two weeks she would begin sleeping with half the village. For, in favour of keeping her, there is this to be said – I have never had a satisfactory physical relation before, I would like to give her a child, and I am very fond of her. She is going to live with her sister in Motril the day I leave here. If she does not get married before I return I shall carry her off to Seville or Madrid, for I am determined never to live with her again at Yegen. The penalty for the seduction of minors is several years' imprisonment, but I think I have now escaped all possible pitfalls and I do not believe I have done any harm to her. How can I have another love affair after this? For this is a culmination, and after it there can be nothing untried or new.

On the 30th I leave Yegen and will reach London some ten days later, that is if London still exists, for I can hardly believe it. Will you keep my letters for me. With love to both.

Gerald

YEGEN, 26 APRIL 1930

Dear Ralph,

Juliana has left. Yesterday morning she set off for Motril with her mother in the company of Paco and other young men who are going on military service. I gave her 700 pesetas and my gramophone. Her character has been developing since Christmas with great rapidity. The sight of almost any young man now turns her head, and since my return from Africa the labour of guarding and surveilling her has become altogether too arduous. Among the other suitors who hang round the doors and throw letters in at the windows there appeared a fascinating lorry-driver who was some relation of Maria's. He first won over the mother, then secured the assistance of Maria, who saw in him an opportunity for compromising Juliana in my eyes. Between them they all egged her on and she, poor girl, being already quite overcome by him, could not resist. I saw perfectly what was happening and told her she must choose, for, if she spoke more than two words to him again, or danced with him, I would break with her. It was Easter Monday, when large swings are put up in the streets and the young men swing the girls. Her mother arranged a meeting at their house and when she left at dusk he kissed her. Before she had got back here I had been told about it and, as there was also an attempt to deceive me and meet him again later, I told her everything was finished between us. She cried – but only, I think, to impress me. Then, when it was time to go to bed, 'You must sleep in your own room,' I said.

At two in the morning it began to rain heavily. I got up as I always do and went to the attic to see if any water was coming in. Juliana's door was open and her lamp burning and, as I passed through the hall, she called to me. She was in an extraordinary state. She jumped out of bed and caught hold of my knees. 'Beat me,' she said, 'if I've deserved it. Beat me, thrash me, for I belong to you – but don't punish me in this manner.' I thought how agreeable it would be to beat her when she deceived me and afterwards to drag her to a bed, and how well she would act her part in such an orgy; but the moment for this had passed and, as I neither felt angry nor desired too easy a reconciliation, I said, 'I shall never sleep with you again,' and left her. I lay awake till four, when the rain began to fall once more in torrents. I rose and crept barefooted to her door. She was sobbing. I put on my shoes and went on to the roof. When I came down she called me and I went in and sat on her bed. The pity she felt for herself she now transferred to me, 'because I must be cold'. She covered my hand with tears and kisses and told me to go back to bed. Next morning she had a temperature. The doctor came and prescribed diet and medicines. Her family arrived. But so much fuss turned her head, and all that she could think of was that her mother should go at once in the pouring rain to Ugíjar for medicine, oranges, etc. and that these should cost as much as possible. Next day she got up, killed a rabbit, which she had not the patience to stew sufficiently, ate an enormous meal and declared that her medicine was undrinkable . . .

The episode with Juliana, you may now suppose, is ended. I have arranged matters with the greatest care so that she will have no hold over me. Yet for all this I have probably committed myself to her irretrievably. I felt such a longing to give this strong healthy body something by which to remember me that these last few weeks I have taken no precautions. I have done all I could to give her a child. If this should be the case,[7] I have arranged for her to go to Granada in the autumn and have promised 150 pesetas a month on condition she does not return to this village. I doubt if I shall ever be able to live with her, but I would visit her, and the idea of having a child by her charms me. Even if its early years were spent in a brothel, it would be better brought up than I was. It would have a taste of the real nature of the world in its infancy. Juliana is devoted to children and it is possible that if she had a child by me some of her wildness will leave her and it will be easier than it is now to have dealings with her. At the moment she is only fit for a brothel.

You no doubt will condemn my action. However, it seems to me that it is not a good thing to follow always the line of prudence and circumspection, as I do; one ought to plunge sometimes. And in this case I have acted of my own free will, without any sort of compulsion, which is a reason for my not regretting it. From last June until now I have steered my own boat through a variety of storms; I have dealt successfully and, I think, decently with several difficult situations and I feel I have a right to my caprice, all the more because a genuine interest in Juliana enters into it. I have not quite the heart to abandon her and I do not see any other way, given her reckless character, of keeping her out of a brothel. She is a whore, with all the wilfulness, laziness, selfishness and lack of resentment of whores; yet there is something in her character – a spontaneity, innocence, lack of malice and resentment – that endears her to me. There are one or two very disagreeable components in the honesty (*honestas*) of respectable women. After all, the touchstone of every one of my love affairs is the likeness and unlikeness to Carrington; that is the current that carries my boat onwards . . . With all love to you and Frances. Yours,

Gerald

GRANADA, 4 MAY 1930

My dear Ralph,

This is eleven o'clock at night in Granada. What shall I say to my only confidant, the relic of so many outworn and faded friendships, the one

---

7. Indeed it was the case – Juliana gave birth to a daughter later that year.

person who perhaps even reads my letters and understands and has some sympathy for what I say to him? The most charming companion, for whose society I would give up that of all the young women at present known to me? I have to tell you that I am in Granada, that it is eleven o'clock at night, and that my heart flutters among a variety of emotions.

The week I spent at Yegen without Juliana was abominable. Her body, the things that had passed between us, obsessed me. I did not know I was so sensual, but now I see that it takes two to make love and that I have waited all these years to find a person that suited me. You will laugh at me if you like (any Spaniard would think I was mad) but I have decided to do the opposite to what any man of the world would do – I have decided to keep Juliana. Before I left Yegen I had a conversation with her family on this subject. I shall not live with her, for she would be unfaithful to me, that being her unalterable nature. But I shall set her up in a cave on the Sacro Monte and visit her when I wish to. I want to keep a caged animal, you understand, but not a tame rabbit and, though her inevitable infidelity (she's a natural whore) makes certain relations impossible, it is not a reason for abandoning her. I find it difficult to give up any woman who has once entered into my life and become *dependent upon me*. And then, as I have never been taken in by those false standards that man's vanity and snobbism set them, I see nothing extraordinary in preferring for my bed a peasant girl to a film star, to a countess, or even to a young lady who reads Bertrand Russell and T. S. Eliot after breakfast. Juliana is not a beauty but then she is abandoned and sensual, which Englishwomen never can be without bad taste, and then it is I who have made her so. These are sufficient motives for the sort of love I have to give. If I hear in a day or two that I have given her a child – as I hope indeed I have done – the matter will be decided.

In a few days I shall be in England and I am curious to see what impression the race of Shakespeare will make upon me. What proportion are human and what monstrosities? For the first night at all events I will accept your very agreeable invitation – you may expect me on Monday. What a pity it is that you are not a slender young girl! Then I could buy you a bracelet, earrings, satins and ribbons, instead of having no choice but to offer you something to eat. A peach-fed ham or a pot of caviar is such a gross distortion of the sentiments I have for you. But never mind, the day following my arrival I invite you both to the best cooked dinner that can be got in London. With all love to you and my dear Frances. Yours,

Gerald

Gerald arrived in England on 13 May and, after a month in London, left for Dorset with a letter of introduction from Stephen Tomlin to the novelist Theodore (T.H.) Powys, who lived at East Claydon. Here, on the day after his arrival, he met a young American girl called Elizabeth (Gamel) Woolsey, a poetess, who had taken a cottage in the village on the suggestion of Theodore's youngest brother Llewellyn. Her rather melancholy, dreamy expression, her air of gentleness and resignation, appealed to Gerald at once and he determined there and then to make her his wife.

There were obstacles in his way, however. In the first place Gamel was already married and, though separated from her husband, not yet divorced. Secondly, she had been having an affair with Llewellyn during the past year and he was still deeply in love with her. She was no longer in love with him – indeed within a few weeks she had agreed to go away with Gerald – but ending the affair was a painful experience. Her health was precarious – as a child she had developed tuberculosis – and her agitation at parting with Llewellyn brought on a slight haemorrhage. The lung specialist who examined her advised Gerald to take her at once to Mundesley Sanitarium in Norfolk.

MUNDESLEY, 2 SEPTEMBER 1930

Dear Ralph,

After three days of heat and roads and hotels we have arrived here and have settled down, I in a little villa above the cliff, Gamel in her beehive-like sanatorium. She is very tired and they keep her all day in bed, which is rather dull for her. I am comfortable and like my villa, but altogether it is a sad beginning for married life.

I do not know that I have anything to tell you about except our visit to Helen . . . She had sent me some days before her 'kindest regards to my wife'. I knew she would not on any account accept Gamel, that she was prejudiced against her beforehand and that her conversation and appearance would satisfy her worst forebodings. But I thought that she might remember that I was her oldest and perhaps closest friend and that even an appearance of friendliness and approval upon such a critical occasion in my life would make me very grateful. This was one of the occasions when a very slight degree of kindness would produce a very disproportionate return of gratitude. I also supposed that Gamel's evident exhaustion as well as her complete defencelessness might disarm her. But one never learns that people are so preoccupied with their own concerns and so completely in the power of their own mental sequences that they hardly ever take in what is going on round them or adapt themselves as they ought to other people's situations.

During dinner Helen was comparatively subdued. Molly,[8] with great

8. Mary (Molly) MacCarthy, *née* Warren Cornish, wife of the literary journalist and editor Desmond MacCarthy.

kindness and simplicity, talked to Gamel. Roger [Fry], who was pre-occupied with his expedition to France, seemed more and more under Helen's guidance. After dinner we moved into the garden. The air was warm, the stars shone over the tiles. The motors swept by along the road, measuring out by the sound of their approaching and receding horns the darkness around us. Molly was in a charming mood and on the very least encouragement broke out into some fantastic flight of fancy . . . I talked a good deal in order that Gamel, who was evidently very tired, should not have to make efforts – also because in Helen's voice I felt some kind of challenge. That patronising and ironic tone we know so well had taken entire possession of it. I had heard that tone so often and with perfect indifference directed towards other people. I was not ready, without striking back, to allow it to be used on me. Perhaps I just showed this, for, when the conversation broke up, Helen said to me, 'You have become so self-confident that I scarcely know you. Is this the effect of being married?' I might have answered that it was the effect of having at last to defend something that had to be defended. She asked me to come into her room when everyone had gone to bed; it was the relic of an old habit of friendship which she had converted to a new use. I was one of those innumerable dependents and confidants whom she *must* listen to and console – very briefly, it is true – since they entirely depended on her. Old habits, too, made her drop her patronizing tone and speak nicely; but she took care in speaking of Gamel to use a doubled-edged compliment: 'She is more subtle than she seems to be.'

I had arranged, because I thought it would please them and make things easier for Helen, to take the children out on the river at Orford for the whole day, then early in the evening to go off to Bury St Edmunds with Gamel. At breakfast Helen rather markedly arranged a picnic for herself, Molly and Roger in another direction. Either because she liked her, or from tact and good manners, Molly continued to make friends with Gamel, which I thought I could see did not please Helen very much. We went off, spent a nice day on the river, came back. It was nearly dinner time; everyone was dressed. As I was strapping on the luggage, Helen came out to me. 'I want to say something you may think rather odd. If you should find Gamel *rather boring, selfish and difficult to get on with*, you must be patient.' I had scarcely time to answer before other people came and we left.

Against these arrows, Ralph, one is always defenceless. For two days I was very angry, ashamed and depressed. I was furious with Helen for such a calculated piece of malice, furious with Gamel for exposing herself to such comments, furious with myself for having been so stupid as not to foresee this . . . I felt, all that day and the next, in that sweltering heat, much as Byron must have felt on his honeymoon. The bottom had dropped out of everything. I was condemned to spend my life with a tiresome woman – very gentle and pitiful, it is true, but whom yet I did not love. In vain I said to myself that in the long run all human chatter and conversation bored me and that a woman of taste and great sensibility such as Gamel . . . was more suitable for me to live with than some more lively and brilliant character, let alone a magpie like Helen; there is an irrational, immeasurable element in love that cannot be dispensed with and I did not believe this. I knew my decision to marry Gamel would not and could not alter, but, finding in my heart a kind of bankruptcy, I wondered what would be the end of it.

Four or five days have passed . . . and once more I am attached to Gamel and look forward to, and believe in, the future. But everything is different and I do not yet know whether I shall return to being 'in love' with her or merely to living with her happily. Perhaps, unless I am perpetually tormented, I am not capable of remaining more than a few days in this state of being in love. Perhaps I am too destructive of my own happiness, too critical, too independent. Or, on the other hand, I may be now merely in one of those interludes of feeling which so often circumstances dictate to one. It does not greatly matter which, since I am perfectly happy and believe that when we set up house together I shall secure both her happiness and my own.

This letter must now be finished. Will you treat it as very confidential and tell me when you see Molly, with all the frankness which our compact demands, what was *her* impression . . . If you will reverse my opinion of Helen's spiteful and insensitive behaviour, you will discover just what I think of yours, of Frances's and of Carrington's. My love.

Gerald

MUNDESLEY, 5 SEPTEMBER 1930

My dear Ralph,

I write again only to bring to a proper close my last letter. The poison has worked itself out. I am once again in love, I think more deeply than before, with Gamel. When I review in my mind what happened, I can see exactly how Helen would justify herself. What do *you* think? Do you smell malice and wickedness? I believe (and after all I can remember her tone, her exact phraseology when she spoke to me) that I could not possibly have been as affected as I was by mere tactlessness. Women's revenge cuts deep. Helen saw how she could pay me out for various real or imaginary slights, and at one blow she did it. Well, the effect was (I am ashamed to say it) to convulse my life for several days and to put back Gamel's recovery by several weeks. She now lies in bed with a temperature. Without bearing any grudge against Helen – for I am now too happy to bear grudges against anyone – I do not feel that I shall ever wish to see her again. She's a dangerous woman, as I've often said, and when she acts she does so very thoroughly. But who'd have thought that another person's malice could move me so deeply? I have fallen several notches in my own estimation. I have also learned more about this wicked world than a whole year of observation would have taught me.

Your confirmation, your honest and frank confirmation through Molly, would very much interest me and I don't mind your giving her a suitable and abbreviated account of this letter. You are off, I think, in a few days.[9] I hope you will very much enjoy yourselves.

Gerald

When Gamel was well enough to leave hospital, she and Gerald moved into furnished rooms at Wells-next-the-Sea.

WELLS, 31 OCTOBER 1930

Dear Ralph,

A letter from Juliana this evening. What a world of happiness one cuts off when one settles down in a regular manner! What journeys, adventures, wine-shops, posadas, boats, cities one says goodbye to for ever! If at this moment I could sail off to Spain, alone, in my car, I should feel the sky was being lifted. My heart is so divided, that's the worst of it! On Mondays, Tuesdays and Fridays I am in love with Gamel; on Wednesdays, Thursdays and Saturdays I pine for my liberty. I should like to revert to the life I conceived when I was 17 – perpetual travel, no companions, no obligations, and then wine-shops and women. But one has to choose and I have chosen, and there's an end to it. Since choice is necessary, I have the consolation of feeling I could not have chosen better. Keep this letter to yourself.

Gerald

For the sake of Gamel's health, Gerald decided that they should winter in Italy. They set off just before Christmas and settled into a small hotel in Sorrento.

9. Ralph and Frances were going on holiday again to Spain, this time to Cadaques in Catalonia.

SORRENTO, 23 FEBRUARY 1931

My dear Ralph,

. . . We lead a quiet regular life – writing all morning, Italian conversation lessons in the afternoon, and Roman or Etruscan studies from tea onwards. The weather is dull and wet and the country round, which is just 'scenery' with only a fair-weather character, becomes perfectly uninteresting. But for the time being that does not greatly matter.

Do you think that married life is that of the seesaw, in which one person is always rather low in order to allow the other to be very high? At present I am the malingerer, while Gamel is more active and energetic than I had thought possible and in continual high spirits. She has been adding page after page to her novel, among them some very beautiful, while I – but it will be too painful for me to finish this sentence. It occurs to me sometimes that I married just in time, caught a young woman just in time, for now my course of life must be all downwards and had I waited a year longer no one would have had me . . .

It is a pity I am so stupid today, for I have a theory of love to submit for your approval – a theory that accounts very satisfactorily for there being, for human beings, two kinds of love. The Greeks knew well of these two kinds, but their explanation has never been thought much of. Mine is far more illuminating. I hold, in short, that there are two kinds of love – the remote and the proximate – to suit two different kinds of spectacles. In one the object is held and focussed very far away and too much proximity is fatal; in the other the object is focussed always within reach and distance is detractive. The one gives a very clear, distinct image and suffering; the other gives happiness with no very definable outline. The one – but you must continue my arguments yourself, for I am really too tired to do so.

Gamel was very pleased at your liking her poetry;[1] she had had no serious notices of it, but one impassioned letter from an Oxford Lesbian. However, Simon & Schuster, the American publishers, have sent a cable asking to see her novel. But now I must stop. Gamel sends her love to you and Frances and wishes she had your Spanish shoes. The Italians know of nothing between bare feet and patent leather. Yours,

Gerald

After leaving Sorrento in March 1931, Gerald and Gamel spent several months travelling about the rest of the country. In Rome they went through a marriage ceremony of their own devising. Standing alone together before the altar of the

1. A collection of poems entitled *Middle Earth* (Grant Richards, 1931).

empty church of Santa Maria d'Aracoeli on the Capitoline Hill, they exchanged rings and plighted their troth. When they got back to England in the middle of June they moved into a tiny thatched cottage in East Lulworth, and here they settled down for the autumn and winter. Towards the end of the year Lytton Strachey fell seriously ill.

HAM SPRAY, 31 DECEMBER 1931

My dear Gerald,

It was very nice to hear from you and receive a delicious ham. Yesterday Lytton was better, for the first time for a week. That means his pulse which before was called 'fairly good' became 'quite good', his temperature remained below 101° for 24 hours, and he snapped a nurse's head off for not leaving his room quick enough. Today he is worse. His temperature at 3 a.m. was 96°, at 10 a.m. 103° – 7 points in 7 hours. The pulse, of which we have had most to complain lately, acquitted itself well for once and is back to 'fairly good' again at 130. The specialist in Suffolk has tried to reassure us over the telephone by saying there is 'absolutely no cause for alarm' in that particular fluctuation. And I am not alarmed particularly, only generally. A week ago everyone but Carrington believed he would die in the next 24 hours. I tried not to, but I felt it would be madness *not* to believe it and that Carrington was almost mad. But she has always managed to do without probabilities and yet get what she wants, and I believe in her now almost as much as I believe in Lytton. The disease is a fiendish one – not typhoid but 'ulcerative colitis', for which there is no anti-toxin and hardly any treatment; with the result that you have no means of getting over it and it lingers on and on until you get bored with it and die or it gets bored with you and leaves you. It runs no 'course' (as every disease should) so that the future is unmapped.

We are buttressed by 3 nurses, 3 specialists and 2 GPs, with a flank guard of Stracheys bivouacking in Hungerford. Frances has got a room at Ham PO. Pippa[2] lives in the house. My responsibilities are the electric light, the water supply, the central heating, and the cartage to and fro between here and Hungerford of visitors and supplies. I do my best to keep Ellie [Elinor] Rendel[3] out of the house, as the only pattern I can detect in the illness is that every suggestion she has made has been wrong and that Lytton always develops a turn for the worse after one of her visits.

2. Lytton's unmarried sister Philippa.
3. Lytton's niece, a doctor, the daughter of James Meadows Rendel, Chairman of the Assam Bengal Railway, and of Lytton's eldest sister, likewise called Elinor.

My love to you and Gamel. Perhaps you'll be in our flat next week. Yours,

Ralph

EAST LULWORTH, 2 JANUARY 1932

Dearest Ralph,

. . . I follow Lytton's health in *The Times*. I wake every morning early to read it and hope to find some improvement. I fear the anxiety, so very long-drawn-out as this has been, is pretty terrible. I hope you keep an eye on Carrington's health and give her sleeping draughts . . .

Our life goes on in the usual way, undeterred (though not unaffected) by these calamities. I spent a happy Christmas. I suppose I have never known any kind of settled happiness before. On Monday we go to Edgeworth[4] for a week, then, if we can still have your flat, to London. If you change your mind about this, you have only to tell us. We shall take your flat by the day; and of course even if you don't want to turn us out, there will be beds if you and Frances come up for short periods.

I don't know whether you'd like me to come over and see you. Perhaps you are too occupied. But I could easily and *would very gladly* come over for a day from Edgeworth, bringing my bicycle in the train and sandwiches in my pocket. You have only to send a wire . . . My fondest love to you and D. C. Gamel sends hers.

Gerald

HAM SPRAY, 5 JANUARY 1932

Dearest Gerald,

Our suspense goes on. Cassidy,[5] one of the specialists, saw Lytton again on Sunday. He had seen him a fortnight previously and found him improved. The only thing is that the improvement must not be too slow, as there is a risk of further complications arising out of the sheer weakness consequent on lying in bed with a high temperature for week after week. Slightly more drastic treatment is to be employed with the hope of hastening the drying up of the ulcers in the upper colon which are responsible for all the trouble. Occasionally despair begins to infect the house. We had a taste of it last Saturday, when the temperature and pulse began to rocket again, but we were all more cheerful again yesterday and today.

Would you like to come over from Edgeworth for the day? I could

4. Gerald's parents' house in Gloucestershire.
5. Sir Maurice Cassidy, the eminent bacteriologist and Physician-Extraordinary to George V.

meet you at Savernake station and with sandwiches; we could have a walk in the forest . . . With my fond love to you both. Yours,

Ralph

EAST LULWORTH, 12 JANUARY 1932

Dearest Ralph,

There seems no end to this illness, but I hope that the new treatment is doing what it is supposed to do and that Lytton's temperature and pulse will really show a marked improvement this week. We have had a great storm here, but today the air is calm and the sun shining and a thousand birds singing in the trees. Gamel has a heavy cold in the head. From the rather jaded feeling I have and the slight tendency to indigestion, I know that my short delicious interlude is over and that I am restored to good health. I am sorry that I am not walking in Savernake with you today. It is probably more complicated getting within reach of you from here – I cannot say, as I have been unable to find a timetable or railway map. But I would gladly come anywhere you pleased on Saturday (the only available day) if you were to wire me giving my destination and my time of leaving Wareham. For you no doubt have a train guide of some sort. If not, I will come down from London, where D.V. we go on Monday morning.

Please give my fondest love to Carrington. I think of you both a great deal, and dream too. I sleep less and dream more, so that though my life is such a quiet one I have the impression of almost tumultuous accompaniments. What would Dr Freud say? . . . My dreams of Lytton are all much the same. There is a little malice – as when he tells me he rather enjoys so much attention – and then he always makes a surprising recovery. And it may be because I have these dreams at night that I have felt so certain throughout that he would recover. I send you my dreams because I have discovered that my thoughts this month are only the palest echo of them.

Gerald

HAM SPRAY, 15 JANUARY 1932

Dearest Gerald,

The doctor thought Lytton was better today – the first time he had said so for a week – and in the mean time he has been worse. He had a good night without a sleeping draught and even admitted it was good this morning. Our spirits have accordingly whirled up, as early this morning they were down – more because of a violent gale in the night, with a hailstorm which ruined everyone's sleep, than because there was any visible change for the worse. Leonard and Virginia drove down yesterday and took Pippa out to lunch. I've been mistaken about Virginia; somewhere she keeps a warm heart, only not on her sleeve.

Tonight Roger Fry has dinner with Pippa, and James rejoins the camp. It is only when things are average to good that one can face visitors, and one can never count on such a condition of affairs at any future date; but I would like to see you and so would D.C., I think, only she always says she doesn't wish to see anyone. What would be nice is a picnic lunch in between the Ham Spray and the Atlantic depressions. I propose to ring you up one day next week, when local conditions are favourable, about 9 a.m., say, and suggest you catch the 10.45 from Paddington. We'll meet you at Hungerford, go off to the downs and have a walk and come back to tea here, and you could catch the 6.30 back. Only I couldn't give you more notice than that and you mustn't mind saying No if you're busy that day – in that case I'll try another day later. Don't throw anything up, promise, or I shan't be able to ask you. With love. Yours,

Ralph

Lytton Strachey died at 2.30 p.m. on 21 January 1932, five weeks before his fifty-second birthday. A post-mortem, carried out at the insistence of his brother James, revealed that his stomach was practically eaten up by cancer.

Gerald had spent the night before at Ham Spray and returned to London that morning. A few hours later he heard that Lytton was dead. Frances, who was now staying at the Bear Hotel in Hungerford, rang him up early next day and asked him to come down again at once. After lunch he went for a walk with Ralph, who told him that Carrington had tried to commit suicide a few hours before Lytton died. He had found her lying on the floor of the garage, with the engine of the car running. She was already unconscious from the fumes of the exhaust. He dragged her out and carried her up to her bedroom. Had he found her ten minutes later she would have been dead.

She stayed in bed for several days, her own grief aggravated by the sight of Ralph's. 'The kindest thing you could do for me,' she told Frances, 'is to take him away somewhere and spare me the spectacle of it.' Frances did so.

HAM SPRAY, 30 JANUARY 1932

My dearest Gerald,

Thank you so much for asking us next week. I thought we might come to you originally, but now I find I must go to London on Tuesday and start dealing with the lawyer and James. I am so sorry. D.C. will go to Fryern[6] either Monday or Tuesday and I shall stay here until Dodo

6. Augustus John's house in Hampshire.

[Dorelia] takes her away. She will be gone for at least a week, I hope. Frances and I had a quiet uneventful 2 days in Wales with Ros and Wogan,[7] while Julia and Tommy were here with D.C. They kept her going for the time, but she is still terribly low in spirits and in health and has embarked on restless activity about the house, which wears her out. The sooner she is at Fryern, the better. I am still most anxious about her and yet I am practically helpless. Nothing really can console her and any attempt to pretend there is consolation must be a fraud. I hate life. Yours with love always.

Ralph.

16 GREAT JAMES ST, 8 MARCH 1932

Dearest Gerald,

I have been observing signs of improvement in D.C. all last week. She came up to London with me on the Monday and went down again to Ham Spray on the Friday, and spent most of her time with James and Alix, Dorelia and the Tomlins, while she was in London. I hardly saw her except for a few minutes in the mornings, when she was still under the influence of narcotics from the nights before. And yet I don't yet feel security about her. She keeps something up her sleeve the whole time, and she gives too many things away compared to what new things she acquires. I have, however, reached the point where I must cease to interfere with her any more. When she tells me to go away I must go, or my staying becomes too unpleasant for both of us. But it leaves me like a lost soul, fluttering outside her life, afraid to venture in and afraid to fly away further – and this must go on until her life takes on some shape and consistency of its own.

The position here in London too has its anxieties. Our tenants upstairs are anxious to leave us and there is a new pair of Nonesuch tenants down below . . . who impair our amenities. So we think of clearing out at the end of June and going elsewhere. But where in the world are we to go? Another London flat? Ham Spray? A country cottage? Abroad? The answer will be in D.C.'s hands.

Now what are you doing about Gollancz's behaviour?[8] Have you

---

7. The novelist Rosamond Lehmann was then married to the Hon. Wogan Phillips, later Baron Milford, the only Communist peer.

8. Victor Gollancz had accepted a novel by Gamel and had even had it set up in type. But since then Radclyffe Hall's *The Well of Loneliness* had been suppressed, and the publishers prosecuted. As Gamel's book was equally 'daring', Gollancz feared that it and he might suffer the same fate. So he decided not to publish it after all.

inspected Gamel's contract closely to see what legs he has to stand on? If you can't get the Woolfs to publish, (a) you can publish it privately yourself; (b) you might get Mrs Kapp[9] to publish from her new press in Brunswick Square (but that would be rather disreputable); or (c) you can drop publication altogether. If you think of (a) and wish to avoid any risk of proceedings, you should do it from a dummy address abroad, where subscriptions should be sent, but the books can be supplied by you in England.

I shall visit you from Ham Spray at Easter, if not before then. I suffer great depression most of the time, and a sort of cynical reconciliation to existence for the rest. I ate some of your caviar and was pleased to see D.C. writing you a letter about it. My fondest love to you and Gamel. Your

Ralph.

Early in the morning of 11 March, three days after Ralph wrote the above letter and while he was still in London, Carrington shot herself with a gun she had borrowed on the pretext of shooting rabbits from her bedroom window. But the wound was not immediately fatal. She was found by the gardener, who called the doctor and telephoned to Ralph. Bunny Garnett, who was sleeping upstairs at 16 Great James Street, drove him and Frances down to Ham Spray at once. Carrington died not long after they arrived.

HAM SPRAY, 20 MARCH 1932

My dearest Gerald,

I have not been able to write, not even to thank you for sheltering me. D.C. is the only person I want to write to – I almost do at moments when my disbelief is strongest. I *cannot* believe it. At times I try to force what it means into my senses, but they rebel. Yesterday when I was in her room it began to come over me. For several hours I felt I could not go on living – exactly what she must have felt about Lytton. There was no alternative; the desire to escape the pain by unconsciousness was overwhelming. Then I went into the garden and sat in her grove, and all my disbelief returned. It was impossible for her not to be there. I have proved to myself her absence repeatedly, but the belief returns under the surface. In some ways I expect letters from her when the post comes. It may be a wise precaution biologically, this stubborn resistance to facts, but it makes me regard myself as half mad and only half eager to be sane . . .

Two nights only here; then we go to Great James St for one, and then

9. Author of the Sapphic novel *Nobody Asked You*, written under the name of Yvonne Cloud and published by the Willy-Nilly Press in 1932.

abroad in James's car. I shall visit Oosthove Farm, Bus, Hébuterne, Pozières and Péronne[9a] before proceeding to Avignon, where I hand the car back to James. Poste Restante, Avignon will be the address until 8 April. After that we may go anywhere, but I have bargained to pick the car up again at Avignon on 30 April and drive it back to England. Do come and stay in the flat for as long as you like while we're away . . . April will probably be horrid in the country unless you enjoy tropical rainfall. We'll leave the keys on the mantelpiece for you.

There will hardly be a prospect of Yegen without you there. Montpellier, Beaumes-de-Venise, or even the Pyrenees? I'll let you know. My fondest love to you always. Your

Ralph.

EAST LULWORTH, 4 APRIL 1932

My dearest Ralph,

I got your two letters and your postcard, and I suppose that by now you are getting near Avignon. We are going to London on Wednesday for a few nights, as I wish to see Alix and Tommy (if he is not too inaccessible) and Gamel to see an oculist.

Your letter expressed what I have also felt – a complete inability to believe that she is dead. Most of the time the words seem to have no meaning. No habits of correspondence or meeting linked us together any longer. As disappointment followed disappointment, I think I had ceased to think of her often. I ought therefore to have pretty well 'got over it', as they say, and yet I see that there are several reasons why I shall never get over it. She was so deeply embedded in my mind and life that every now and again the superficial layer is uncovered and then the realization that she is dead – not merely that I shall never see her again but that she is herself non-existent – comes home to me. At night sometimes, following evenings when my own forgetfulness has astonished me, I have terrible dreams which show me that in one part of my mind at least I have understood her death only too well. One or two that I remembered I wrote down and will show you.

I feel tired and unable to write coherently tonight. I only wished you should have a letter on reaching Avignon. I will write again from London. With fondest love to you and Frances from us both. Always yours,

Gerald

9a. It was Ralph's idea that the best antidote to present anguish was a return to the scenes of anguish in the past – namely the battlefields he had known in the war.

AVIGNON, 10 APRIL 1932

My dearest Gerald,

I was very pleased to find a letter from you here. I hope you will stay in the flat in London as long as you like. We are going today to the Hôtel du Château at Beaumes-de-Venise, recommended by you and Helen Anrep – your recommendation outweighing hers. We shall stay there for at least a week and that will be our only known address. We had a look at the place in the car and it seemed suitable for walking about and looking at flowers, though many of them seem already over. The sun came out as we reached Orange and not a moment before – nothing but rain from Arras to Verdun, to Metz, to Nancy, to Dijon, to Lyon, even to Valence.

Last night James and Alix arrived punctually and took over the car. They have driven off in the direction of the Bussys.[1] It is possible we may go to Cassis[2] to see Duncan [Grant] and Vanessa [Bell] for a day or two; otherwise we have no arrangements after Beaumes. Driving a car is a sort of mild drug; it prevents the mind from diverting itself very far from the immediate present in time and space. I have no object in this voyage except to pass the time until it is less oppressive. I have not succeeded so far. She accompanies me everywhere and yet she is nowhere. Please write just a line to me again at Beaumes. I should like to hear news of Alix and Tommy. We hardly had any talk with her and James except about motoring. My fondest love to you. Your

Ralph

EAST LULWORTH, 11 APRIL 1932

Dearest Ralph,

We arrived back from London an hour ago. I was a little disappointed at not finding a postcard awaiting me from you. Though I have started this letter I do not know what to say. I never saw London so sad and dismal, nor felt myself so cut off from everyone in it. One meets people, one talks, without being able to say what one is thinking. Afterwards one hates them, whilst they jump to all sorts of erroneous conclusions about one's character. I may have been a simple, honest man once; now I feel myself such a jumble of thoughts and feelings, and in other parts so numb and paralysed, that I am not sure I have any right to my name and existence. Can it be this – that the most important event in life is

1. The French painter Simon Bussy and his wife Dorothy, Lytton's second sister. They lived at Roquebrune on the Mediterranean coast.
2. Cassis had long been a favourite holiday place for Bloomsbury.

unintelligible? I can neither think of *that*, nor think for long together of anything else . . .

There is no doubt I do not feel in love with the world at the moment; no one satisfies me; I should like to fall asleep and remain asleep for a long time. But as I do not know what I feel, why write about it? By the way, Alec [Penrose] complained at lunch today that this had been a pretty bad winter *for him also*! He has come into £100,000, that's his trouble. I can't blunt my eyes to the fact that if I were to come into, say, £10,000 tomorrow I would feel very much better. I would take an overland ticket for China at once, and two more for you and Frances. We would not come back till we had grown pigtails down to our waists and got to like boiled potatoes better than lychees in syrup. As it is, here we must stew and let our bank balances make a kind of symbol of our fortunes – down, down, down, perpetually, till nothing of either them or us is left.

Illness meets one now at every step, in every letter. Tonight Gamel heard that her first – should I say, 'late'? – husband had congestion of the lungs, whatever that means, following flu. As he had no money at all and no one to look after him, she is very upset. Then last week Llewellyn [Powys] had a haemorrhage, after two years' intermission, and (characteristically) walked twelve miles the next day. My old nurse, who has been very ill since January, just keeps going. Gamel, however, is well, which I am thankful for – for my life would fly to pieces without her. Now I am sorry to have written in this strain; it will only depress you when you are bathing in mountain streams and picking spring flowers. Don't forget you are both of you my dearest friends.

Gerald

16 GREAT JAMES ST, 12 MAY 1932

My dearest Gerald,

I hope you saw from the wire what I meant. I only want you to come to Ham Spray if *you* like. If you'd rather, I'll come over to Lulworth one day at the weekend. I suppose you'll drive over if you come. Now I'm back I shall have to make some plans, but I'm going to see what Ham Spray is like first.

We had a wet drive back through France. I went to Serre and Hébuterne – they were still finding bodies in No Man's Land – Sailly-au-Bois, the *épicerie* vanished – Bus, squalid as ever – Anthie, and the bakery – and spent a night at the Quatre Fils d'Armon at Doullens, kept by a sour old spinster. I visited a good many cemeteries. Nothing could be more English than the English ones – croquet-lawn paths and daffodils, with gardeners touching their caps. The Somme was a waste of pale green wheat and grey tombs in alternate fields . . . I don't dread tomorrow at all – a Friday, the ninth of the series.[3] How many more? My fondest love always. Yours,

Ralph

HAM SPRAY, 26 AUGUST 1932

Dearest Gerald,

I am very glad the operation[4] is over at any rate and that they found nothing malignant. That excludes the main anxiety. The minor anxieties, however, are less readily tolerated by the human system and some of these must remain until the whole breast situation returns to normal; so I am very sorry that you will be pinned to London for 3 weeks, with further X-rays to follow . . .

I have been in low spirits down here for the last week – plenty of sleep at night, but great depression all day long . . . I have no aptitude for life left; nothing holds my interest more than a page of *The Times* – and yesterday's *Times* at that. I would persuade myself it was my health, only I have no symptoms to improve upon. I have no desire to go away from here; in fact any suggestion that I should do so rouses all the determination I have left in opposition. Four months have passed, an English summer, in a flash . . . I have done none of the things I had hoped to do in that time. There is no one I particularly care to see any more, though it is never wise to confess to hostile feelings. I cling to Frances more and more, and I never waver about you. The rest go up and down like a seesaw. I seem to wish to see them only for the purpose of disliking them and wishing them away. My fondest love to you always.

Ralph

Gamel's operation, though completely successful, left her very run down; so Gerald decided to drive her out to Yegen where, he hoped, the sun and mountain air would do her good.

HAM SPRAY, 3 NOVEMBER 1932

My dearest Gerald,

What is your child like?[5] In your letter you never refer to it. I should have thought it would have been your first enquiry on getting to Yegen,

3. i.e. the ninth since Carrington's suicide.
4. Gamel had developed a tumour on her breast and it had had to be removed.
5. Miranda, as the child came to be called, was then just beginning to toddle. Gerald and Gamel had decided to adopt her in a year's time.

even before a garage for the car. The length of the upper lip is the test feature to exclude Paco and the lorry-driver from paternity, in case you weren't aware. There are any number of other features as well, but they won't have developed far enough to show as yet . . .

The most humble cottage-pie life goes on here, and that is the best I can do for myself. Every fortnight we go to London for three days, but I never know what to do there. I'm a confirmed misanthrope; I never expect to make any new friends and I can never make up my mind whether I can stand the ones I seem to have. Last week there was one of those dreary features of London life, a cocktail party at the Meynells. The drinks were powerful, but that hardly seems to me enough to build upon. The girls were familiar by sight and in manner, yet what on earth's to be done with those old faces and those old bodies? Were they ever worth having? I have no desire to have them now. You see how I feel – very extenuated and dimsy about everything except Ham Spray and Tiber[6] and the aspen-tree. And am I to lop that or not? There were two gales about a week ago, when I hardened my heart, and yet . . . Now it is so calm and still and the yellow leaves flutter straight to the ground, so why do anything? There are such excellent reasons for action and equally good ones for inaction that I'm tempted to leave it to the tree to decide how long it shall stay there.

I've started to sort out D.C.'s letters, having at last finished Lytton's. I can't find any from Lytton to her – can she have destroyed them? It doesn't tally with her character to do that; but I've searched the studio and her room and I don't believe they're in the house unless she hid them, and in that case they're 'buried treasure'. It is very depressing. I can only do it for an hour or two at a time and then I have to go out for a walk or do some gardening . . . You have principles on these questions. What do you say? Ought I to keep everything or make a bonfire of all the rubbish? Barbara kept on whining steadily for 12 years, for instance. My own letters make such a wretched impression on me that I'm tempted never to write to anyone again. They are utterly unsympathetic, and yet there was never a time when I didn't feel as if I was inextricably involved in her. Not a trace of that feeling appears; they're just jaunty or silly or off-hand or resentful. Where did my love for her go? Did she have to deduce it always from my criticisms and abuse? – for she certainly knew I loved her. I cannot help being ashamed of myself that I could contribute so

6. The Ham Spray cat, named after Matthew Arnold's lines: 'So Tiberius might have sat, Had Tiberius been a cat.'

little to her happiness while she was alive; it convinces me that I am a hopeless character, as I can never hope to become more agreeable as I get older and I haven't been at all agreeable in my youth. I even think I don't want to be agreeable ever again, even if I could be.

I wish you had left copies of your MS with me before you went, as you once said you would, or will your book come as a pleasant surprise instead? My means of communication with you are only these vile letters which I can't manage, but at least I can stutter out that I love you.

R.

PART THREE   1934–1941

Ralph and Frances were married in February 1933, and visited Gerald at Yegen in March. Three months later Gerald and Gamel returned to England. They were now determined to live permanently in the south of Spain, but somewhere more accessible than Yegen. Gamel's health required that they should again spend the winter abroad and, since they had let the Yegen house, they decided to try Portugal. But no sooner were they settled at Praia da Rocha in the Algarve than Gerald developed bronchial pneumonia and was bedridden for several weeks.

Dearest Gerald,

Your letter has just come. I am extremely sorry to hear you are so ill. It is a bad thing to have a temperature for so long on end, but in the end it may be a guarantee that you will still be at Praia da Rocha when we arrive, because for every day of high temperature you have 3 days of convalescence later on. If it would be any help to you and Gamel we could start earlier, but we are thinking of coming on the Dutch boat sailing from Southampton on 16 February, reaching Lisbon 19 February and Praia da Rocha on 20. This plan we shall carry out unless you'd like us to hurry . . . We may bring somebody with us, but I've no idea who it may be so far – perhaps just a squad of hospital nurses to have round our beds. Have you any idea how you caught your disease? Is influenza rife in the country? It sounds to me as if you'd got a touch of bronchitis and aggravated it by driving 200 miles in a day and that there may be a danger of Gamel catching it too . . . Fondest love always to you.

Ralph

By the time Ralph and Frances reached Praia da Rocha, Gerald had recovered sufficiently to drive on to Yegen where he had agreed to spend a few weeks with his tenants, an extremely attractive young man called Mark Culme-Seymour and his still more attractive sister Angela.

Dearest Ralph,

The weather is now so marvellously fine, the sun so hot, the air so light and clear, that I feel very sad to think that we must ever leave Yegen. But indeed we must. A thousand reasons urge it. One of the principal ones came up today when I went down to Ugíjar to put in an application for

the adoption of the child. Its new name will be Miranda Woolsey y
Brenan – for Helen and Rose, family appelations, are to be expunged. It
is a sweet little child and I am delighted with it . . .

I have been very happy and working. Angela brought a flood of high
spirits. She's a *most* charming young woman – no mistake about that –
but you mustn't imagine I had an *affair* with her. No one is attractive to
me in that way except Gamel; and if anyone were, she must have a
darker skin and foreign language to draw me. 'So you're in a rut, it
seems?' I am, and have no wish at all to get out of it. That is why the total
effect of Angela was to make me more in love with Gamel than I have
ever been before, but not to the disparagement of Angela for whom I
have a different, almost brotherly feeling – difficult for a 1000 per cent
he-man like you to understand . . .

Gerald

YEGEN, 26 APRIL 1934

Dearest Ralph,
Cold winds have returned – yesterday a shower of snow fell – and we
crouch again over the fire . . .

I have just had Chatto & Windus's receipts. About three copies of
J[ack] R[obinson] seem to have sold since Christmas. I shall have made
£105 from English and Colonial sales, including the advance of £50
which I have spent. It is certainly a gloomy business. The wolf is now just
outside the door; we must settle in Spain and give up all hopes of living in
England till better times come. We have found someone who will
undertake looking after the child for 25/– a week and we shall leave it
with them soon after we get back, as from us it will never learn either
English or manners. I have been going into the question of adopting the
child. After paying for various documents I discover that we cannot
adopt it until one or both of us has reached the age of forty-five; to make
up, we can then adopt any person of not over forty! A house has been
found for Juliana for 1000 pesetas and I shall not continue to be
responsible for her. Miranda, Oriana, Persecaria, Pauperina – what
names do you favour for the child? Miranda suggests its origin and lack
of education; it has not yet learnt to blow its nose.

I do not know why I began this letter, seeing that I have nothing
whatever to say. My fondest love to you and Frances, who wrote a very
nice letter.

Gerald

After a long reconnaissance of the coast between Algeciras and Malaga, Gerald at last settled on a house at the entrance to the Coin Valley as a substitute for Yegen.

MALAGA, 3 JUNE 1934

Dearest Ralph,

Well, we have bought the house and are off. £1120 at present rate of exchange, including fees and taxes. Then we shall have to spend £70 on doing it up, something on the garden, and more on knocking down three houses and doing up that required for Antonio.[7] I am a little alarmed by it. But the house is extraordinarily lovely, early 18th-century, views of mountains and sea from every upstairs window, and the garden magnificent. Gamel is really enchanted by it, and that I consider the most important thing. Then I like the country round very much indeed. It is beautiful, open and suited to ordinary life. We got the house cheap and, if things went badly, could always let it at a high rent to the English who now swarm at Torremolinos and Malaga.

There is no more to say. We get back to Yegen tonight and go on almost at once to Almeria with Maria and Miranda – an introduction to new life. (We shall stay, though, at a 7-peseta pension – we do things on the cheap now.) Then, after packing up and a last hunt for plates, and so on, we catch the Dutch liner on the 23rd. Fondest love to you both.

Gerald

P.S. The name of the village is *Churriana*, which means *whore*; and the name of the person from whom we bought the house is Don Carlos *Crooke*, which means –? However, he is a very nice man.

Though they had signed the deed of purchase, Gamel and Gerald could not obtain possession of the house till the end of the year; so they spent the intervening months at Lulworth before returning to Spain in November. They moved into Churriana on Christmas Eve, and an army of masons moved in on top of them. It took five months to make the house habitable. Meanwhile Ralph and Frances, who were to be the first visitors, had to change their plans.

HAM SPRAY, 19 DECEMBER 1934

Dearest Gerald,

Frances has got herself into trouble with some pig's ovaries, which were highly recommended to her. A quantity of her urine was handed to a messenger, who took it to Paddington where it was injected into a mouse. Five days later the mouse delivered its little oracle and she is

7. The gardener, husband of Maria's sister Rosario. So Gerald now had a staff of three.

officially, and with all the authority of modern science, with child. As a possible father I feel very out of it. Nobody wants my urine; I wasn't even given a pig's testicle for supper. As Frances is so quaintly constructed, she must not go on buses, trams, trains or boats for the next two months, for fear of miscarriages – there has already been a faint attempt at one, which has been beaten off with large yellow pellets . . . Most probably she will not be allowed to travel after the 2 months, so you mustn't count on seeing us in Spain after all . . .

I can't think of any present for you, so I hope you and Gamel will put up with my fondest love for this Christmas. Yours,

R.

HAM SPRAY, 5 JUNE 1935

Dearest Gerald,

Is it true that I haven't written to you for several weeks? Not since the Caesarian question came up? Well, I never. I thought it was only the other day and that I must have already told you all the pros and cons. Frances has a bunch of fibroids inside her. I don't know what they are exactly, but they're always described as benign but uncomfortable and if they reach a certain stage of size and discomfort they ought to be removed. Surgeon Ellison, when he saw Frances three weeks ago, suggested that although she was getting along nicely enough during gestation, the actual birth of the child might be impeded in the natural course by some of the fibroids and lead to delay and haemorrhage, and that if he did a Caesarian about ten days before the due date he could remove the fibroids at the same time as the child, thereby obviating the possibility of having to have another operation in a year or two's time to remove the fibroids and making sure of the child's birth not being interfered with. It is not yet decided on finally, as she is to see him again next week and ask a few questions. For one thing I've heard from Lionel Penrose that a Caesarian is the slightest operation if done quickly, and rapidly becomes more severe according to the time it takes, owing to special operational shock. If these fibroids are going to delay the operation beyond the crucial period we will reconsider it. But if he can guarantee to do the whole thing within 15 minutes it will be safe enough. In other ways it has advantages – 1) certainty of time of birth; 2) avoidance of possible damage and horror of birth of the child; 3) no laceration of female genitals with consequent frigidity (such as every normal mother seems to suffer from for years if not permanently); and 4) removal of the horrid fibroids so that one need never mention their name again. If it is fixed up it will be for 10 July (within a day or so)[8] and we go up to London to prepare for it on 1 July. In any case that's the day we leave Ham Spray, even if we have to hang about London till Nature functions . . .

As we haven't been to London for 3 weeks, I've no gossip. We've had some foul weather and no prospects of better. If you get back about the 21st of this month you'd better come and stay here pretty quick or we shall be flown. Any time in June will suit us perfectly, but nothing later.

The death of Colonel Lawrence[9] has fluttered England more than the earthquake at Quetta[1]. 'The loss to literature' is so severe. But I can bear it, can't you? Ours is the Lawrence epoch, in which D.H.[2] and the Colonel seem to be expressing the spirit of the age and idealizing it. The sooner it's over the better, unless there is only a Hitler–Stalin age to follow and no more literature, only politics and economics. Fondest love to you both . . . Yours,

Ralph

By the time the workmen had finished with the Churriana house, Gerald and Gamel found themselves in possession of one of the most beautiful properties in the area. So they returned to England to fetch their furniture before hurrying back to Spain and settling in.

EAST LULWORTH, 25 SEPTEMBER 1935

My dearest Ralph,

I have been making my will and, as before, have left you, Bunny and Gamel executors. In the event of Gamel's death before myself I leave everything to Miranda and appoint Blair and Rhoda[3] her guardians. As you know, I think, she is not my adopted daughter and cannot be by Spanish law until I am 45. But I have called her so and I wish you to maintain that she is if English lawyers should make enquiries. Forget her past name and Juliana's name and everything. She has no documents except her Spanish passport, which is never used and should on our death be destroyed. If we should die together in an accident in Spain, our servants have instructions to take her at once to Mrs Bush, Villa Sol y Mar, Torremolinos, who should hurry her off to Gibraltar. For, as you'll

8. The child, a boy, was in fact born by Caesarian section on 8 July, and named Burgo.
9. T. E. Lawrence – Lawrence of Arabia – had just been killed in a motor-cycle crash.
1. Which occurred on 31 May 1935, burying some 20,000 of the population in the ruins of their homes.
2. i.e. D. H. Lawrence, the novelist.
3. Gerald's brother and sister-in-law.

see, if Juliana were to hear of our death and get hold of her, she might be able to keep her and get her money. She must therefore be spirited out of Spain and not allowed to return there until legally free.

You would have the house at Churriana on your hands. I would suggest letting it through the Malaga house agency, keeping on Antonio and Rosario, and getting rid of Maria who is useless. I would not like it sold if that could be avoided. Maria should be given a good present, and something sent to Juliana from time to time to keep her quiet if she bothered you.

I don't pretend this to be a letter, so I stop with my best love.

Gerald

HAM SPRAY, 1 OCTOBER 1935

Dearest Gerald,

I suppose you have signed this new will of yours and left it with a lawyer, but I can't believe you took anyone's advice over it or you would realize what the result may be. Juliana has given you custody of the child for cash. On your death she is entitled once more to the custody of the child by Spanish and English law. You are not even registered as its father, so you have no power to dispose of it. The fact that you do dispose of it, to Blair and Rhoda, amounts to kidnapping. You cannot kidnap children with impunity alive; far less, after you're dead, can you do it at all. You can leave instructions and people will promise to carry them out, but of course they won't dream of doing so when you're not there to tyrannize over them. If the child were to get as far as Gibraltar, which is most unlikely, all your estate would be consumed in paying lawyers and the end would be the same – Miranda, when penniless, would be returned to her mother.

The simplest and obvious thing is to leave 1000 pesetas a year for 20 years to Juliana, provided she allows the child to live in England and be brought up by Blair – *nothing*, if she won't, and in that case nothing to Miranda until she reaches the age of 21. If Juliana is more maternal than mercenary, she can always get the child – even tomorrow if she wanted to – from you. But if, as you believe, she prefers money, Blair will get the child without fail. If you leave the money to Miranda and try any tricks from the grave, Juliana will certainly get her and what money the lawyers leave, which won't be much but Juliana will think it more than it is. Still, as you're not in any danger of death, the whole question is academic. And remember, you are the final incarnation of Machiavelli; nobody is going to emulate you on your decease out of respect for your memory. We shall all remain as humdrum and unadventurous as ever . . .

I shall spend the winter doing the index to Greville,[4] or so I say, but I expect Frances will do most of it . . . Fondest love to you both.

Ralph

CHURRIANA, n.d.

My dearest Ralph,

You are entirely right in your remarks upon my will and I wish I had asked your advice before. I shall draw up a new will as soon as possible, leaving Juliana about 500 pesetas a year for 20 years. At present she gets only half of this. Should I die before this has been done, please do your best. I am telling her that the child has been adopted by English law, and she is easy to deal with if a small present is sent. But I hope to live at least through the present month, and if I live for three years she can be formally adopted. Though I have none of your belief in my longevity, that is a reasonable expectation . . .

I hear that war has broken out [in Abyssinia] though I have not seen a paper. Churriana is greatly perturbed. Maria and Rosario begged me to buy them gas masks, and my old soldier's stories of 1915–1917 find an eager audience. The Catholic papers say that it's all a Soviet plot against a great man (Musso[lini]) who is trying to bring a little civilization to Africa. The Left are all for the League [of Nations], and the more Left they are the more warlike. But as fidelity to the League is incorporated in the Spanish constitution, the Right will not be able to act very openly. I don't anticipate anything very dramatic occurring before Christmas and, whatever happens in the Mediterranean, I see little danger of a *general* European war for some years. The chief outcome of this will be a new arrangement of forces. I hope that if Mussolini cannot be stopped we clear out of European affairs altogether. What I feel is that we shall be caught in some quite useless and dangerous compromise; for it is a difficult thing to make a *volte face* in foreign policy, especially when there is such a clever man as Laval[5] on the watch to prevent it. You don't

4. After Lytton's death the task of editing the Greville Memoirs had been carried on by Ralph and Frances, who also undertook to prepare a full index volume. The edition, with a preface by Roger Fulford, was eventually published in 1938.
5. Pierre Laval, foreign minister and Prime Minister of France. He and Sir Samuel Hoare, the British foreign secretary, signed a pact aimed at settling the conflict – but at Abyssinia's expense. The consequent storm of protest that burst in Britain and France led to Hoare's resignation and Laval's dismissal from the premiership.

give any inkling of what you think. But really how tedious and stupid all these schemings and plannings are, and yet everything we care for depends upon guessing right!

Our house and garden are a paradise. Trees and plants grow by magic here, but if I say this too often the great Mussolini of Ham Spray will begin to envy me my Abyssinia and I shall have all the pleasure I get in it taken from me. Please give Frances my fondest love and let us cry quits on our last letters. Your devoted

Gerald

HAM SPRAY, 7 NOVEMBER 1935

Dearest Gerald,

For a month I have been having bronchitis and not enjoying it at all. The after-effects are depression and complete loss of the senses of taste and smell. And depression takes the form with me at once of disliking everyone for very good reasons, but particularly everyone who wishes to close the Suez Canal. In fact I refuse to vote for anyone who is so stupidly bellicose and, as I have a horror of voting for the Government,[6] I see that I need not bother to vote at all but shall go up to London for the day instead . . . The general election is duller than any election in my lifetime, simply because there is no chance of a change of government and no question at issue between anybody. The sort of thing that happens is a violent dispute about what Lord Snowden said when he was Mr Snowden in 1931 and whether it is consistent with what he said in 1932. A desperate hunt round for personalities in default of politics, and such dull personalities! Not even Sir Stafford Cripps[7] dares accuse Mr Baldwin of being a bugger or telling a lie. Dear old Lansbury[8] is the man I would vote for, but the Labour Party are too ashamed of him even to mention him.

I hear that the Sheppards[9] have taken a house in Churriana with one table and nothing more in it. I make my private forecast of your behaviours to that ménage, but it remains an *absolute secret* until it is confirmed by events. The little girls and Miranda are so suited to each

---

6. Stanley Baldwin, the Conservative leader, had succeeded Ramsay Macdonald as Prime Minister on the latter's retirement. In the election he was returned with a majority of nearly 250.

7. Sir Stafford resigned from the Labour Party's executive when the party supported economic sanctions against Italy.

8. George Lansbury, leader of the Labour Party, also resigned as his strongly pacifist views were not accepted by the majority of his followers.

9. Clare and Sydney Sheppard, both sculptors. She was a niece of Molly MacCarthy.

other that they are almost bound to hate each other at sight . . . Fondest love to you and Gamel.

Ralph

CHURRIANA, 22 JANUARY 1936

Dearest Ralph,

We have had rain, fog and cloud nearly every day this month and I'm glad to think you've not had any better. The chief pleasure of living abroad is saying to oneself how much finer weather one is having than other people. We now have workmen in the house; two coke stoves are being installed; there is to be an apparatus for heating water, and an arbour in the garden. The patio is to be tiled in a pattern of black and white pebbles. I get up late and most of the day seems to go in talking to Sydney [Sheppard] and in reading.

My new book, however, holds its own and has even made progress. That is to say, of the hundred pages I wrote, about thirty remain. I can look at them five days out of seven without actual repulsion, and sometimes with approval, which means that I shall go on with it. I became, as I told you, a novelist overnight – that is the part I have to check, for I dislike and distrust the plot spinnings of novelists above everything. The discovery of the plot and characters is the most elementary part of the business for me and simply gives a framework within which one must pick and choose and create incidents.

I have always disliked the unreality of almost all novels, especially of English ones. The predominance of the plot-character convention, the obviousness and dullness of the development, the mass of tricks that have to be used, the almost complete severance from actual experience, have made them, in my mind at least, utterly tedious. In J[ack] R[obinson] I tried to avoid some of this unreality by presenting actual sensations with greater fullness than is usually admitted into novels. This can only be done by rhythmical arrangements of words – 'poetry'. The dialogue had to be keyed up to accord with it. I found the management of these rhythms very troublesome; I was continually slipping into rhetoric and false feeling. Owing to the absence of metre, prose rhythms are less pliant than those of poetry; it is difficult to arrest or moderate any emphatic rhythm that has been set up. My ignorance, or a lack of interest in the material, also tended to throw me more into portrayal of sense impressions – i.e. into poetry. Hence the vices of that book (for which, by the way, I feel such horror that I cannot open it or see it lying about without a wish to hide it).

My new book is in the form of memoirs; these memoirs will be more or less parallel to the course of my own life. The style is plain, with only rarely any approach to poetry. The general tone is rather gay than sad. To write it, I sink into myself like another Descartes. I put away all thoughts of other books and try to discover what I actually do remember. Then, taking these atoms of memory, I change them and combine them into little incidents and then into anecdotes, which I try to make amusing and illustrative of some general tendency. These anecdotes are my units, which are connected to one another by links of various kinds. Such is the form I am aiming at, then, suggested, as you will see, by Zeno. I do not suppose I shall be able to keep very closely to it or that I shall be able to avoid *all* the fictions and empty inventions of novelists. Since I do not aim at absolute consistency of method, that does not so much matter. Novels are steeplechases where one has often to get over the ground as best one can. But I shall *test* the incidents as often as possible, by examination and introspection, in what I suppose I can call my pseudo-memory. I hope in this way to produce at the end of four or five years what Montaigne would call *un livre de bonne foi,* an honest book.[1]

I need scarcely say that I do not consider memory to be a well of truth; on the contrary, it distorts nearly everything and then it creates as well. It requires a great many checks to be applied to it. But by returning to actual memories (as in *J.R.* I returned to actual visualizations) one escapes the danger of novelizing – a danger as great and as universal as is the danger of rhetoric in poetry. Novels, for example, such as [E.M.] Forster's, are entirely composed of it, and even in better novels it forms a large percentage of the total.

But this must be a tedious letter to you. The rain has come again; the workmen with their dirty boots, the children who collect round them, have an unsettling effect. And even a cold in the head (that magic carpet for carrying one back into the past) fails in its usual spell. The Russells[2] (duly married) arrive on the 4th. I hope the weather will have changed by then. I wonder if you got your aspen down before the storm; I read of it in the *Sol* and felt some anxiety. Now that Edward-Eden[3] reigns, the astrologers prophesy a new epoch of brotherly love. I shall be satisfied if it helps to put everyone with pre-war mentality on the shelf . . .

1. This novel, provisionally titled *Segismundo,* never saw the light of day. After writing more than 200,000 words, Gerald abandoned it in 1946.
2. The philosopher Bertrand Russell and his second wife Patricia ('Peter'), *née* Spence.
3. Edward VIII had succeeded to the throne on 20 January. Anthony Eden had been foreign secretary since the previous December.

My father speaks of coming out in April; he seems really decided to leave Edgeworth this summer. He doesn't generally come to this decision before June or July; but this winter the hunting has been bad and the weather worse, so he may do it. Fondest love to you both.

Gerald

HAM SPRAY, 10 FEBRUARY 1936

Dearest Gerald,

... I've been reading Samuel Butler's life and I am struck by the resemblances to yours, but I don't expect you to be. The clue to his character is his relation to his father, whom he hated and admired passionately. His whole life was spent longing for his father to die, and after his father's death he felt thwarted and unappreciated because there was no one to quarrel with, because even Darwin was dead too – his father substitute. So he concocted another synthetic father out of the whole body of elderly classical scholars and wrote *The Authoress of the Odyssey* to annoy them. But his fury knew no bounds when they didn't even bother to answer him and refute him. He continually appealed for appreciation to posterity, and the last years of his life were devoted to preparing all his papers for posterity – and what has posterity done for poor old Samuel Butler? Paid rather less attention to him than his own generation.

Maynard [Keynes] has written a new book on money[4] which upsets the whole classical theory of economics. I am delighted with what I have read, though I already see I'm not going to agree with his own new theory. So far no one has dared review it for fear of saying the wrong thing. The franc still hasn't gone, but I still hope to go to Paris before Easter ... The Sheppards seem to like their house and intend staying until July, I hear. With fondest love to you both.

Ralph

CHURRIANA, 19 FEBRUARY 1936

Dearest Ralph,

We have had four days of warm Atlantic winds and rain – very disagreeable. The election[5] took place in a downpour. The Right expected a great victory and have had a great defeat. It was the 30,000

---

4. *The General Theory of Employment, Interest, and Money* (Macmillan, 1936).
5. The election of 16 February had resulted in a victory for the Popular Front; and Manuel Azaña, leader of the Republican Left, was officially elected President on 10 May.

political prisoners, most of them still untried, who decided the issue. There has been much alarm that Azaña has taken over the government without waiting for the second election (which will decide a few seats) to take place. In my opinion the victory of the Left is a very fortunate thing. Had they lost I should have expected another revolution, or Fascism, or more likely both.

I am sorry Mrs Marshall[6] has been ill and glad to hear you wish to make her life more comfortable and contented. I wonder, however, if you set about it as you do about me. If so, I expect her not to live much longer. But though I see you are anxious to depress me as much as possible, by showing the futility of my writing another line, I'm not going to be drawn into expostulation. I'll only say you chose your example badly, for Samuel Butler was little known during his life and has become very famous since his death. His ideas have influenced even the people of Malaga. So you see you have had the fate of Balaam, and your comparison – meant to be injurious – has done for me far too much honour . . .

We had a luncheon party today – 8 people. Maria wore a white apron she had made expressly and everything went without a hitch except that the coffee was served in a butler's tray. We get very cheap and good *pâté-de-foie-gras* out here and Gamel has learned an Italian macaroni with olives and peppers that is quite delicious. I wish you were here to teach us how to make good mayonnaise, and I would read Samuel Butler aloud to you whilst you did it. Otherwise our life is very quiet: a walk after lunch; and after tea Bertie [Russell] reads aloud diaries and letters of the year 1860, for he is writing a memoir of his parents . . . My fondest love to Frances.

Gerald

CHURRIANA, 15 MARCH 1936

Dearest Ralph,

. . . Why not come and stay with us for a bit? My parents are definitely not coming out and we should very much like to have you. There is plenty of room for Burgo and Nursie too . . . You'll see a lot of old friends out here . . . And there is Angela's sister Janetta,[7] aged fifteen, who has set my heart on fire.

There have been rather severe riots at Granada; they only lasted half a

6. Frances's mother.
7. Angela's half-sister, the daughter of Reverend Geoffrey Woolley VC and Jan, *née* Orr-Ewing, widow of George Culme-Seymour.

day, but the chief cafés and the theatre were burnt down and 40 people are said to have been killed. At Cadiz they are said to have broken into the convents and driven the nuns out naked. Mrs Balfour[8] is living in a convent in the heart of the poor quarter and I have advised Clare to go in and get her out. But she longs to be a martyr and will not move. Tomorrow there will probably be rioting in Malaga, and anything may happen. These things do not appear in the papers.

I think the situation in Spain rather critical. Azaña now represents the Centre, for the Socialist party are so elated by the elections that they wish to impose a Dictatorship of the Proletariat. I do not exactly know what that means; but more and more newspapers of the Left come out with larger and larger headlines and less and less information, and political passions are stronger than ever. But I do not think anything will happen for some months. The Right are squabbling among themselves. The Fascists, though very few in number, act as a kind of leaven as in France; they have unpleasant habits of shooting from balconies at processions of workmen. Azaña, by English standards, belongs to the extreme Left, but he has become suddenly the bulwark against economic revolution. Even the Jesuit party is to support him. And I dare say he will succeed, until a European war comes and makes everyone in Spain prosperous.

The weather is delicious. In the garden our tulips are in flower. Why not take the next boat out? I think that in such a lovely climate you are likely to be in a lenient mood and to overlook the ten thousand glaring faults of your always devoted

Gerald

CHURRIANA, 20 MARCH 1936

Dearest Ralph,

We shall certainly be very offended if you *don't* come and see us . . . I should not pay any attention to the reports of riots in the English papers. The elections passed off in perfect order and the *Daily Mail* had to apologize to the Spanish Government for the stories it told. It had hardly done so when there were severe riots in Granada, Cadiz and Logroño – all places where the Left had lost through, it is said, the bribery of the Right. It certainly seems odd that Granada, which is fanatically Socialist, should return only Right candidates. These riots were put down after a few hours and then came the burning of a church in Madrid. That produced a great effect; the Government issued the severest orders; and

---

8. Clare Sheppard's mother, a staunch Roman Catholic.

as the Cortes have now met I do not think anything will happen. All the Left parties are obliged to support Azaña until his United Front programme is carried out. Then the trouble will come, for the Socialist party will choose the first moment to have a revolution. This summer, then, is likely to be perfectly quiet in Spain . . .

After ten days of lovely weather we have again had torrential rains – very good for the tulips, but bad for everyone else. But the country is looking lovely, so be sure to come here as soon as you can . . . Incidentally, you may meet Señor Largo Caballero,[9] the expective Lenin of Spain; we have a common friend and he expects to be taking a holiday here in April. I think it is a good policy to make up to the man who has the power to cut your head off. Spain is my country, revolution or no revolution, and if it goes red I must try and change my colour too. Fondest love to you and Frances.

Gerald

HAM SPRAY, 25 MARCH 1936

Dearest Gerald,

You may be regretting your warm invitation, but I hope you haven't done so as we are accepting it and coming out by the next boat, the Dutch boat that gets to Gibraltar on 7 April, sailing on 3 from Southampton. If you would allow us to stay with you for a week, we ask nothing better . . . But how on earth does one get to Churianna from Gibraltar?

. . . I had an idea that Seville after Easter, when the *feria* is on, might be delightful and I hope to persuade you to come there with us if the rioting is not too fierce. Ibiza we washed out as it takes too long to get there. But we fancied going home via Barcelona and Paris. We shall only be out of England 3 weeks, and leave the old nurse in charge of Burgo here with her sister to keep her company. As he lies flat on his back or stomach all the time, I don't think he would get much education out of Spain this year. Besides, he's growing teeth, which absorbs all his attention . . . It will be very nice to see you both again so soon. With fondest love.

Ralph

CHURRIANA, n.d.

Dearest Ralph,

A bombshell. My father is coming out after all – arrives Gibraltar on 28 April and leaves 14 May. It is inevitable and unavoidable and I

9. Largo Caballero was to head the Popular Front Government later that year.

suppose we shall support it somehow. Will you come earlier? I should be very disappointed if you came to Spain without coming here; indeed I doubt if any part of Spain except just round here is safe to travel in. We will make an expedition to Antequera. That is a very nice town with very large prehistoric tombs, the largest in Europe except for Mycenae. There is also El Torcal, a natural granite maze in the mountains, which it takes 3 days to explore. One cannot go there without guides, for one is lost in a moment – so they say, for I have never been there, but the mountains are very fine.

The local syndicate rules all our affairs here now; but they seem surprisingly moderate and I am on good terms with some of the leaders, so I don't think they'll cut my head off. We have had a terrible week of rain and the country is waterlogged. Much love, and send a wire when you come.

Gerald

HAM SPRAY, 29 APRIL 1936

Dearest Gerald,

We whizzed back from Barcelona in 24 hours in considerable comfort and thus completed my plan on the exact day originally intended. It is a burden to me, this resolute adherence to plans once made. If I deviate from the plans I'm precipitated into anxiety and bad temper, and if I stick to it I get no positive satisfaction whatever, only the bare escape from vacillation. Thus my life gets less and less elastic as I wear blinkers of my own manufacture and go trotting to my destinations like an old tram horse.

Seville was delightful ... Rosamond and Wogan turned up by bus from Gibraltar and stuck to us until Barcelona. Ros thought the Guadalquivir inferior to the Thames, but otherwise was not too lady-like ... Ros, Wog and I went to the bullfight alongside the new President of the Republic, and saw some terrific feats by very young matadors. For once they were on their mettle and took risks; one got a slight toss and a picador had a horn through his leg. The fair went on every day and was a dream of beauty, and the royal apartments at the Alcazar were wonderful. I'd never been since the Republic, nor had I seen the Zurbarans in the Belles Artes before.

I am sending you 770 kilometres on our kilometric ticket. I watched to see if our photo was ever looked at by anyone and it wasn't ever, so there is not the least difficulty in using them before they expire in August. Tell me what news there is of my house next door and how your trip back

from Antequera passed off. I saw that a man was killed on that road a
day later by falling over the cliff. Burgo never missed us and is quite
unaffected by our return ... The weather here is perfection, but I
understand it was worse than midwinter while we were in Spain.
Fondest love to you and the deepest gratitude for letting us stay so long in
your lovely house. Yours,

Ralph

CHURRIANA, 8 MAY 1936

Dearest Ralph and Frances,

We sit cowering after breakfast over a large fire, with the rain pouring
down – coldest weather, I do believe, since February. However, it has
been delightful till a day or two ago. I bathed at Torremolinos and stayed
in half an hour and it seemed as if summer had really come. You, I
suppose, are shivering in a snow-storm.

I'll go back to when we said goodbye at Antequera. We visited the
Torcal. To do this we had to climb 1500 feet to the summit of the
mountain, and there we found a very strange landscape. I won't describe
it beyond saying it was extremely beautiful and much to be recommended to all tourists. Should Ralph ever wish to put an end to his life,
there is the Cisma de la Mujer – the Woman's Abyss, three thousand feet
deep and only three yards across – into which he could hurl himself. A
poetic ending. We threw pebbles down and had to listen so long as they
rattled down that we were quite terrified.

My parents are here. As they are sitting opposite me chatting away in a
most agreeable manner, I will only say that we are having a *very*
enjoyable visit and that we shall be *extremely* cut up when they go. They
seem to like everything they see, even our cooking, and my father has
given me £30. They leave on Tuesday and we go with them to Gib, where
I have to carry out a little transaction on the Black Bourse. After that we
shall have no visitors for a long time ...

You may have seen we had a strike. It looked for a moment like being
serious, but the Governor filled Malaga with troops and the strikers gave
way. The Right party here are all very optimistic. But Allen's[1] explanation is not reassuring. Azaña has been manoeuvred into accepting the
Presidency. The present government will thus lose its driving force and in
a year or so, it is thought, be worn out. Then the Socialist party will step

---

1. Jay Allen, the star correspondent of the *Chicago Tribune*, who was then living at
Torremolinos.

into its place. Once in power they will arm and drill the workers and have a revolution. Allen declares they mean to have a terror – for a month or two workers will have *carte blanche* to murder whom they please and burn churches and houses. Then, when the middle and upper classes have been liquidated, the government will take control of the situation again. It sounds almost incredibly stupid and barbarous, but I feel that in these days anything may happen. I shall send out a lorryload of books and furniture when the arming of the workers begins. Our plan is now to settle in *Jamaica*. However, the present government is getting on fast with the settling of peasants on the land, and I think it may well remain in power until the end of its natural term . . .

Thank you for the kilometric ticket; we may use it later on to take a jaunt to Granada. I wish you were using it to come and see us again. With fondest love to you both.

Gerald

HAM SPRAY, 7 JUNE 1936

Dearest Gerald,

I am very sorry to hear you have had the flu again and been in bed. Do you think the disease is endemic in Spain, because people get it there all the year round while in England it is confined to 6 months of the year? We are very well and toiling away in the garden, Frances planting, I attacking the perpetual foes of man – nettle, thistle, ground elder and couch grass, the malignant fraternity who ought to have subjugated the entire vegetable world by this time if Darwin's 'survival of the fittest' were actually true. I never go near London because it gives me a headache and I have got over all the heartaches it once produced in me.

Ros and Wog have been having the Lindberghs[2] to lunch and the Colonel is described by Ros as 'completely impervious to women', by which one concludes he didn't capitulate to her full-blown charms. We had dinner with Ros and Wog last night and met Elizabeth Bowen, the authoress, and rather a good authoress to my mind but also a horse-faced woman of about 40 with an engaging stammer and an active mind . . . Yours with love.

R.

2. Colonel Charles Lindbergh, who made the first non-stop flight between New York and Paris on 20–21 May 1927, and his wife Anne, *née* Morrow, daughter of the American ambassador to Mexico.

CHURRIANA, 12 JUNE 1936

Dearest Ralph,

... We live very quietly here, undisturbed by the vendetta that has broken out between the UGT and the CNT.[3] I do not know whether *The Times* mentions it. Every day in Malaga the Communists and Anarchists kill one another. Last night a Communist patrol from Malaga tried to burn down our Anarchist Centro here, but we beat them off. Anarchists were seen fighting side by side with Guardias Civiles, a thing that has never been known anywhere before. The origin of the quarrel was whether rotten fish should be sold to the Municipal Hospital or not. The Fishermen's Union (UGT) had raised the price of fish very much and the Fishvendors' Union (CNT) complained that the poor could no longer afford to buy them. Then a Communist town councillor exposed this great scandal of the fishvendors: they sold their best fish on the market and their worst to the lunatics and the sick. Next day the Socialists shot up a prominent CNT man and every day someone fresh is killed. It is only a part of the furious quarrel going on all over Spain between these two revolutionary parties and I think that till it is healed the chances of revolution are greatly diminished ...

I have been reading [W.H.] Chamberlin's History of the Russian Revolution. It is painful reading, but extraordinarily interesting. Though the aims of Communism are sympathetic to me and I should prefer to live in a world where work and property were fairly equally shared, their methods, beliefs and frame of mind generally are abhorrent to me. I hope that Blum[4] will prove that a serious step towards Socialism is possible by a government working within a democratic constitution. Tell Frances I recommend her to read a Spanish revolutionary novel, *Seven Red Sundays* by Ramon Sender, just translated. It has some merit as literature. Fondest love to you both.

Gerald

CHURRIANA, 4 JULY 1936

Dearest Ralph,

... I was in Malaga yesterday and met three landowners of my acquaintance. The first beckoned to me in the Calle Larios and in an audible whisper said, Don't be afraid; all this *canalla* will be put down. In two weeks Calvo Sotelo will be King of Spain.'[4a] (C.S. was minister

3. Unión General de Trabajadores and Confederación Nacional de Trabajo, two of the biggest trade unions in Spain.
4. Léon Blum, the Socialist politician, who had become Prime Minister of France that year.
4a. In fact he was murdered by the Socialists on 13 July.

for finance under Primo de Rivera). The second went a little further, but
it was the third informant who was most circumstantial. 'There is to be
an army rising before the 15th, in which the Air Force will take the lead.
The Government will be overturned and the Right will form a dictatorship. Largo Caballero has gone to England to keep out of the way.'
'But if it fails?' I asked. 'Oh, it can't fail; for that would lead to
Communism.'

If this rumour is true it is most dangerous. An Army coup would
certainly fail and might well produce a Left revolution. That must be
what Caballero, who has steadily been losing influence in the Socialist
Party, is hoping for. But perhaps if everyone at Malaga had heard of it
the Government may hear of it too and at the right moment pounce on
the ringleaders. If nothing of this sort occurs, there will probably be a
Socialist-Republican government, on the lines of Blum's but more
drastic, in October. But the situation in the villages is anarchic – strikes,
persecutions, shootings, battles with the police, a breakdown of authority. It is very difficult for any party to govern. However, as I said, unless
there should be an attempted Fascist coup, the danger of revolution is
past. If you wish to buy a house here I recommend waiting till November
. . . Fondest love.

Gerald

On 16 June 1936 the Army in the Spanish Zone in Morocco rose and occupied Ceuta
and Melilla. That afternoon the revolt spread to Spain itself and fighting broke out in
Cadiz, Seville, Malaga and Saragossa. The Civil War had begun.

Gerald and Gamel decided to stick it out and refused to join the British residents
and tourists who were evacuated from Malaga by the Royal Navy, although they did
send their daughter Miranda home in the care of Jan Woolley. But by the beginning
of September their local bank account was almost exhausted and they had no way of
getting money from England. They therefore gave their servants all they could spare
and left in an American destroyer for Gibraltar, from where they eventually sailed to
Plymouth. Back in England they took lodgings at East Chaldon in order to be near
Llewellyn Powys who was about to leave for a sanatorium in Switzerland, from
which he would obviously never return.

From the end of 1936 until the beginning of 1953 no letter from Ralph to Gerald
has been preserved. Over this period, therefore, the correspondence becomes
one-sided.

EAST CHALDON, 28 NOVEMBER 1936

Dearest Ralph,

We left our very cold farm yesterday for this very lovely cottage and
here, in our sitting-room seven feet square, warm at last, I sit. I've been in

London engaged on *cosas de España* – can't settle down whilst Madrid hangs in the balance . . . I've promised to address 4 bishops and 200 clergy on Tuesday, but expect to rat. It is such a business going up to London. However, I have been deputed to write to Winston [Churchill] and may have to see him – again, I hope not.

I had a fearful dispute with Bertie [Russell] over his peace plan. I think the conclusions are absurd. Pacifism can only be a private religion at the moment. As soon as you organize it against the Government there will be a reaction. Love of peace must *infiltrate*, I say, and not be aggressive. Now we've made it up again; I proved more pacific than he did. I saw nothing about Don Carlos[5] in *The Times* and feel very anxious. For God's sake send me two lines by return and tell me. Perhaps you can send me the cutting.

I was present at an armaments deal in London; saw thousand-pound notes handed about like postage stamps. The armaments agents were the two most villainous-looking people I ever saw in my life; might have been selected for their part in a League of Nations film on the wickedness of arms-dealers. Then I spent the evening with 4 Americans trying to work up their vitality to champagne heights. Fair gave me a headache. Arthur Waley is coming for the weekend and I must do my letter to Winston. Llewellyn sets forth on Tuesday. Our plans are to go to Edgeworth about the 18th for Christmas. We could pay you a visit after if you thought you wanted us, but we have Miranda. Fondest love.

Gerald

Cosas de España, i.e. propaganda for the cause of the Spanish government, occupied Gerald throughout 1937 and 1938. He and Gamel had rented a furnished cottage at Aldbourne called Bell Court, which they eventually bought. It was close to Ham Spray, so that they could see the Partridges easily, and not far from London where Gerald spent much of his time reading in the British Museum. Summers and autumns were spent at Ley Park, a modern villa at Welcombe in Cornwall.

LEY PARK, n.d.

Dearest Ralph,

Why don't you come and see us? We have a Hungarian professor of sociology[6] coming for a few days, no one else. We can put you up *here*.

5. The former proprietor of Gerald's house in Churriana. As a Falangist in Leftist Malaga he was in danger of his life and Gerald had not only sheltered him but also helped him to get to Gibraltar.
6. Franz von Borkenau, author of *The Spanish Cockpit*, a brilliant book on the early months of the Civil War.

Besides, I have a project. We found near Newquay the most romantic cottage in Cornwall, all alone in a little valley, with a little white sanded bay of its own, very inaccessible yet close to Newquay. It has the most divinely beautiful garden, with tall waving tamarisks and rose-trees and hydrangeas run wild. Not a house in sight. It is probably for sale for not very much and by letting for August one can always get £20 or more of the rent back. Let us buy it between us. It is in perfect condition except that a window needs enlarging. In the garden is a large hut with a glass front, large enough for Burgo and six friends. Remember, property down here is appreciating fast. Come and see me and we will look at it. I guarantee its *perfect* beauty and solitude, and all the country round – sand dunes and common land – is lovely.

I was never very perturbed about the Czechoslovakian crisis.[7] I only thought there would be war if we ran away. There will be no war, I believe, this year. Next year it will be quite a different matter. I am not optimistic – I fully expect the worst – but it is *possible* that the Czechoslovak business can be arranged this year. It will be if the Germans are at all amenable to reason; and if they are not, then war is inevitable.

. . . Chamberlain[8] is living in daydreams. I approve his feelings and wishes – so far as I understand them – but it is all wishful thinking . . . To say that the termination of the Spanish War will bring appeasement is the exact contrary to the truth. However, I am trying to spend our few remaining months of peace on thinking about other things. One has to learn philosophy as one grows older. Please consider this house seriously and don't down the project simply because it is my suggestion. Anyhow it would be great fun going off to see it and this lovely part of Cornwall. Fondest love.

Gerald

NEWQUAY, n.d.

Dearest Ralph,

Your letter gave me the first whiff of war hysteria – 'all your friends are longing for war; France and Czechoslovakia are just as bellicose as Germany.' When war breaks out you will say that Hitler and Goering

---

7. Hitler's recent annexation of Austria had set the seal on the fate of Czechoslovakia, which was obviously Hitler's next target, and the British government's policy of appeasement only postponed the evil hour.

8. Neville Chamberlain, the British Prime Minister, kept acceding to Hitler's damaging demands and deluded himself that he was thus achieving 'peace with honour'.

are most peaceable men and that England and France are the aggressors. This seems to me a pity. If pacifism is simply a form of war hysteria *à revers*, what influence will it be able to exert during a war or after one, at the critical moment when a settlement has to be made? It is merely one more militant and aggressive body such as Fascism and Communism, prepared for any distortion of the truth to attain its ends; it will simply produce a reaction against itself. Not that I take your pacifism seriously. It provides a magnificent excuse for disagreeing violently with everyone else; it provides you the best possible motive for a private war of your own. Still, as we have begun to live in very unpleasant times, I think it is a pity to throw reason overboard as you do and go on in this way. If you are going to tell people who are not pacifists that they are 'longing for war' they are going to keep away from your company. The passions roused by war are so unpleasant that one shirks from meeting anyone whose judgement is not under some control; for violence and exaggeration are infectious and it requires a double effort to keep sane and cool. So if there is a war I daresay I shall regard you as a leper till it is over and approach you with great caution and circumspection, for I am sure you will keep a volcano temperature so long as it lasts. I shall aim at preserving not my life especially but my reason, which I see will be a far more difficult operation.

There is an acute Czechoslovak problem in our own house. Gamel has chosen this moment to declare she is pregnant, or thinks she is. I see a thousand traps and pitfalls. But please ask Frances *not* to mention this to Gamel, as it may be a false alarm. She does not see that if there is a war, in order to provide money I shall have to take a job and that job will most likely be a commission in the Army, to which I have the very *strongest* repugnance. I had decided to volunteer for London A R P but that will not be paid, and if the child appears I shall have to change this. As I said before, I doubt there being war this year, and if it comes it will be because they think they can take any risks with this Cabinet. But I think war almost certain in a year or two. With love.

Gerald

ALDBOURNE, 3 OCTOBER 1938

My dear Ralph,

I do not know what reflections you have made upon our last quarrel. I see it as the *finale* of a series of altercations which have always been upsetting and sometimes painful. You have, it seems to me, fits of aggressiveness which are brought on simply by my presence ... No doubt there is at times something definitely provocative on my side, but often I am conscious of having to use every kind of resource of retreat and subterfuge in order to escape your attacks. I realize of course that this is simply one side of our relation; but as I really hate being attacked in any form and dislike all arguments which have any feeling in them, I have often felt hesitations in going to see you.

This last occasion followed, it seems to me, the usual channel. – The attack, under form of joke, comparing me to Hitler, my too provocative reply, and the final assault on your part, which caused me to lose my head completely. I very much regret, as I am sure you have already realized, everything I then said to you and Frances. These last weeks have been a very great strain to everyone, all the more perhaps to those who have not, like the pacifists, the refuge of a cut-and-dried principle and who are therefore tormented with scruples and conflicts. I am sure you have seen by now what it means to accuse anyone at such a moment of having always longed for a war and of being innately bloodthirsty.

But is it of any use for us to meet again if our meetings lead sooner or later to scenes that are painful and humiliating to all of us? I think not, at all events until the world is in a better state than it is at present. I daresay that you and Frances agree with me. But I would like to say that I do not and never shall, I hope, bear you the faintest grudge or bad feeling, whatever you may feel about me. We have been friends too long for that. After 24 years, to revise our opinions of one another would be too ludicrous. But since the effect of this nightmarish state of the world is to increase your aggressiveness to me and my sensitiveness to attacks (which sometimes drives me half way to meet them) the only sensible thing to do seems to me to separate until the horizon lightens. In that way we may be able to keep better opinions of one another. And I repeat – I can't emphasize that too strongly – that there is no change whatever in my old feelings towards you.

Gerald

ALDBOURNE, n.d.

My dearest Ralph,

Thank you very much for your letter. I have felt *very* deeply our quarrel, if that is the word to use for it. And I have felt ashamed of the part I played in it. I don't think that anything that any of us said on that occasion had any real meaning. Now we have become two touchy old colonels who can't meet – an absurd situation! Well, I hope you will write to me sometimes – nature notes, gardening hints, scandal about friends, anything but politics. I will reply in the same tone. Then cautiously, guardedly, we might manage to meet occasionally, well chaperoned, on some neutral ground. When we have settled in our cottage I should like to show it you. I suppose the air can be kept clear of sparks for a few hours whilst the great powder magazine that we make when we are together is assembled. Will you please give my love to Frances and ask her to forgive me for anything I may have said – I don't know what. Yours affectionately,

                                                                        Gerald

                                              LEY PARK, 27 OCTOBER 1938

Dearest Ralph,

I haven't heard a word from you lately. As for us, I have been poisoned by eating tinned oysters and we both have bad colds. My book[9] has made bad progress; I have at the moment distaste for *cosas de España*. As a relief to them I have been reading [Sir Basil] Liddell Hart's Life of Foch. That and his History of the War are the *Bouvard et Pécuchet* of our time. When one tires of everything else, one can read books on mass stupidity. Another fine volume is being prepared now for future historians on the policy of the British Cabinet since 1918. It has reached a high-water mark, I consider, this last fortnight. 'Defend to the last ditch every inch of British territory or protected territory in the Mediterranean, and hand over the control of the Straits to Musso.' That is an infallible receipt, I say, for war. We are now beginning a new £600,000 graving dock at Gibraltar. If it were not so horribly dangerous, it would be pathetic.

I suppose you did not see (*The Times* carefully omitted it) that there has been a great round-up of the English at Malaga and Torremolinos. Even Hawker, the owner of the Santa Clara Hotel and a great pro-Francoite, is in gaol. I get envelopes from Antonio without any letter inside them. Well, well, well, well. I daresay you will be seeing us before very long. Fondest love.

                                                                        Gerald

Despite his distaste for *cosas de España*, Gerald went on with his propaganda for the cause of the Spanish government and found an unexpected ally in the Duchess of

9. Since his return to England Gerald had been reading what he could find on recent Spanish history, because he wanted to get a better idea of how the Civil War had come about. Franz von Borkenau had encouraged him to put down the result of his discoveries in book form. This was the origin of *The Spanish Labyrinth*, perhaps Gerald's most important work, which was published in 1943.

Atholl who, though a right-wing Tory MP, shared his views. Towards the end of 1938 she resigned from her constituency of West Perthshire in order to recontest it as a protest against Chamberlain's policy of appeasement, and she asked Gerald to come up to Scotland and help her.

DUNKELD, 9 DECEMBER 1938

Dearest Ralph,

My fears about evening dress were unnecessary. So long as I have been at Dunkeld I have had no dinner at all. Hardly have we finished our lunch than a car is announced at the door and the duchess and I whirl away to one meeting after another. A quarter of an hour for tea, sandwiches and coffee in the car at 11, and back to Dunkeld to a late supper after midnight. Some of the meetings are in the schoolrooms of tiny hamlets in wild Highland glens – blank Scotch faces, wild tinkers' eyes (the tinkers, having no vote, are enthusiastic supporters); other meetings in towns and 500 or 600 are present. When I first saw posters announcing that Captain Brenan would speak on Spain, I felt rather alarmed; but I was so tired from the night journey and had such a headache that I blundered through my speeches (no notes, no real preparation) without any stage-fright. The hecklers spoke in broad Scotch and were incomprehensible, and at one small meeting there was a drunk who interrupted the whole time with 'I'm no voting for yae, mon, I'm voting for Hitler.'

Between every meeting there were long drives – 20 or 30 miles through country as wild as Spain: snow-covered mountains, torrents, flooded rivers. As it is dark by soon after 3, we saw it by moonlight. These *têtes-à-têtes* with the duchess, I liked; she is a sweet, charming woman. As an Australian reporter, Noel Monks, who is assisting, remarked, 'What I should like my mother to be.' But her speeches were uncontrollably long – all about Czechoslovakia – and she sleeps only 5 or 6 hours and works all the rest of the time. The duke rallies the Murray Atholl clansmen from the telephone by his bed. There are 2 professional electioneering agents, a certain Dame Eleanor Livingstone, the organizer of the peace ballot, and 3 or 4 voluntary helpers.

Yesterday they took me off speaking after a particularly dreary speech I made, when I felt my head was coming in two, and I am now organizing the local committees. I go off in a car and move by bus from village to village. I find this very interesting and amusing, and enlightening too. For example, the lairds are all against the duchess, and everyone who works for them fears he will be dismissed if he comes out for her. But most of them are secretly for her, and today the proposer of a vote of confidence in Snadden[1] came to me in secret and told me he was heart and soul for the duchess. In one village the laird has even got round the secrecy of the ballot – a real Spanish situation. At one moment I sit by the coffee-room fire in a hotel that is Snadden's HQ, and his staff are compelled to go and sit in the fireless dining-room when they want to talk. Tomorrow I go back to Dunkeld and expect to be sent off to work up enthusiasm in North Perthshire glens. Now that I am rested and have found my bearings I think I could begin again to talk . . .

The situation at Dunkeld is full of comedy; the ménage is that mixture of middle-class vulgarity, cheap furniture and unconventionality that one comes across in Ireland. Lunch is a solemn affair, but the butler and footmen are ex-stable-boys who have red hands and have never left Perthshire. If the duchess wins (as she is sure to do) the duke is to open Blair Castle[2] and give a great entertainment to all the workers in the election. The duke's own militia regiment will attend, his pipes will play in the gallery, and we shall drink whisky and play roulette. Blair is said to be an extraordinary place, a castle in the mountains hung with suits of armour, and, I am sure, furnished in the shoddiest Victorian style. This will be on 23 December and I daresay we shall lie under the tables on the rush-strewn floor all through Christmas. I suppose I shall have to stay and see it.

There is a romantic side. We cross a river (the rivers are terrible things here) and the duchess says, 'At this ford my husband's ancestor, the Earl of Murray, was stabbed in 1634!' At the Pass of Killiecrankie we have to plough through snow. Of Lochleven I remember only a distant black spot (the castle on the lake) and hecklers on the means test. The constituency of West Perthshire is the second largest in the British Isles. I have learned to pronounce Aucherlochry and Farquahar – both harder than you would think – and . . . but it is time to go to bed and I must get up early. But how agreeable is this return to *active* life! Unfortunately, like all other forms of hard work I have known, it does not gain me anything, but on the contrary costs a great deal. I am sweating day after day at my own expense to help a duchess, one of the largest landowners in Britain, earn £500 a year.[3] Alas, poor Robinson! With fondest love.

Gerald

1. W. M. Snadden was the official Unionist candidate.
2. The family seat, Blair Castle, was normally opened only during the summer months. For the rest of the year the Atholls occupied a large modern house on the edge of Dunkeld.
3. A Member of Parliament's salary at that time.

CHELTENHAM, n.d.

Dearest Ralph and Frances,

Thank you very much for the pretty tie. It will cast a moonlight shade over my pink frostbitten complexion. I am sorry that the Perthshire highlands provide nothing but haggis and scones. I had a chilly journey back on the night train. The steam radiators froze and couldn't be melted with blow-lamps, and we crawled through a blizzard and snow drifts over Shep Gap. The Paddington-Hungerford was late too – 4 hours – and when I got to Aldbourne new difficulties began. However, we got through in a taxi to Swindon, passing marooned buses and lorries all the way. We were to have lunched today near Edgeworth, but the drifts at Bisley are 40 feet deep and they have to dig a tunnel through one of them, so we are staying here. Fortunately my father's new house is comfortable and warm.

The duchess lost because her cars, coming from Edinburgh and Glasgow, were held up by the snow. Also because the Liberals got huffy and did not vote. Generally speaking, the young and the poor were for her. The genteel classes were hostile, especially the women between 35 and 65. But for the new Italian claims, Franco would now be getting belligerent rights and the 12 millions in Government Spain would starve; for Mr Hemming's[5] report was 100 per cent favourable to Franco. They chose him of course because they knew it would be. I feel rather upset on the duchess's account; she was so certain of victory. Now she is finished. And those terrible Scotch lairds, with their Fascism and their antisemitism and their disagreeableness, are triumphant.

I think there may be a minor crisis in January; the screw will be put on Poland and Rumania. But the most serious development seems to me the growing *rapprochement* of Germany and Russia. If that comes off this summer, and the Republicans win the Presidential elections in America next autumn, I see every probability of a war in which we shall be defeated. But there seems to be an increasing tension inside Germany, which may hurry things up a little. Meanwhile we hear that Bertie Russell is lecturing in support of Chamberlain in Chicago, although he is privately convinced that Munich[5] has made war and the triumph of Fascism inevitable.

4. Francis Hemming, Secretary to the Non-Intervention Committee, had been to Burgos to explain the British plan for the withdrawal of all foreign combatants from Spain.
5. i.e. the infamous Munich Agreement of 10 September 1938, whereby the Sudetenland was ceded to Germany. This was the last stage of the futile policy of appeasement, and was conclusively proved worthless when Germany occupied the whole of Czechoslovakia only six months later.

We are going back to Bell Court next week. With fondest love to you both.

Gerald

When the inevitable war broke out, Ralph remained true to his pacifist convictions. His belief in the sanctity of human life and the brotherhood of man was firmer than ever, and he refused to 'take lessons in murder' which was what military service would have been for him. He did not object at all to civil defence, as he regarded his neighbours and fellow-countrymen as companions in a common misfortune; but he considered he was of far more use to the community producing food in Ham Spray.

Gerald, on the other hand, put his name down for the special reserve of officers with a recommendation by his sister-in-law's uncle, General Gwynn. He also got in touch with the Foreign Office, who offered him a post as Press Attaché at the British Legation in Nicaragua.

101 GLOUCESTER ROAD, SW7, n.d.

Dearest Ralph,

My spirits go up and down and round and about in this awful vacuum. For some days I have sat alone in the mausoleum of the British Museum Reading Room with a Ministry of Information pass[6], reading books on Central America. Bald-headed old gentlemen came and bowed before me till I almost felt young, useful, a soldier once again. Now I have read every book they possess back to 1550 and have nothing more to do. Yet I don't really *want* to go to Nicaragua; there seems something really too shoddy and frivolous about the whole affair; only this is the one kind of job I could get and I can't settle down to spending the war at Aldbourne. The army is the only profession that offers peace in war and I cannot see a uniform without longing to join up. But that is just what one cannot do; even by faking my age it would not be possible. Then I think I will become a munitions worker and sink into factory life – anything not to sit about and fuss and wait and fidget. But as Kenneth Grubb[7] tells me he has strongly recommended me for Nicaragua or Guatemala, I suppose the odds are I shall be sent there in spite of my notoriously red opinions. I took the bull by the horns yesterday and wrote him a long letter about this. My father has written me a friendly letter, offering me a pair of gaiters and riding breeches he wore in India 40 years ago. As he explained, 'you needn't mind taking them, because they are useless to me and I have no place to keep them in.'

I went to the films this afternoon, but Chamberlain got a volley of

6. The Reading Room had been closed to ordinary readers.
7. Kenneth (later Sir Kenneth) Grubb was then Controller in the Ministry of Information.

hisses. In Hyde Park the Communist speakers were active and not in the least at a loss in defending Stalin.[8] The Mosley speakers were also there, but concealed their flag and their name. Their speaker professed loyalty to the Government 'in spite of its containing so many Jews' and said that his programme was to 'break Germany up into little pieces'. But this could not be done, he said, unless Mosley,[9] the great German-hater, came into power. But one sentence later he was saying that Hitler was a man of peace and that the German colonies ought to be restored. I found myself agreeing with the representative of 'British Israel', who said that we had brought this war on ourselves by our moral iniquity. But the particular iniquity he objected to was our desertion of the Negus in Abyssinia who, with the King of England, is the only remaining descendant of King David.

Blair has already been given two posts in the Ministry of Information and found the posts disappeared next day. Many other people seem in the same state. Some with incomes of £1000 a year are now drawing a salary of £250, and others have had a considerable rise. Half the advertising trade are on the dole . . . Arthur Waley spent two days filling sandbags. He knows Lord Perth[1] and offered his services in any capacity; the next day Perth went and his services were politely refused. He is terribly downcast and says he can't go on with his work. But he refuses to leave London. The war – I won't talk about it. Goodnight. My fondest love to you both. I would like to know how you get on.

Gerald

The Foreign Office finally decided not to appoint press attachés in Central America for fear of offending the United States, so Gerald first joined the Home Guard and then enrolled as an air-raid warden in London.

42 ADDISON ROAD, W14, 27 OCTOBER 1940

Dearest Ralph,

This life I am leading is a very mild imitation of an extremely quiet spell in the trenches in the last war – the long tedious waiting in the dug-out, the little bumblebee overhead, then, every few days, the

---

8. On 23 August 1939, Stalin had concluded a pact of friendship with Hitler, which enabled the latter to launch his *Blitzkrieg* on Poland.

9. Sir Oswald Mosley, leader of the British Union of Fascists, was arrested in May 1940 and interned.

1. James Eric Drummond, sixteenth Earl of Perth, a diplomat by profession, was then chief adviser on foreign publicity at the Ministry of Information.

'incident'. That means a quarter of an hour of melodrama, half an hour of standing about or more rarely rescue work, and then the talking over the incident afterwards. One returns covered with dust (a bomb falling on a house makes a dust like a volcano) and saying, 'Whew, what a lucky escape those people had!' For London is full of lucky escapes and one has to search far indeed to find anyone killed. I sometimes think I am the only person about *not* to have had a near shave, though I have once had to fall on my face in the road. I have seen four houses smashed to cocked hats, hundreds of windows broken, a railway hit and a gas main set on fire for only one casualty – a man with a broken arm.

A commonplace experience seems to be this. A bomb hits a house and knocks it flat. Mr Smith sleeping in the basement is dug out unharmed; Miss Smith, who was upstairs powdering her nose, finds herself lying in the laurel bushes with all her clothes pulled off. The rescue squads start to dig for Mrs Smith, who suddenly arrives from the neighbouring pub where she had gone to have a drink. 'But where is Juju, my precious treasure?' The wardens search for Juju without success. Then three days later his tail and hind paw are discovered hanging on the laburnum tree three hundred yards away. The danger to life is less than that provided by the mildest of influenza epidemics, whilst the danger to property is impressive and on the whole gratifying.

I write as a tourist. London is an invigorating place for a week or two. I recommend those people who usually go ski-ing in Switzerland to take on a warden's job for Christmas. But more than a month would be tedious, and three months would get one down a great deal unless one simply made one's job of it. For apart from the personal reaction to bombs (and there are just as many people who sleep upstairs as there are who go down the tubes) one's comfort in London depends on having windows and gas, on not having to fight one's way home on buses and tubes, and so on. The majority of people need a basement which has been strengthened a bit and which has electric light and heating to spend the evening in. But only the middle classes have this and many of them have been very slow in organizing their lives; the panicky will leave London and the others will acclimatize themselves.

People are on the whole putting up with the dangers and discomforts very philosophically. I don't say courageously, for I do not think the danger sufficient to require courage, except in people who have already passed through an 'incident'. But they show commonsense in refusing to be impressed by the ruins or by the little buzzing bees who circle about every night overhead. Some are quite heroic. The other night a couple of

Dent's[2] patients, an elderly couple of over 70, rang up at three in the morning. Their house had been destroyed – could they come for the night? They came – a man with white hair, rather tenuous-looking, and a jolly old girl who might have been on the stage. They wore dressing-gowns lent them by the dressing station. Their story was that a bomb had hit their house when they were in bed and buried them. Mrs H. blew a whistle which she wore round her neck for that purpose, and was dug out covered in blood. But she was only scratched. They spent a day and a night at Dr Dent's and then set up in Blair's house on the first floor. Nothing would induce them to leave London, though they could easily have done so. 'I always think the country so boring,' said Mr Hooper. Yet he didn't look the type of hero.

Last night there was a very horrible incident. A bomb hit the back of a pub in Shepherds Bush where a sing-song was going on. There were 15 killed and 12 badly wounded – one of the worst smashes London has had. Fortunately it was just beyond our sector, so I did not have to get them out. I am returning to Aldbourne tomorrow week; I daresay it will be nice to return to a regular life again. This life certainly has its attractions, but one needs an incident every few days to keep one's interest up – and that, if one comes to think of it, is not a very rational state of mind, since this incident is likely to be unpleasant to someone else. And I don't stand in need of excitements, whether of danger or sex, though this slight renewal of old sensations has been interesting. But there is no doubt that to tens of thousands of Londoners these bombs are giving a great deal of fun. Young and old, men and women, get a real kick out of them. After all, the pleasure of knowing that one is not afraid of these rhinoceroses that fall from the sky and scatter destruction is one of the greatest and most liberating anyone can know. But it is a pleasure that palls with time. Before this winter is over, Londoners will be very tired of their adventure. At present they are still full of it and of a sort of surprised elation that they have become heroes so easily. I must stop. With fondest love to you and F.

Gerald

ALDBOURNE, 23 JUNE 1941

Dearest Ralph,

 . . . My father and his new wife[3] came to tea yesterday. She is a plain,

2. Dr John Dent shared the house in Addison Road where Gerald's brother and sister-in-law lived.

3. Gerald's mother had died on 7 January 1938. His father's second wife was Mabel Constable Curtis, three years younger than Gerald himself.

sensible, kind young woman who neither smokes, drinks, bicycles nor drives a car – I imagine because she has never been allowed to. What surprised me was to find that she was a bit of a rebel – one of the Oedipus tribe in fact. So what possessed her to marry my father? He told an extraordinary story about the publication of the banns. The curate couldn't read the writing and gave out her approaching marriage to a different man. The vicar tried to hush this up and lied about it. My father, deeply offended, paid him a visit and offered the curate the alternative of a written apology or a horse-whipping! He arrived with an awful assemblage of rubbish he is trying to get rid of. Last year it was 6 pairs of polo breeches, dated 1890. This year it is dozens of frames, awful little silver objects worth 6d each, and – my sword!

The Russian news is strange and, like the commencement of all new ventures, rather breath-taking. I feel sad at the thought of the Russian people, who have suffered so much during the last thirty years, being invaded and devoured by these mechanized savages. Will this be Hitler's Peninsular War? I imagine he will occupy Southern Russia and the Caucasus without much difficulty. But how will he organize it so as to get both corn and oil? And will he be drawn on to the Urals? The new version of the burning of Moscow should be the destruction of the oil wells at Baku. Or will there be some surprising event such as the capture of Baku by parachutists?

I hope that meanwhile we lay the German towns in ruins. Every German woman and child killed is a contribution to the future safety and happiness of Europe, for the worst thing about the Germans is not their character or their aggressiveness but the fact that there are 75 millions of them. The only satisfactory solution to the war would be the reduction of that figure to 45 millions. We cannot, when we have won the war, do this systematically, because then the licensed days of taking human life will be over and we shall have to treat them as our friends. To bear hatred then would be madness; but now, whilst we can, let us bring this war, which they have started and in which they glory, home to them so that they never forget it.

This will shock you. I see your pained clergyman's expression. However, I care little for the theological doctrines of pacifism which, it would seem, do more to provoke wars than to prevent them, and want to see practical measures to secure *peace* for the world. Today – death to every German. When we have won – forgiveness and brotherhood.

Pacifism in present circumstances is an extremist position. When I see pacifists who are prepared to demonstrate their belief in the power of brotherly love by abandoning their possessions, by devoting their lives to preaching what they believe, as the monks and the Communists both used to do, I shall take off my hat to them. But those I know seem to me people who, for some reason or other, are bad at arithmetic. They can't add up even very simple sums . . . Poor creatures, I think; and when I see that they feel sad because they are cut off by their beliefs from other people, that they have to work up their own feelings as clergymen do about sin, that it is often a strain to be natural and at ease, I feel sorrier than ever. And I also feel a morbid curiosity about them – the same curiosity that makes me attempt to draw my clergymen friends upon the subject of the Trinity. How, I wonder, whilst they put up this front to the world, are they dealing with their own Fifth Column? And then – this is bound to happen in the end – my curiosity makes me write a letter which is likely to annoy them. But still I hope it won't. With fondest love.

Gerald

ALDBOURNE, 28 SEPTEMBER 1941

Dearest Ralph,

I am sorry we have not been over to see you. The only reason is that I have been working hard[4] – this is my usual season for work – and that the shortness of the days makes afternoon visits difficult. It is not really true, as Julia told me you thought, that it is our divergent views on the war that keeps us apart. We have been going out very little. At the same time I must say that I should be more eager to see you if I felt I should not have to be put through it in heated tones by you over the war. *It's not pacifists I dislike* – on the contrary, I feel that if I could live on a more mystical and less factual plane I would be one myself . . . But your particular brand of calling yourself a pacifist, and at the same time associating yourself with the aggressors rather than with the attacked, is very disagreeable to me, just as is the contrast between your total indifference to very terrible wars such as the Chinese and the Spanish and the high moral principles you invoke when this country is involved. I think your ideas need sorting. We are none of us rational people, but when we fail to give a certain colour of plausibility and reason to our ideas, we find we lose contact with other people and isolate ourselves. You would feel better if you had some work to do and left your seat in the stalls. And if you served a turn as fireman or ARP warden in a town during air raids, you would feel better still, because danger is a tonic to

---

4. Gerald was then working for the BBC, giving regular broadcasts to Spain.

you and the tremendous warmth of your feelings in this war is in part, I believe, due to a repressed desire to be an actor in it.

However, you can be certain that I am *not* going to quarrel with you or take against you over your opinions, whatever they may be, though I may have sometimes to defend myself against them. Indeed I don't regard them as deliberate opinions at all but just as fragments of lava thrown out by your volcano. We all have volcanoes, we are all liable to go into eruption. This war is a strain on everyone and whilst it lasts is a perpetual struggle for calm and sanity. Nothing therefore I say here is said *de haut en bas*. All I really would like is that you shouldn't talk to me about the war unless you are feeling calm and detached about it. There are plenty of other things to talk about and in fact when I go out to lunch or tea I rarely hear it mentioned at all. For since all the deciding factors are unknown and even unguessable by people like ourselves, there is little or nothing to be said about it. Besides, we have an insufficient common ground for discussion. Catholics keep the subject of the Trinity up their sleeves when they go out lunching with Protestants or agnostics, and so we ought to act with one another.

You have strong opinions about people who resist aggression; remember that I have equally strong opinions about pacifist-isolationists, who I consider by their folly and shortsightedness have helped to produce this war, just as in certain countries diminutions of atmospheric pressure bring on tornadoes. But argument between two people holding such opposite opinions is useless, because neither can possibly prove the other wrong. Though I wrote this letter to say that there is not the *slightest* diminution of my affection for you and Frances, I see I am in danger of beginning an argument. I will therefore stop, with fondest love to you both.

Gerald

This last letter led to an estrangement between Gerald and Ralph, and they ceased to communicate or to see one another until the end of the war.

1. Gerald and Ralph at Watendlath Farm

2. Lytton Strachey and Ralph

4. Carrington and Lytton

3. Ralph and Carrington

5. Gerald, shortly after settling
   in Spain

6. Frances at Ham Spray

7. Carrington, Boris Anrep and Frances

8. Julia Strachey and Stephen Tomlin

9. Rosamond Lehmann and Wogan Phillips

10. Carrington, Roger Senhouse and Frances

11. David Garnett and Ralph

12. Yegen landscape

13. Gamel, Gerald and Ralph in the *granero*

14. Frances and Ralph

15. Gerald's daughter Miranda

16. Frances and Burgo

17. Roger Fry, Helen Anrep and Ralph

18. Ralph, Maroussa Volkova, Frances, Boris Anrep and Raymond Mortimer

19. Raymond Mortimer and V. S. Pritchett

20. Helen Anrep and David Garnett

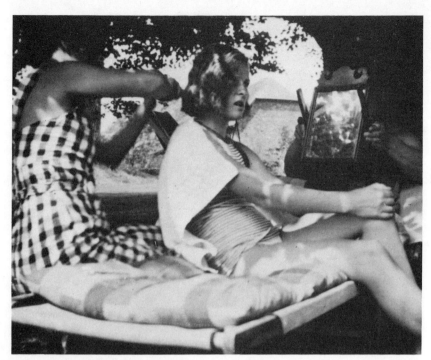

21. Frances cutting Janetta's hair

22. Gerald at Bell Court

23. Robert Kee and Janetta

24. Gerald, Gamel and Ralph

25. David Garnett and Ralph

26. Janetta and Ralph in Spain

27. Gamel

28. Gerald and Ralph in the mountains above Yegen

PART FOUR 1946–1954

Dearest Ralph,

I liked your talk.[5] It is always of great interest to know exactly how writers write. I put down both the clarity of Lytton's style and its lack of vitality to his meditational method. Useless to imitate Voltaire if the pen doesn't race along the page; Shaw's style is far purer and more Voltairean than his.

In my view Lytton's great contribution to biography was his sense for what to leave out. Sieve after sieve, one feels, has sifted the heaps of material and left only the finer essence. It is that that gives his books *form* – something rare in English literature – though hardly *style*, which is the spontaneous thing exuded with the ink, though perhaps patched and mended after. And it makes his books, as you say, enormously readable. I used to say, I remember, a little maliciously, that reading *E[minent] V[ictorians]* was like walking through a magnificently designed house where everything necessary is there and nothing else. Lytton had an admirably regulated mind and gifts that were well arranged and get-atable. He knew just what he could do and just what he couldn't, and just how to do it and when. In literature that is a rarer thing than having 'genius'. Yet I wonder if in the process of writing he didn't kill, as so many of the 18th-century writers did, more of his spontaneous qualities than was necessary. His conversation and gesture showed he didn't lack them. I feel that the ironic clichés you speak of are a tired, over-neat way of writing.

I enjoyed seeing you and Frances so much. With fondest love.

Gerald

Early in 1949 Gerald and Gamel went back to Spain on a short trip which led to a travel book, *The Face of Spain*, published by Hamish Hamilton in the following year.

Dearest Ralph,

Here I am in Malaga, recovering from flu, sitting feebly in one of its 200 cafés among the din of foreign voices and noises. We came through

5. Ralph had given a talk on Lytton Strachey for the BBC on 8 October 1946.

Cordova, spent some days there, and on by motor-bus and car among the towns of the *campiña*. Then here. Outwardly Spain is the same as ever. You do not clap in cafés.[6] A few girls ride bicycles. There are more street sellers and beggars. Food in the hotels is wonderful. But talk to anyone and one gets a different impression. The drought this year is the worst for years, and since in the craving for autarky the Government has given up using coal in factories and employs only electric power drawn from waterfalls, there is a great crisis and factories are working only one day a week. Even in the best years wages are lower than they have ever been, while luxury in the form of expensive foods, dresses and huge American cars is greater than before. So one sees everywhere hunger, women and children begging, poverty, whilst in the towns of the *campiña* the misery was so dreadful we hurried away. There, about a third of the population has given up washing and one sees half-naked bodies with rags pinned round them, coated with dirt, and with expressions of despair and hatred on their faces. It is Belsen, but few of these creatures are allowed in the large towns. I feel I can speak openly of this in a letter because I am going to urge that Spain be given Marshall Aid,[7] with certain safeguards to prevent the money being spent on champagne and Chrysler motor-cars. There ought also to be a complete British Embassy in Madrid,[8] that is to say if the FO can find an ambassador tough enough not to be corrupted by the dukes and duchesses.

The day before I fell ill I went to Churriana. The beauty of the country seemed even greater than I had imagined it. Everything in the garden was better, taller, finer. Antonio has done wonders. They had a long story to tell. They have been through a great deal – it would take pages to tell – and I felt that their loyalty and devotion were something one could never repay. They said – and it was clear that they meant it – that they only wanted us to come back as before. Rosario has grown large and almost square. Antonio's kind freckled face has hardly changed. There are two blooming daughters. And Maria? Left to herself, she started a stall of black-market foods. Twice a week she goes up by train to Coin, buys her produce and comes back here. She looks so severe and stately that the

---

6. i.e. to attract the attention of a waiter.

7. When General George Marshall became the American Secretary of State in 1947, he had produced a plan, named after him, for the financial and economic rehabilitation of war-shattered Europe; but Spain did not benefit from this for several years.

8. At that time Britain was represented only by a chargé d'affaires. It was not until 1951 that an ambassador was appointed.

police never take the cover off her baskets. And now she has bought one of the best shops and houses in the village. Her clever, pretty daughter has helped her. Rosario says her success is due to her being a good woman who treats everyone fairly. She will end up one of the *ricas* of the village, and if she went back to Yegen her daughter would be a *doña*. This is what is happening all over Spain.

I have had extraordinary conversations, meetings, adventures, without looking for any of them. But I still have flu on me and my head is tired, so I cannot write more. I keep a diary and when this is written have little energy left for writing. We shall probably stay here till after Easter. And we have decided to come and live in Spain ... With fondest love.

Gerald

CHURRIANA, 14 MARCH 1949

Dearest Ralph,

Here we are, living in Rosario and Antonio's house. I can't tell you how happy I am to be back. It seems as if these last 12 years I had not lived at all. This is the country for life and it is also unbelievably beautiful. The garden is full of arum lilies and freesias in flower. The oranges are just coming out. So we are making all the necessary arrangements for coming back in 1½ years' time, when Miranda is a little older. She, I suppose, will stay a good bit with us. I thought that we might keep some hold on Bell Court till the world is in a quieter state, and of making a gift of it to Miranda and letting it furnished by the year. We should probably come back every second year and try to arrange to spend 2 months there. Considering all that has happened – and a great deal has happened – the house, books and furniture are in wonderful condition. The Italians carried off my MSS. of St Theresa and St John of the Cross, thinking it was dangerous red material, a photograph of you which they took to be that of Johnny Churchill, and a small but select collection of picaresque novels. A Fascist family who rented our house broke into the room where I kept my clothes, under the pretence that bombs were hidden there, and went off with them and the sheets. But the garden is in superb condition. Antonio and Rosario have been I can't tell you how faithful to us. Today they are quite important people and exchange visits with the bailiff and butler of the Duque who lives in that big fancy estate which I think you went to once. In case we should be killed in an air crash and the house is sold, will you please remember that I want a considerable sum, say £500, to be given to Antonio and Rosario for their services, and £50 to Maria who has a little shop. The value of the house has gone up enormously.

We start back in a week, but we shall take a month or so on the journey, jagging about on motor-buses and local trains. I am writing a book out of the diary I keep, but the sort of life we lead – continual visitors and walks and conversations – doesn't put me in the mood for letters. And many things cannot be written down. I expect to get back either immediately before or after Easter . . . Forgive such a dead letter. With fondest love to you and Frances.

Gerald

ALDBOURNE, n.d.

Dearest Ralph,

We are off to Cornwall on Friday. I had meant to get in touch with you and Frances – a new variety of *Suspiria Railwaycoachia* has turned up in the vicinity – but I have been labouring like a mole at the confounded corrections of my book.[9] Now I'm just finishing – hip, hip, hooray! – and shall be able to return to the human world once more. 200,000 words in 2 years, 8 months. It's been a labour of Hercules. Now I feel able to undertake *anything*. Only I want to do something very, very, very difficult. A short story without characters or plot. A poem that has no words. Something all impulse and improvisation, spun by the lucky spiders that inhabit the brain but rarely peer out. Above all, no *suite*, so spadework . . .

When we come back from Cornwall about the 10th we must meet . . . What a silly letter! With best love to you both.

Gerald

WELCOMBE, 7 AUGUST 1949

Dearest Ralph,

How nice to have a letter from you. Your Wiltshire parties sound very amusing, though they wouldn't suit me. I fear these gatherings of crustaceans. In my rock pool there must be pale waving seaweeds and anenomes – and that, I suppose, is why I haven't got one to plunge into; just the puddle of *la vie intime*.

We have had a nice schoolboyish week. Gamel stays at home writing poetry or talking to Ronnie,[9a] who is her great favourite. We – that is

---

9. *The Literature of the Spanish People*, at which Gerald had been working since 1946. It was published by the Cambridge University Press in 1951.
9a. The poet Ronald Duncan, who lived in a mill-house near Welcombe.

Miranda, Vero[1] and myself – go off with rucksacks and cameras and a huge supply of bad jokes and puns. On Wednesday we walked to Hartland Pier for lunch, then bused to Clovelly, then walked and bused back, stopping at pubs, dodging storms, and in the end getting wet through. Ten hours of hilarity. Then we have twice been to Gull Rock, bathed naked in its little bay, investigated the cave of the seal, and taken a great many photographs. Vero is such a nice man, simple, lively and extraordinarily kind and unegoistic. And fathers are always happy when their lovely daughters smile on them and take their arm. But today it is raining. The wind howls, the branches wave, the rain streams down, dripping and lashing and spitting and splashing, and so we all sit round the big square table like good schoolchildren, writing our Sunday letters. As I haven't got a father or mother,[2] I write to you!

How odd it is. I believe I could set off tomorrow, as I did when I was 17, with a little hand-bag, for Italy, for the USA or South America, and forget my past, forget everyone except a friend or two in England to write to from time to time, above all forget books and literature and be happier than I am at present because I had got rid of so much ballast. I daresay too that everyone would be the better for my going. Gamel would settle down to her secret, spinsterish concerns, and *Horizon*[3] would be free from a lot of boring rubbish of a different kind. I have always wanted to disappear, to cease to leave any trace of my passage, to be beyond all human relations, to be just a pen, a notebook and sensibility. And so, by shedding all the shams and politeness of life, and all its artificial aids and protections, to get nearer to the pulse and heart of it. That's my philosophy – which I practise as the Archbishop of Canterbury practises Christianity. Everything except getting away and uprooting myself bores me. I am a bad writer because I am a fraud. And all the other so-called good writers are frauds too. *Je conspue les littérateurs.*

Well, this has been an introspective letter, providing rich material for Ham-Spraggian psychoanalysis. Meanwhile the rain pelts down and the sycamores squirm and writhe in the wind. How wonderful life is! And how we waste our opportunities! One will be dropped into the grave

1. Vero Richards, a middle-aged friend, who with Gerald's encouragement seduced Miranda in the interests of her sexual education.
2. Gerald's mother had died in 1938, his father in 1947.
3. The literary magazine, edited by Cyril Connolly, to which Gerald had contributed two articles on the life and poetry of St John of the Cross.

without having tasted more than a fraction of what was possible to one.

Gerald

Early in 1951 Gerald and Gamel went on a two months' tour of Calabria and Sicily, on which he later based an article called 'The City of the Sybarites', published in *Encounter* in October 1957.

16 FEBRUARY 1951

My dear Ralph,

As you are my executor, I would like before going to Italy to express three wishes in case I and Gamel are simultaneously killed in a motor-bus. I am sure that Miranda, who is my heir, will respect them.

I owe a great debt to Hope-Johnstone. Apart from the fact of our being life-long friends, it was he who persuaded my great-aunt to give me an allowance and make me her heir. I feel a deep regret that I have not done more for him. It should be understood, therefore, that he cannot be asked to leave his cottage[4] and that if Bell Court is let, it must be stipulated that he has the right to have baths and to use the kitchen sink. This is very little to ask, as few tenants would object to this. He also has the full use of the garden.

Any of my friends who want books should be allowed to take them, and there are a few Spanish books which should be offered to the London Library. H.-J. will be able to guess which they are. Blair will be your fellow-executor, and I should of course wish you and him to take books you like.

Further, I would be grateful if you would take over all my letters and papers, burning those which are rubbish. If you should ever move to a small house, Blair no doubt could take them. If the house at Churriana is sold, I would like you and him to bring back any china, rugs, etc. you want for yourselves and also a box of letters, especially those of D.C. and Virginia Woolf. If the house is sold, *at least* three hundred pounds should be given to Antonio and Rosario for their faithful services. Ever yours,

Gerald Brenan

Gamel's mother died in Florida, and in December 1951 she and Gerald flew to New York so that she could claim her inheritance.

---

4. A tiny annexe to Bell Court, where Gerald had allowed Hope-Johnstone to live rent-free.

My dearest Ralph,

. . . I go with some forebodings, but Gamel has agreed that if she wants to linger beyond 20 February I may return by myself. But I do not think that she will want to linger. Then, when we get back, Ruth[5] will motor us out to Malaga.

Life, life, how awful life is when one passes 40! I only enjoy the sleep of literature, with an occasional jaunt to make a change. The desire to write – every year a little better – simply eats one up and leaves no room for anything else except a few old affections and friendships. Writers aren't human beings and I wonder anyone else can stand them. They only give out warmth and light when they are dead.

I fear my autobiography[6] will seem to you a pale affair, but I believe that I shall without much work infuse life and interest into it. I improve everything, I find, when I let it lie a little and take it up again. And then the themes of the book only emerge with adolescence. Its point will lie in its themes. *Mr Fisher*[7] is more difficult and hazardous, but I believe I shall end by making something of that too. It is my own autobiography, *and* my father's, *and* H.-J.'s, all rolled into one and turned inside out. The presentation of a *rentier* Hamlet, half Oblomov and a quarter Lear – a great fusion. In the fragment you have, there are some hopeless passages, but now I think I have discovered how to replace them. So far I have only put in 3 months' work on it, and I find the fusion of old passages and new rather difficult . . . Now I must stop . . . With fondest love.

Gerald

Dearest Ralph,

How nice to get a letter from you. Out here we think a great deal of our friends. One of the pleasantest things about living abroad is that one feels a constant nostalgia for one's own country. Here we sit in this delicious climate, but I am haunted by the drip-drip of English rain and the sight of grey mossy clouds. And then by the sight of a big man with a Regency face walking down the High Street. You will be welcome when you bring it out here.

Yes, the weather is delicious. In the heat of the day a wind gets up and

5. Ruth Lowinsky, a near neighbour.
6. Gerald took several years to complete the first volume of his autobiography, *A Life of One's Own*, which was not published until 1962.
7. Eventually published by Hamish Hamilton in 1961 under the title of *A Holiday by the Sea*.

the yellow bamboos creak like the shrouds of a sailing vessel. Seventeen different kinds of birds chirp or sing, and the nightingale has had the inspiration to make its nest above the ground in a catalpa tree. I never want to leave the garden, but Gamel, who grows younger as I grow older, drags me out for walks. Yesterday she insisted on our going after lunch to the beach. We walked 2½ miles down a dusty road, bathed (the water was really warm) and then walked 2½ miles back with the sun in our faces. I was glad to find that she disliked it as much as I did and was tired. I learned long ago that if one wishes to walk in Spain one must choose high altitudes.

On Monday we start a grand *obra*. Lime, *yeso*, sand, cement lie in great heaps in the patio. Our head mason, José el Catalan, comes and throws his shrewd little eyes round him. The problem we are anxious to discover is – has the long beam over the landing window rotted, or has it not? Then most of the roof tiles will have to come off and the boards under them be replaced with *racillas*, which one might translate as under-tiles. In England the bill would be £500; here I doubt if it will exceed £60. In the cruel lands labour is cheap.

The cigarette problem has been serious. I have been smoking myself to death. Twenty cigarettes for 7½d! To cure myself I now buy a better and milder tobacco from Antonio. He gets it from the military aerodrome where he works every morning as head gardener. A military aerodrome has to go in for commerce too, so each week a plane flies to Morocco and comes back packed full with contraband tobacco. The Air Force, who cannot live on their pay, sell it in Malaga and make quite a bit out of it. I love these arrangements by which one government department cheats another, don't you? They seem the last word of refinement in our Byzantine civilisation. However, to continue my story, I get this tobacco and make it into cigarettes in a little machine that costs 23.30 pesetas. As it takes me several minutes to make one, I smoke less.

There is another side to our military aerodrome which pleases me. As they have no serviceable planes to amuse themselves with, they have put up an exquisite little building, all white patios and elegant facades, like a lotus-eater's convent. A garden too, with flowers and fruit and rare South American trees. A pond, a fountain, gold fish, and so on. You'll agree with me that this is just what a military aerodrome ought to be.

My book[8] has been getting very encomiastic reviews in Spanish literary journals. One came out with the headlines *Un amigo de España*.

8. *The Literature of the Spanish People.*

This does not make me anticipate with much pleasure our projected meeting with Spanish writers in Madrid. (As I am to write on 'Spanish books of the year' in the *New York Times*, such contacts will be necessary.) But it may prove the decisive point in our lawsuit to recover our house.[9] And now the frogs in the garden next door are warning me that I must get back to my work. With fondest love to you and Frances and my respectful compliments to Burgo.

Gerald

HAM SPRAY, 22 JANUARY 1953

Dearest Gerald,

A letter from Gibraltar and one from Churriana were most welcome. I can see you're going to have an epic struggle with the Spanish temperament before you can call your house your own. In the three weeks since you left[1] we've hardly stirred. There has been fog for days on end, broken for a single day at a time by brilliant sunshine. Burgo went back to his London tutoring in a very tractable state, with a bank account to himself and a smile on his face. We shall see where it lands us.

I've had the final proofs of Broadmoor[2] to go through and don't like the look of the book at all – prosy, sententious, and with long boring passages. I know exactly how I should crack down on it if I had it to review.

We went to Bell Court to lunch with the Japps.[3] They appear to have settled in and to be very pleased with all the arrangements . . . Darsie wanted to dig, but I warned him that the soil was packed with plants and he'd better wait until he could see what would show above ground in the spring. He is very vigorous and has bought a bicycle from France on which he intends to scour the country . . .

V.S.P. and Dorothy[4] came to dinner and we had the usual tour de force by V.S.P. acting in turn the 36 literary folk who turned up at the Trocadero to do honour to John Lehmann[5] and the 80 similar gentry

---

9. During the war parts of the house had been let furnished to various tenants, including an Englishman and his French mistress, who had rented the ground floor for the ludicrously small rent of 125 pesetas a month. Since they showed no intention of leaving, Gerald was obliged to sue them.

1. Gerald had just been on a short visit to England.

2. Ralph had just finished *Broadmoor: a History of Criminal Lunacy and Its Problems*, which was published by Chatto & Windus later in the year.

3. Darsie Japp, a painter, and his wife Lucila had rented Bell Court.

4. The writer V. S. (later Sir Victor) Pritchett and his wife, *née* Roberts.

5. The author and publisher.

who did honour at the Savile Club to Compton Mackenzie's 70th birthday. I particularly enjoyed V.S.P.'s impersonation of [Arthur] Koestler, whom I continue to think one of our most interesting writers. I've just read his *Spanish Testament*. The description of Seville gaol is superb, and what a contrast to his French internment camp three years later – the Spaniards can never forget that they are human beings. V.S.P. was in high spirits because the *New Yorker* has just taken another of his stories for £400, but there were groans about the cost of educating children and the arrival of income-tax demands . . . He had a terrific financial bait held out to him by the B B C. They offered him £55 a week for one 20-minute talk a week on books on Sundays for a whole year, *but* he was to give up the *New Statesman* except for occasional reviews. Eventually Dorothy and he decided against the offer and he goes on with his 'Books in General'. Kinglsey Martin,[6] however, has raised his salary, so some good came of it . . .

I'm having a slight slap this week in the Mag[7] at Cyril Connolly over the Missing Diplomats,[8] which he has dressed up as a pamphlet with a preface by [Peter] Quennell to sell at 5/–. Mrs Maclean[9] has gone to live in Switzerland near Geneva, and I have hopes that Robert Kee[1] who has gone to Geneva for 6 months may go to see her and extract some authentic information. My objection to Cyril's article is of the either-or kind. Either he was as intimate an acquaintance as he made himself out to be of Maclean and Burgess, in which case it was bad taste to trot out their private lives in public. Or he was not, but then he shouldn't have posed as such in order to sell his article in *News of the World* style . . . Fondest love to both.

Ralph

HAM SPRAY, 17 FEBRUARY 1953

Dearest Gerald,

Delighted to get your letter. Have you had a call from Cyril Connolly yet? He's supposed to have flown to Madrid with a car and the intention

6. Editor of the *New Statesman* from 1930 to 1960.
7. i.e. the *New Statesman*, to which Ralph too was a regular contributor.
8. i.e. Donald Maclean, Head of the American Department at the Foreign Office, and Guy Burgess, a former second secretary to the British Embassy in Washington, who had disappeared from England on 25 May 1951 and were believed to have defected to the Soviet Union.
9. Melinda (*née* Dunbar) Maclean was to disappear with her children from her Swiss home on 11 September 1953 in equally mysterious circumstances.
1. The writer and future television star, who had just been given an assignment with the World Health Organization. He was married to Janetta Woolley and they had recently been divorced.

of visiting you. I called at the Spanish Tourist Office in Jermyn Street the other day and there again your name came up. The little toothbrush-moustached Francophil at the desk (whom I quite like really) asked if I was thinking of visiting you and then broke out into an indignant protest against *The Face of Spain* – so unfair; it should have been 'One Face of Spain'. All the same he was full of respect for your talent. I went there to find out about travel by car in Spain, as we are thinking of leaving this country for April. But please don't be alarmed. If we drive down by the coast road to Malaga, we shan't expect you to put us up; we can stay at Torremolinos or Malaga itself. I thought of going on to Gibraltar 'for a refill',[2] as my Jermyn-St friend called it, and back via Merida and Estramadura if the roads are possible there. We should start at the end of March and be away 4 weeks about. I thought it possible that I might get a refill for you too at Gibraltar in this way. If you have any advice about the coast road, derived from your journey with Ruth [Lowinsky], I'd be very glad to have it.

I've seen James [Strachey] in hospital in London. His eye is under bandages and it won't be known for some weeks whether any sight is left in it. He is wonderfully stoical and reads Braille under his bed-clothes. Simon Bussy is the latest Strachey calamity; he has been going off his head for the last year and took a turn for the worse at Christmas. French sanatoria are famous for their brutality, so it was decided to ship him to England. In the plane from Nice to London he became fidgety, got up, and started to leave the aeroplane. Janie[3] was in despair as, if he was obviously mad on arrival, he'd have been refused entry; but he cuts up rough if thwarted, so she fell back on the impersonal 'It is not permitted to leave the machine in flight' and got him to sit down again. The Bussys are now looking for a permanent 'home' for him near London and living at No. 51 Gordon Square meanwhile. They'll have to let their villa at Roquebrune as a source of income.

V.S.P.'s first broadcast about his tour of Spain last autumn was good; next week we shall hear him on Andalusia. We saw them on Sunday for drinks – in tearing spirits and not sleeping a wink. They are inscrutable. Fondest love to you both from us both.

Ralph

2. Gibraltar provided a useful loop-hole in the currency restrictions, then still in force in England, which limited the amount of money travellers abroad were allowed to export.
3. Bussy's daughter.

Dearest Ralph,

Those snows and rains that, to judge by the papers, you are suffering from have thrown out an arm here. We have had three of the coldest days I ever knew at Malaga and this morning there was a ground frost. As we have no fireplace, I feel outraged, though in the evenings with oil-stove and *brasero*[4] we manage to keep warm

The cold has brought emigrants. Cyril Connolly turned up with his sweetly smiling wife[5] and two Americans called Davis.[6] Mrs Davis is the sister of Cyril's first wife and they have a flat in Madrid and worship everything Spanish. I can't help liking them very much, because they show so much admiration for a certain old friend of yours . . . I don't think I have had time to disappoint them yet, so it has all been very pleasant. They gave us a delicious lunch today at Antonio Martin's[7] and Cyril promised to make [George] Weidenfeld publish my autobiog. and advance me £500. More, they want to buy La Cónsula,[8] Sir Herbert Barker's house just a stone's throw from our garden wall. Lady Barker is said to be asking £7000 and tomorrow we go over it. Cyril wants to buy a house too, and a lot of olive trees, and we have found one for him about a mile away. However, I doubt if this comes to anything. He, Cyril, has been in his best mood, amusing, flattering, friendly. We agree about literature – that it ought to be life-enhancing and that egoism is the writer's best quarry to hew from. As I have always said, one gets to know England and English writers out here. On my native heath all my social difficulties are overcome . . .

What with the cold and our domestic difficulties, life is still rather inconvenient. We have to have 4 people to lunch in the one room we can keep moderately warm; Rosario has only a tiny fire to cook it on and the dishes have to be carried 100 yards. I need warm weather and the whole house to feel like Philip II in the Escorial, which is the feeling I want to give myself. We came out here to expand, not to contract . . .

Frances's letter came this evening and we read it with great enjoyment. To end this I can only say that we are spending money rather reck- lessly and have just bought a fine mother-of-pearl inlaid bed from the Philippines to honour you with on your approaching visit. If Weidenfeld

4. A brazier, holding burning charcoal or red-hot coals, usually placed beneath a table.
5. Barbara, *née* Skelton.
6. William and Anne, *née* Bakewell.
7. A fish restaurant on the waterfront at Malaga.
8. They eventually did so.

refuses my autobiog. we are done for, since Gamel is unlikely to produce anything. Her native indolence has returned and she is doing everything possible *not* to translate Galdós, though she keeps up the pretence that she is going to translate his longest novel. Anyhow she has successfully avoided getting pinned down by Weidenfeld. . . I have to do everything, down to seeing that flowers are picked for the table and things properly laid. But there, husbands musn't complain or perhaps they'd do nothing else. One moves in half an hour from thinking everything is wrong to thinking everything is perfect, and the happy marriages are those in which each party keeps its complaints to itself. No wonder no novelist ever painted marriage, for there is nothing solid or objective in it. I am lucky in that all my private complaints run upon practical things. A good secretary would blow them away in a moment. With fondest love to you both.

Gerald

HAM SPRAY, 7 MAY 1953

Dearest Gerald,

The journey is over and now we sit in the garden under a hot sun, brooding over the past and hardly giving the future a thought. I am afraid that we were rather too many and too much and too soon for you,[9] but if you live in a Garden of Eden you must expect visits from snakes at all times. After we left Gibraltar the weather deteriorated and in Portugal we picked up a little diarrhoea and a raking cough. We saw Franco in Seville – just a fat white hand waving behind the bullet-proof glass of a limousine, to the tiny applause of a row of schoolchildren clapping their hands; no shouts of praise from anyone. Botanically, we caught a flash of the wild arums in the cork woods east of Tarifa, found the wild peony in flower near Jerez, and a sheet of hoop-petticoat daffodils in Asturias just below the snow line. After the Magdalenian bison at Altamira we drove straight to Lascaux to compare them with the Aurignacian; the Magdalenians were the better draughtsmen, as the Abbé Breuil[1] admits. By a strange coincidence, just as we were entering the cave at Lascaux, a familiar figure emerged – Morgan Forster, whom I hadn't seen for many years, travelling round France in a car with two American admirers . . . Fondest love to you and Gamel.

Ralph

9. Ralph and Frances had motored out to Spain with their son Burgo and also Pippa, Richard Strachey's daughter, to keep him company.
1. Henri Breuil, the expert on Palaeolithic Art.

Dearest Ralph,

Yes, your book is a very able one. I always knew it would be interesting, but the tact and restraint you have used throughout has been a surprise. I know well the temptation to use strong, outspoken language, but in a book intended to exert influence that is fatal. It rallies the like-minded, but alienates the cautious and judicial. One excessive phrase, and the secret bent of the mind, the dangerous warmth that the writer is trying to hide, is given away. As I know that you have very strong feelings on this subject, I am all the more surprised that you have been able to conceal them. I could never have done so. Or rather, I might have done so for a few chapters, but would have shown my hand at the end. I tend to have Hitlerian – or Shavian – views on the question of the permanently demented and imbecile, but I thought your last chapter admirable . . .

Hope [-Johnstone] is here. He arrived with a very unbecomingly projecting tummy from Switzerland – top flies undone, edge of drawers showing – complaining that his feet wouldn't carry him because he had put on weight. He felt the change of climate, the austere food, even the heat, though the thermometer never reaches 70°, and looked very miserable. However, now he has begun to cheer up and his conversation is often, what you wouldn't believe, very delightful.

As to St Theresa, it may well be that I shall never get more than Knopf offered me for it, but in these matters the writer's psychology must be considered. I should feel less enthusiasm for a book I was selling outright and for such a mean sum. I also want to be free to let the subject choose its length, which I imagine will be 70,000 to 80,000 words. Further, I dislike extremely being exploited. St T. is a large subject, involving a lot of reading and a knowledge of the background. I believe I can write an interesting book on the subject, because I will come to it with precisely the right sort of ambivalent attitude. Theresa was a very complex, very paradoxical woman and her 'mysticism' is a perfectly natural and explicable thing. Imagine a poet like Mallarmé or Auden, or a novelist like Flaubert, devoting his life to forcing out of himself every scrap of deeper or finer feeling he possessed and organising it to a purpose; imagine a more or less solitary person endeavouring to lead a fuller life, to exist on a higher level, and you have something analogous to this mystical business and to the discipline and asceticism of Carmelites. To a biographer, the interesting thing about T. is that she was so fond of analysing herself and her states of mind, while remaining a very able woman with a good deal of wit, charm and feminine appeal. When I see what Utilitarianism has led to, I turn gladly to philosophies that aim at improving the quality and energy of human life rather than stupefying it with bread and circuses. The mystic-fanatics of course sacrifice everything to achieve this, and the completeness of their sacrifice makes their lives extremely dramatic.

We are off to Madrid in a day or two. All night sitting up in the train, then heat, noise, ambassadors, foreign intellectuals, an attack of Beethoven.[2] Out of sheer cowardice I have been putting it off all month, and if I get in one of my bad moods we shall probably come back without having seen any of the big bugs. There is nothing I detest more than being socially out of my element and, as a Hispanist who talks Spanish badly (I talk it every year worse), I feel dull and ridiculous. I hate the formal meeting, the request to show off, the look of curiosity directed on me. I should like to have a title – to be Lord Pimpoon – which would oil one's social path for one and give one nothing whatever to keep up. If I had that I would dress very well, learn by heart one or two phrases of magnificent imbecility, and enjoy social life. As it is, I only enjoy very simple, very quiet, rather intimate conversation, when there is a possibility of good things being said but no pressure to try to say them. But this letter is becoming a bore. I hope to hear soon that Burgo has got over his last hurdle and is at Oxford. That is the atmosphere he needs, and if he doesn't try to work too hard it will be all the better for him. With fondest love.

                                                                 Gerald

                                              HAM SPRAY, 12 MAY 1953
Dearest Gerald,

Your words of praise for my book quite bowl me over – too kind! too kind! Yet there is no one I wanted more to like it than you. My fear was that the stodge I had to introduce to gratify the Super[3] would effectively bog down anyone trying to read the thing. But you appear to have got through to the bitter end. And I think the end *is* bitter – it is uncomfortable to think what a small platform of sanity one is standing on and how much one depends on nothing rocking us off our perch into the surrounding sea of unreason; one is at the mercy of events more than one presupposes and yet instinctively one guards against them by a private

2. Gerald's code name for diarrhoea.
3. i.e. the Superintendent of Broadmoor.

system of tabus. The days of the great State tabus are numbered, I'm inclined to think (the Ten Commandments, for example, because it would be mad to believe in God chatting to Moses on Sinai) but for social intercourse there must.be fly-buttons, or more would pop out than others could tolerate. All children are a bit mad and the great lesson they spend 16 years in learning is how to act as if they were rational beings, by a process of trial and error as often as not. Then what about our heredity? We don't meet mad mice or mad budgerigars; the human race is singled out for insane behaviour. Are we all descended from a mad ape? Isn't painting an arrow on a painted bison in the recesses of a cave a pretty mad proceeding (this comes from a visit to Altamira) as a way of getting bison for dinner? Playing with fire, too, is a lunatic trick – no other animal has ever tried it – but that's how civilization must have started. I don't believe we know the first thing about our minds, and yet we have to live by means of them. I ramble on with unanswerable questions, and that in itself is not a sensible activity. By the way, the canvas suits[4] are not to aid masturbation but to impede it to some extent; the private parts are accessible to the hands but only with considerable difficulty . . . My fondest love to you and dear Gamel.

                                                                R.

                                          MADRID, 5 JUNE 1953
Dearest Ralph,
    You're going to enjoy this letter because it will make you say, 'Just like Gerald!' And I fear you'll be right.
    I begin with the railway journey. Instead of being an expeditious little affair of 17 hours, it lasted 26. An accident occurred on the line and we sat in a fly-blown, dust-riddled café at Baeza station under a hot sun. Three acacia trees and nothing else standing out of the ground within many miles. I enjoyed this because I always enjoy the unexpected, and used up all the writing-paper in the station in a letter to V.S.P. Then we reached Madrid, black all over with the smoke of the train – bad Asturian coal – because one has to travel with the windows wide open.
    Chapter Two. To save money we decided to go to a pension. I had a list, but as the first three were full we took our chance at a small, rather primitive place. The proprietor shaved in the bathroom and kept his Sunday trousers in our bedroom, but it would have done us well if they hadn't begun dismantling the kitchen range at 7 a.m. and putting it

---

4. i.e. those worn by certain inmates of Broadmoor.

together with hammers at 8. Enraged at this loss of sleep – for we hadn't done more than doze for an hour or so in the train – we rushed out and took a room in an expensive hotel where we pay 95 a day and get little back. However, by keeping our window tightly shut all night we manage to sleep.

Chapter Three. As my reason for coming here is to get information on current Spanish literature for the *New York Times*, I wanted to meet writers. So I went straight to Walter Starkie, who runs the British Institute. He gave me a formal interview in his office hours, though once in 1935 he lunched with me at Churriana. A round, fat, smiling man, dressed in a shiny black silk suit, white tie and Franco decorations on his lapel, looking like a defrocked pope. He beamed all over when he saw me and began to talk immediately. At every name mentioned he came out with, 'I know him.' Then when I asked him if he could arrange for me to meet some Spanish writers, he performed a very skilful evading action. His position was extremely delicate, the authorities were always attacking him, and so on, and so on, ending in a string of anecdotes but not answering my question. Then I understood that my interview was over and when I got up he invited me to have a drink with him at the British Club, where, he said, he would introduce me to some 'interesting people'. When three years ago I met him there, he introduced me to the President of the Club, the representative of a firm of sanitary apparatus, WC basins, etc., who instantly told me that his Spanish wife was descended from a famous medieval nobleman, and practically insinuated that he was a grandee himself. So my hope of meeting Spanish writers dwindled away, though I couldn't help remembering that he had given a party specially for Ronny [Duncan] and that they had all shown great curiosity when he spoke of me.

I lunched with John Marks, the *Times* correspondent, a very attractive man who talks bull-fighting as other people like him talk cricket. He would have done something for me if he had not had every evening full up. And I also met a kind Irish woman who works in the Spanish BBC and has taken me under her protection. She promises to pull strings when my case against my tenant comes up, but I haven't got much confidence in her ability. This evening we are meeting her chief – a Falangista. The Ambassador was too taken up with official dinners over the Coronation to be abordable, so we gave him the miss. So when we get back we shall have spent all the money we counted on for my article, and I shall still have all the bloody books to read and the thing to write. This is the moment for your comment.

Madrid has been hot, dull and expensive. I felt too discouraged with life to go to the Prado, but yesterday, Corpus Christi, we went to the Escorial which Gamel wanted to see. A boring visit, four guides and a lot of waiting, but after seeing it we went for a walk by a little stream bordered with green grass and granite boulders. Elder and roses in flower, peonies just over, and parties of Madrileños picnicking and bathing. I found an exciting new flower, which I think is *Dictamnus fraxillenus* or dittany of Crete, and a number of other attractive ones – spiraea, iris, orchid, genista, white thrift – whose first names I knew. The detail in the Guadarrama is charming, so different from the awful treeless barrens on every other side of Madrid.

Then today the weather changed. It is dark, cold and inclined to rain – delicious after the hot, bright weeks. Tomorrow we return to Churriana . . . Time moves slowly here in this dull city. Nothing to look at but the women – not even New York puts so many beauties on the streets where everyone can look at them. So you get this letter. And now back to Hopie with his tin-pot cynicism and his stories which I've heard 20 times before. And to work and earn money. That's all I really care for. With fondest love.

Gerald

PS Here's an instance of how my dear compatriots load the dice against me. The Ambassador made a speech at Cordoba in which he spoke warmly of my interpretation of Gongora and quoted at length from my book. The British Council printed his speech in English and in Spanish and circulated it to British residents and eminent Spaniards. But in doing this they omitted all mention of me and Gongora, since they couldn't include the Gongora part without bringing me in as well. I shouldn't care, if the success of my lawsuit didn't depend to a great extent on my reputation.

HAM SPRAY, 9 JUNE 1953

Dearest Gerald,

Your disillusioned letter from Madrid has just come. It is not so much 'just like you' as just like Starkie, a horrid self-seeking little bounder whom we once met on a Greek cruise, with a phony enthusiasm for folk-dance and a poor hand at a guitar; he's one of the deathwatch beetles who burrow into culture and undermine it while getting fat on the process . . . It is possible, of course, that respectable Spanish writers in Madrid fight shy of him and that's why he was so reluctant to sponsor you; or was he afraid of forfeiting another decoration, as you surmise? I wish you could have met the Ambassador and his wife[5] (Jock and Dolly,[6] as they are known in this part of Wilts). He's beyond reproach and has very informal habits – gets into his shirtsleeves in public when he feels hot, and that sort of thing. I suggest you invite him to call on you at Churriana when he next goes on tour, as he must occasionally. Poetry is his subject, as it is yours, so there need be no question of politics involved . . .

I have not yet started on insulin, but it can't be long delayed as the reduced carbohydrate diet shows no sign of turning my urine the right colour. I hope to avoid, however, a preliminary period of seclusion in a clinic; I can imagine nothing more boring, when I don't feel ill. Frances is trying her hand at a chapter of autobiography for the old Bloomsbury Memoir Club,[7] which still meets 2 or 3 times a year but is now almost entirely composed of Charleston representatives – Clive [Bell], Vanessa [Bell], Duncan [Grant], Quentin [Bell], Bunny [Garnett], Angelica [Bell], and the latest addition, Olivia Popham, because she's married to Quentin [Bell]. Julia, Janie Bussy and Frances compose the outside element. The resemblance to the Royal Academy is striking, but the Charlestons don't seem to realise that. Fondest love always.

Ralph

CHURRIANA, 23 JULY 1953

Dearest Ralph,

What a wonderful moment when the parting guest – the two-months guest – leaves! The water can be heard flowing again, the birds sing. Up above the tall trees the sky looks blue. One forgets whether one has ever listened to an argument, conducted on furious Russian-student lines, as to whether the Americans drink chocolate or cocoa which they *call* chocolate. In other words, Hopie has left for Gibraltar and the white cliffs of Bungo-Bungo Island . . . He spent his whole visit complaining of the climate and the food. In the end he provoked Gamel into a very un-Southern answer. In a weak moment he said, 'You see, I don't get enough to eat here'; and she answered, 'Isn't that rather a good thing?'

---

5. Sir John and Lady (Frances, *née* Van Millingen) Balfour, a very charming and civilized couple.

6. A generic term for such couples, invented by the writer Philip Toynbee.

7. Founded by Molly MacCarthy in the hope of inducing her husband Desmond to write something other than journalism. The members – about a dozen old friends – were expected every month, after dining together, to foregather in one or another of the members' houses and each read a couple of pages of what was to become a full-length biography.

For when he arrived he had put on so much tummy that he complained his feet wouldn't support him.

As I think our food is on the whole *fairly* good and anyhow very abundant, I felt a bit indignant, seeing the frightful meals on which he supports himself at Aldbourne. We were a little mollified when he went to Antonio Martin's restaurant and said the food was equally bad there. The truth is that he has developed a sort of senile greed and, having come from staying with a rich Italian-Swiss family where they eat very well indeed and have clotted cream at every meal and rich sweets and Bolognese *pastas*, he felt injured. After all, why else does one pay long visits to one's friends except to save money and eat very well?

People's eating psychology is very interesting. When we had straw-berries, as we did every day for three weeks, Hope took about four helpings. But then cherries from Ronda followed. He would scarcely touch them. Although they were in fact very good cherries, they weren't Swiss Morellas. Then came figs, bananas, plums, apricots – of course, not eatable. His spirits rose with melons, though we had to listen to a lecture on how much better French melons were; but if a water-melon, Gamel's favourite fruit, turned up, he crossed his arms like an angry child. It was the same with octopus. He adores octopus (*pulpo*) and shovelled into it every day, but when the season ended and various sorts of fish followed – among them whitebait – he played about with it like a spoiled child and left most of it on his plate . . .

Another irritating habit was his complaint of the weather. The thermometer never rose above 80°, and he has spent ten years in the tropics and has recently applied again for a job there. He said this was 'damp heat'. For weeks he either lay on his bed or sat in an armchair and refused even to go into the garden in the evenings. He didn't like the garden, he didn't like anything. He had a theory, too, that when one was 70 one ought to lie down all the time. However, when he discovered he could get a boat he developed immense activity, got up at seven every morning, went into Malaga, packed books, took photographs of little girls and was quite untirable. In reality he is as strong as a horse; it's his character not his body that has deteriorated with age. Some obscure jealousy prevents him liking any house where I live; and very good, rich food is his panacea and his opium – the thing that consoles him for the sadness and loneliness of his life.

I feel sad about it both on his account and on my own. We had both expected to enjoy his visit and hoped that he would come out every year. His company is often delightful, and for us he had the great merit of occupying himself and not needing to be entertained. He has always been the only man I could live with, I suppose because I am so accustomed to him. His habit of repeating his stories I don't mind, for I like monotony. The only thing I have ever disliked about him has been his habit of argument. A good argument every day is a hygenic necessity for him and he has become very clever at trailing his coat and catching either me or Gamel. But that could be endured; what neither of us can stand are the continual complaints. I wonder if he will ever come out to see us again.

I grow more disagreeable myself with age, more impatient and irritable. Perhaps the elderly should never consort with the elderly. Otherwise I have greatly enjoyed this long summer. It is many years since I have been in such good health, and I sit all day from breakfast to 7 at my desk, sometimes taking an hour off for a siesta. I enjoy the peace, the big rooms, the sound of water flowing and of birds singing, and the emptiness. I think that Gamel, whom I rarely see except at meals, enjoys them too. I don't want anything. There is always enough going on to prevent one feeling one is a hermit . . .

Our American neighbours at the Cónsula[8] are confirming all my hopes. They live for their own peace of mind and are very anti-social. We are going to become great friends and to see little of one another. His slow, droning Californian voice is like a force of Nature, soothing to the ear but difficult to understand. She is very nice to look at – a sort of human geranium. Now write and tell me how the injections go and how you feel. With fondest love.

Gerald

HAM SPRAY, 14 SEPTEMBER 1953

Dearest Gerald,

. . . I forget where my life had got to when I last wrote to you. Had Mr Montgomery Hyde, MP pinched large chunks of my book and published them in the *Evening Standard*? Had Burgo passed his last exam to get to Oxford and his medical exam to exempt him from the army? I'm sure of one thing – we hadn't gone to Edinburgh for a week of the festival, so I'll begin with that.

Colin Mackenzie[9] invited F. and me to stay in Robert Louis

---

8. i.e. Bill and Annie Davis.
9. An old friend of Frances's at Cambridge, where he had won the Chancellor's medal for English verse before getting a first in Economics. During the war he commanded Force 136, which was responsible for special operations in the Far East.

Stevenson's house in Heriot Row for a feast of culture. And so it proved. *Hamlet*, T. S. Eliot, Molière, the Vienna Philharmonic, the Roman virtuosi, Menuhin on the fiddle, Irmgard Seefried in *Lieder*, Mozart and Beethoven, Bach and Bartók – 3 times a day the dose was repeated and really it was magnificent, nothing petty and provincial like the Aldeburgh festival. We came away saturated with art. In the short intervals when social intercourse was allowed we were introduced to crowds of people with Scotch names and faces (both of which I found extremely hard to remember) but one queer fact I discovered was that almost everyone was Roman Catholic and that one had to modify one's conversation in consequence. We drove up in the car with Raymond [Mortimer], seeing the sights of the North as we went – Kedleston Hall, Chatsworth, Durham Cathedral, the Roman Wall, Fountains. Unfortunately Raymond, who was staying in splendour at Dalmeny with Lord Rosebery for the festival, soon fell ill once again and had to fly back to London to have yet another stone removed from his bladder. He seems doomed to frequent doctors for the rest of his life ever since that unhappy prostate operation. Burgo stayed at home with a motoring friend whose name we never discovered and had a high old time by all accounts. I suppose he felt liberated by our absence . . .

And now I must tell you about the *Evening Standard*. I just happened to buy a copy . . . and there I saw my own prose staring me in the face in an article called 'Broadmoor after Straffen'.[1] I rang up my solicitor from the Paddington hotel before catching my train and he tackled the *Evening Standard* next morning. There were five articles published and two of them came straight from me, with a lot in the others paraphrased. Fortunately Mr Hyde had hardly bothered to alter a word in my sentences, and the *Standard* collapsed at once when I served a writ on them for breach of copyright. So now I am to have an acknowledgement printed and they pay £300, which I shall share with Chatto & Windus. I've never derived so much profit from anything I ever read in that paper.

My insulin treatment went very well for the first 6 weeks but now seems to have reached the stabilization point. The condition of my feet has greatly improved and they don't wake me up at night any more; on the other hand I fancy that the injection makes me a little light-headed in the mornings and rather depressed. I wake up with a gloomy disposition,

---

1. A young man called John Thomas Straffen had been committed to Broadmoor for murdering two little girls in October 1951. In April 1952 he escaped for a few hours, during which he murdered another little girl.

which hangs on me until the afternoon. I see my doctor again in another 3 weeks and shall try to elucidate this mental state.

I wonder whether V.S.P. has sent you an account of the christening ceremony, when his 2 children were dipped in baptism. We were in Scotland so couldn't attend, but what are our friends coming to? Or rather, where are they going? With best love to you both.

Ralph

CHURRIANA, 18 SEPTEMBER 1953

Dearest Ralph,

It is a long time since I last wrote to you. August has passed into September, summer into autumn, and heavy misty days into clear bright ones. For it is the opposite in this country to what it is in England – the mists come in late summer, drawn out of the sea by the sun's heat, and the clear weather comes as soon as it cools off. September is a delightful month. One lives in shirt-sleeves yet can sometimes imagine a coat; one sleeps under sheet and bedcover and can almost conceive of there being such things as blankets. The muscatel grapes are very abundant, and every night before going to bed we go out into the garden and grope about among the rough fig leaves for some figs. I am still enchanted by this life, and though summer got Gamel down a bit she has now revived.

We've had the emptiest of times – nothing, no one. I have been working with a horrid obsessionary hatred on the revision of my autobiog. vol I. I am against leaving anything in a rough state or unfinished. This correction has been terrible. In writing the part dealing with adolescence I did not realize the tact and restraint needed. I have cut out reams of stuff, sewn and joined together, and made it what it has to be, though whether anyone will want to read it is another matter. So dated. Sometimes I think I remember the Battle of Waterloo. Now I suppose I must get going on Saint Theresa. I have the choice between biography, criticism and another travel book. Biography offers the least difficulties . . .

Your letter came last night. I feel so sorry to hear of your depressions. Can the dose be too large? Let me know how you go on. There is nothing worse than being depressed. I often get it, but not from physical reasons but only as the usual consequence of the literary life. But Gamel is a melancholic who suffers from long bouts of it, and these react on me as I feel I ought to take her on a trip or do something to amuse her. Being a writer's wife is a sad fate. One is eaten alive all the time by one's husband's egoism . . . I should like to write an Aristophanic play in which all the writers' wives get together while their husbands were groaning and scribbling and groaned out their complaints on them . . .

And what do you say to the disappearance of Mrs Maclean?[2] Your theory is knocked on the head. I see no alternative to believing that they are all Communists. And I have another theory – that Senator McCarthy[3] is an agent of the Kremlin too. Do you know that he speaks excellent Russian? I like Colette's political comment best. Some one spoke to her of the atom bomb. '*La bombe atomique? Qu'est-ce que c'est donc? N'est-ce pas une espèce de glace?*'

I have just had a short note from Hope – two months after leaving us. Not a word of thanks to Gamel or indeed any message to her for the two months he spent here. I do not think I can ever have very friendly relations with him again. I can easily forgive the continual disagreeableness, though Gamel says she can't, because he is growing old. But the meanness was too repulsive. This showed itself partly over the book question. He left in Yegen in 1922 a lot of books, half mathematical, half on other subjects. As soon as he got here he began to go over them and to make a sort of catalogue of them. This was his principal occupation for several weeks. As he told me that he had duplicates in England of nearly all the non-mathematical books, I offered to buy these from him. Then I saw that some of my own books were beginning to vanish and that a large canvas bag in his bedroom was beginning to bulge suspiciously. One day when he had gone into Malaga I found a key (he kept it locked) and opened it. It was full of my books – recently bought books, Spanish books that he knew I would need for the Cambridge [University] Press anthology Gamel is doing. One was a presentation copy from the author. I took out two and left the others and decided that the best thing to do was to take a generous line. So when he got back I brought up the question of the books he was leaving and offered him £15 for them. This was a good deal more than he could have got if he had sold them, and he said himself it was more than they were worth. Only I added the rider that I would like him to give me a list of all the books he was taking because it was inconvenient to think one had certain books and then to find them missing. He agreed at once and put out in a pile the books of his that he wished to take. I gave him two big wooden cases to pack them in and, partly as a sign of good faith and partly that I should have the

2. See note to letter from Ralph, dated 22 January 1953.
3. Senator Joseph McCarthy was responsible for investigating persons presumed to be Communists or subversives, in which he used means that caused nationwide disagreement.

expense of sending them to Malaga, he left them open for me to deal with. As he had asked for these cases because he wanted his hand luggage to be light so as to avoid expense with porters, I supposed that he would leave my own books behind. But not at all. His hand luggage – four pieces – was so heavy when he came to leave that one could barely carry it in four journeys. And ever since he left I have been finding more and more of my books missing.

I must say that I found the meanness of the whole proceedings too repulsive. During most of his visit he had been thinking of nothing else but how to lift as much as he could off me. One could almost see his mind working on this. He hadn't liked the food or the climate – he has never liked Spain – and saw he wouldn't be coming out here again or having any farther use for me. So he would make the most of his last chance. I've no doubt he'll do his best to pinch any of my books at Bell Court that he happens to fancy, but he is cautious and knows I have a catalogue of them, and I think that if Darsie takes certain precautions he will not push matters too far . . . But please do not repeat this story to Darsie; he and Hope are neighbours and I do not want to prejudice Darsie too much against him.

What has shocked me about this affair has been the *degree* to which Hope's meanness and calculating spirit have grown on him. He has always played for his own hand, has always seen himself against the world, has never had any scruples. I have excused this because he had no inherited income to rely on and because he led what I thought a good and disinterested life. But now in his old age he has lost all sense of measure, and only the meanness and the greed for rich food are left.

This boring letter must end . . . Write and tell me what the doctor says and if the injections are to be modified. With fondest love to you both.

Gerald.

HAM SPRAY, 9 OCTOBER 1953

Dearest Gerald,

We took Burgo to Oxford yesterday and deposited him in his college. He has a huge sitting-room and large bedroom and a man-servant – a princely habitation, but I hope he won't try to live like a prince. Already Oxford shop-keepers are writing to know if I'll guarantee his credit. I drove back thoroughly content and woke at 3 a.m. a mass of anxiety (these are the tricks our modern Cagliostro, Dr Freud, plays on us). I felt certain, as in a nightmare, that no good would come of Oxford and, in that emptiness of courage and hope that comes in the small hours, I foresaw the future as a grey wall of despair with nothing on the other side. After breakfast I have recovered some composure. The experience was a warning, not of course of the future itself but of the fears about the future which I am so successfully repressing most of the time and which can only pop up when my guard is relaxed – the keg of dynamite I sit on while pretending I think of that paltry squib, diabetes. I'm going to London next week to see the expert about that, by the way. I want him to ginger up my feet if he can.

Your letter about H.-J.'s delinquencies – there are senile as well as juvenile practitioners – is a sad story. Your sense of obligation to him for the past has made him your pensioner *ad infinitum*, and it is not the situation that irks him; he has always felt that the world owed him a pension and a gratuity – he used to chase after legacies – and I suppose his grudge against you is that your pension is inadequate and therefore he must supplement it by surreptitious additions. The alternative supposition is worse – that he gets some perverse pleasure in biting the hand that feeds him and is determined to deprive you of any satisfaction in your behaving handsomely towards him by making sure that the consequences are disagreeable. I don't think that is true, for he applies his principle of extortion indiscriminately. The Japps have a story of his baths. He asked them if he could have a bath at Bell Court against payment. Darsie did a sum, calculating the time the geyser was used for a normal bath and the cost of the gas; he told H.-J. that it took 10 minutes and consumed 3*d*. worth of gas. H.-J. came over for his bath and forgot that the gas meter was visible down below; he ran his bath for over 20 minutes and then tendered 4*d*. magnanimously. Darsie was offended and refused to accept any payment at all. A silly trifle, but it shows that his bland manner carries no weight, for Darsie is a most unsuspicious man and expects good of all comers. I have not spoken to the Japps about their continuance at Bell Court after Christmas, but Darsie has planted a number of flowers which will not bloom until next summer, so I assume they mean to stay for another 6 months at least on the present terms. I'm sure they wouldn't buy the house even if it were offered to them, because of H.-J.'s presence! They said so in so many words . . .

Melinda Maclean's disappearance, heading East, has made me look foolish in my scepticism. Cyril sent me a triumphant message on his 50th birthday, when he was entertained with lobster, champagne and *partridge* by ex-Lady Rothermere.[4] But why has Moscow at last spoken on

4. Mrs Ian Fleming, *née* Anne Charteris.

the subject and said they aren't 'over there' and that it is all a piece of capitalist rhinoceros slander to say they are? Have they all slipped down a crack between the Curtains or gone off to Venus in a flying saucer? I redouble my scepticism.

Sebastian Sprott has been to China and seen the Germ Warfare exhibit. Asked whether he believed in it, he replied, 'Why not?' but, when pressed by some of us at Ham Spray, he had to admit that he couldn't and would need a lot more evidence before he could. He sat beside a Chinese schoolmaster at a do and squeezed his hand. 'I like you very much,' said Sebastian, and asked the interpreter to translate. 'Let us hope there will always be peace between our countries,' replied the schoolmaster as he squeezed back. Fondest love to you both.

Ralph

HAM SPRAY, 19 NOVEMBER 1953

Dearest Gerald,

To compensate for the savagery of last year, we're having one of the mildest autumns ever known; there has not yet been enough frost to blacken the sagging dahlias and one can sit in the verandah all morning in the sun, reading the books that come pouring off the presses. Virginia's Diary[5] can only be compared to Flaubert's letters – that's what the critics have decided, and I agree. She was a remarkably heartless woman, living in an auto-erotic world of her own imagining and engaged in a lifelong struggle with words in preference to people ... My name appears as having sent off *Jacob's Room* to *The Times* for review without enclosing the date of publication – a reprimand from the grave. It's rather strange that *The Years*, about which she took such endless trouble, should *not* be such a masterpiece as she expected. There have been some condescending reviews, Angus Wilson kindly announcing that he doesn't think as poorly of her as do the best authorities in America. Bloomsbury prestige has sunk into the trough along with George Meredith.

Morgan [E. M. Forster], however, has an O M and his reminiscences of India[6] have had a pat on the back. It's a slight affair: letters to his mother when he was the Rajah's secretary, edited by him with comments – some characteristic Morgan touches, both funny and sentimental. The latest of all the autobiogs. is Bunny's,[7] which he has probably sent you. If

5. Virginia Woolf: *A Writer's Diary*, edited by Leonard Woolf (Hogarth Press, 1953).
6. *The Hill of Devi* (Arnold, 1953).
7. David Garnett: *The Golden Echo* (Chatto & Windus, 1953).

not, I've a spare copy in brown paper cover which I'll send you. There's a note of self-glorification about it which grates a little. The next volume, already announced, covering Bloomsbury, will start the old survivors from their lairs. The hero of the hour of course is Dylan Thomas, who by dying young has received an obituary in *The Times* worthy of Keats. I've just read his collected poems and can recognize an authentic poet navigating sublimely that rarefied atmosphere where the subconscious and the conscious join, which I suppose is the only stuff of poetry. His constant mood of exaltation reminds me of Walt Whitman, but he flies far higher and never condescends to come to earth for an occasional rest. But the printed words are only a libretto; they need his rapturous voice to intone them to produce their intended effect . . .

So much for literature. Life has not been very exciting; our weekend visitors have not been stimulating; and Burgo, who can generally be relied on to keep us on the hop, is tranquilly reading the Venerable Bede in his lofty rooms at Christ Church . . . With fondest love to you and Gamel.

Ralph

CHURRIANA, 21 NOVEMBER 1953

Dearest Ralph,

We have had a little excitement here of an unpleasant kind. Antonio's dog has developed rabies. You may remember this gentle, affectionate little mongrel with its terrible sense of guilt. Three days ago some children came into the yard and shooed at it. One of them fell down, and it bit him. As the dog seemed perfectly normal, we all thought that this was due to a sudden attack of bad temper. All dogs hate children, because they tease them . . .

. . . That evening Rosario brought rather disquieting news about the child; it had been bitten not in one place but all down both legs. A chain was procured to tie up the dog – that's the law – and the doctor sent word that it must be watched carefully. But still the dog wasn't tied up. Next morning we overslept and were not up till after ten. On going out, Rosario told me that the dog had torn to bits the two bantam hens which run about the court and with which it had grown up . . . I said, 'Tie it up,' but she put off doing so and half an hour later it had disappeared.

We still didn't believe in rabies . . . Then that night news came in that the dog had been seen making for the sierra, and next morning Antonio set off to find it. It was essential to produce it safe and sound if the child was to be saved from the anti-rabies injections, which are very severe and even slightly dangerous. He came back at lunch with some news of it and went to bed, as he always does when he is upset. But something had to be done, so after lunch I made him get up and we set off in torrents of rain to trace the dog's path. In the highest of the *cortijos*[8] we came across bad news. The dog had run into the yard, given a slight bite to their female dog, and continued on its path to the sierra. Evidently it was mad. When I got home I opened the Encyclopaedia, which I ought to have done before, and saw that every act of that dog was consistent with its being in the early stages of rabies.

And now? The child has started its inoculations. A young man whom the dog nipped in play on its last night here has also had them . . . Often, when a dog goes mad, the whole family takes the injections. But they are not pleasant things to take and occasionally they give one the disease. We are still wondering what to do. Certainly life in Spain has a quality of its own. I must stop and post this. Fondest love.

Gerald

CHURRIANA, 23 NOVEMBER 1953

Dearest Ralph,

Your letter came tonight. I would love to have that copy of Bunny's book. Autobiography brings out the worst in one, and even (in one's desire to make the most of one's material) traits of egoism that aren't really there. The more you delve into the personality of anyone, the more you find he hasn't one. People only look coherent when seen from a distance.

I shall buy Virginia's book. But you are wrong in saying that she had no heart. She had a great deal. What other famous writer would sit down to write his friend's biography, as she did Roger [Fry]'s?[9] Like the rest of Bloomsbury she loved her friends and was unjust to her acquaintances.

We are now all of us taking the injections. Before that agonizing question, 'Can I be certain that I never got a drop of the dog's saliva on my hands?' no one can stand firm and refuse . . . The inoculations turn out to be harmless. The Encyclopaedia says that 4% catch the disease from the inoculation; an American book says that 1% develop total paralysis; but the doctor says he has never heard of a fatal case. One feels at first stimulated, then a little tired. Nothing more. The case has other sidelines. Rosario threw the remains of the two chickens that the dog had

8. Farmhouses.
9. Virginia Woolf: *Roger Fry, A Biography* (Hogarth Press, 1940).

killed into the street gutter. Every dog and cat that eats this and has a sore mouth or nose is likely to catch the disease. Out in the sierra, where the poor animal is lying in some *barranco*, the hawks and the eagles and crows will eat its flesh. If they have a scratch on the mouth they will develop it too and will then attack their mates. I thought it would make a good *New Yorker* story but I fear that the Spanish Government would dislike it, so I shall not write it. Rabies discourages tourists . . .

It was sad about Dylan [Thomas]. A nice baby-face, frightened of being alone, frightened of dying, but with a Dionysius element in him one rarely finds in our drab island. But I can't help feeling that his poetic explosion was over.

Now I must stop and return to my assignment. The amount of work before me is a little depressing. I am so tiresomely conscientious. And the executive part of my mind is so weak. But I must make money and I have not the slickness necessary for potboilers. With best love to you both.

Gerald

CHURRIANA, 16 DECEMBER 1953

Dearest Ralph and Frances,

First I must thank you for the Bunny biography. I read it at a sitting with great enjoyment. However, I do agree with you that it does not cut very much ice as 'literature'. There are so many people in it that what must be the real theme of every true biography– the developing life of the hero – gets lost. It seems to me that his life, so free from difficulties, so rich in friends and pleasures, would be very difficult to turn into a 'literary' product, but he might have done better if he had gone more slowly at it. He fails to create the atmosphere of his childhood at Cearne or to make his parents' life vivid and convincing. He should have spread himself more in a poetical way, in a mood of nostalgia and reminiscence, in describing those delightful walks and picnics and tree-climbing feats with other youths and girls. But I make these criticisms rather diffidently because I know by now how difficult it is to make anything good of autobiography. Also in Bunny's book there are many good things. His eye for people is excellent. The portraits are shrewd, generous and true, and they improve towards the end of the book. Only he hasn't taken quite enough trouble.

We have finished our injections. We met in Malaga a man (Colonel Wynter-Wagstaff is his name) who told me that in India he had had injections against rabies four times. A routine affair, he called it. That has left me rather disappointed; I thought we had been privileged.

It is raining again. We have had nothing but cloud and rain and rain and cloud for a month. How is it, then, that Malaga has 307 cloudless days every year? Opposite me hang the dates, ripe for picking, on the palm tree; on the other side the oranges and tangerines, ripe too. Yet the climate is Cornish.

I am posting you a French book called *l'Espagne du Sud* by one [Jean] Sermet. It is a book that one reads in short bits at a time, for it is dully written; but it is crammed with new and exact information of all sorts, mainly *unhistorical*. The photographs are superb and my hope is that it may tempt you to come out to Spain again in a more leisurely manner. I enclose a specimen of an exquisite little plant – *Arum arisarum*. Do you know it?

I hope you all have a very happy Christmas in Paris. What a sensible idea to go there and escape the Yule-log! With fondest love to you both.

Gerald

HAM SPRAY, 18 DECEMBER 1953

Dearest Gerald,

. . . I spent 3 days this week at Winchester Assizes at the trial of Lord Montagu of Beaulieu for buggery – the first trial of a peer for felony before a jury in English history; the law was changed in 1948, putting an end to trial by the whole House of Lords. He was acquitted of buggery, but the jury disagreed as to whether there had been gross indecency; so his case has been put back to be tried again for that at the next Assizes. It was a *cause célèbre* all right. The newspapers could only make a mess of it, as they couldn't print the real evidence and weren't allowed to give the boy's name. I went there representing the *New Statesman*, who entered the lists of homosexuality at the behest of Morgan Forster and on behalf of John Gielgud[1] 6 weeks ago, but as the case is still *sub judice* I can't write a thing to print – not that it would have done the homosexual cause much good. Seducing 14-year-olds is not a good wicket on which to bat, even if the umpire gives you Not Out in the first innings, as occurred at Winchester.

Lord Montagu is a willowy young man of 27, with an obstinate little face and a quick way of talking, reminding me of Eddie Sackville-West.[2] He was charged with buggering a boy-scout in a beach hut after bathing on August Bank Holiday. It comes as a surprise to hear the *gros mots*

---

1. The distinguished actor, later Sir John Gielgud.
2. The Hon. Edward Sackville-West, later 5th Baron Sackville, music critic and novelist.

bandied about so loudly in front of a gaping audience of middle-aged women, old gentlemen and Negroes, who represent the public on these occasions. 'Anus' and 'penis' are all very well, but 'cocks' and 'cock-stands', 'backsides', 'bums', 'bottoms', shouted loudly by gentlemen in wigs with considerable (false) emotion, quite take one's breath away. Any printer who set up in type what was said in that Court would be sent to gaol immediately by the same gentlemen in wigs who uttered the words so juicily. The boy was a tartish type of grammar-school boy, and he reported when he got back to his fellow scouts, 'I've been bummed by a lord'; but the one thing you never seem to get evidence about in law-courts is the tone of voice in which words are uttered. In this case I don't doubt that it was a mixture of surprise and exaltation after seeing the boy in the witness-box – he had certainly undergone no traumatic experience. Lord M. in the box cut a very aristocratic figure. 'I will not shirk the issue,' he had said to the police, and he didn't; he brazened it out like a lord and the prosecution couldn't trip him up. 'I gave him my towel but I didn't touch the boy,' was his reiterated defence. The doctors who examined the boy afterwards declared that he could have been buggered – and then again he might not have been: nothing to tell either way from the state of his bottom. (They were very funny in the box. The Harley Street specialist kept shaping the two cheeks of a bottom in the air with his hands for the benefit of the jury.)

I can well understand why the jury disagreed on the minor count. It was a fair guess that *something* happened in the beach hut and that 'I've been bummed by a lord' was not an idle daydream. All the same, one couldn't accept the boy's evidence as he kept changing his story and admitted telling a pack of lies under cross-examination; whereas Lord M. stuck to his 'I didn't touch the boy' like a limpet to a rock. The Judge summed up in favour of Lord M. and couldn't make anything of the jury's failure to agree. 'The prosecution have to *prove* this case,' he repeated to the jury; and it certainly wasn't proved . . . To make sense of the boy's lies one can only assume that he was an agreeable party to the proceedings, but that was the last thing he intended to admit and neither prosecution nor defence wanted him to say so. As for the future, I doubt whether the Crown will offer any evidence when the case comes up again and Lord M. will have to go through life with a slight blot on his escutcheon.[3] I am sorry to have wearied you with so many details, but one comes away from a Court bursting with undischarged emotions of

3. Lord Montagu was in fact eventually convicted and sentenced to twelve months in prison.

one sort and another. Why must the lawyers use the English language with such insulting floweriness (the Judge talks plain English) – 'honour unsullied', 'the tongue of rumour has been busy,' etc., etc.? But I won't go on . . . With fondest love.

R.

CHURRIANA, 3 JANUARY 1954

Dearest Ralph,

I got a wild scribble from Beryl [de Zoete] tonight, telling me that Molly [MacCarthy] was dead. She is one of the people who ought to have lived for ever. Life, as one grows older, gets more and more sad till at last one becomes reconciled to leaving it. Can you tell me how this happened?

My bank has refused to allow me another overdraft, though of course I have securities with them. A new Treasury policy? . . . This is going to be extremely inconvenient unless they relent . . . I think I shall have to consider putting the cottage up for sale next summer to strengthen my reserve in the bank . . . These worries eat into my mind, but unfortunately they do not make one write any faster. I jog along – have only done 80 pages in 3 months. The mass of material to be incorporated kills my spontaneity – my only gift – and I have to take to pick and shovel like Flaubert. But the subject is grand – austere, dramatic, monotonous – and no one can do it but I. I am trying to write a book which will continue selling for ten years.

I hope you all enjoyed yourselves in Paris. We brightened our Christmas repast by imagining you eating *escalopes à la Milanaise* and *glaces Napolitaines* and filling your glasses with the best vintages of Margaux. Then, with a cigar in your mouth, with your deliberate Regency walk – or shall I say West India Company nabob's walk? – I saw you taking a beautifully preened Burgo to the most undressed of shows, while Frances went to bed with a good book. (How much easier I would find it to give you your own news in my letters than my own!)

As for us, we spent a very quiet Yuletide. A Christmas tree for the girls – Antonio carried a very big one a mile and more from the aerodrome – a drink with the Davises, and a tea-party for them here. They tell me they don't believe in entertaining, and as their terrifying wolf-hound now has the free range of their grounds – their theory is that they will soothe its passions by keeping it loose – we dare no longer go there. As they never come here I don't think we shall see much more of them, though I like them very much and I believe, in spite of all appearances to the contrary, that they like us. I am disappointed.

Our life, then, is work from breakfast to midnight, and Gamel works about as hard as I do. We are two moles tunnelling for our food like V.S.P., though with so much less power of earning it. But work is my life and I only curse my incurable dullness and stupidity. Not even my best friends know how stupid, except in flashes, I am.

We got Virginia's *Journals*. I have not had time to read them yet, but I have had a look at them. I find them altogether delightful. We did Virginia an injustice in thinking that because her amusing conversation was so fanciful, and her novels set out to destroy and break up 'character', that she did not understand people in an ordinary way. The *Journals* show that her range of feeling and observation was wide. She was a writer all through in a way in which no one is today, and how consistently alive and intelligent! There was something crystalline about her mind that makes her, like Keats, a sort of embodiment of genius. Had the reservoirs been greater, the roots deeper, she would have been a very great writer indeed. I imagine that there is a connection between her madness and her living so close to the surface.

I was sorry that her visit to Yegen was left out. I saw her very busy scribbling at her diary there. No doubt there were some comments on myself – how boring I was, and so forth – which caused Leonard to suppress it. But I don't think I should have minded too much anything she said, for I know well that I was very stupid and quite intolerable. I care less than most writers do about what is said of me, because I know that in a way, as a writer, my weaknesses and limitations are my strength. And anyhow one has to get accustomed to living with oneself. The marvel is I have been able to emerge at all. Fundamentally there is a gross arrogance, inseparable from intelligence, which cuts off most of the great from human life. Dr Johnson's humanity came from his weaknesses. I feel about my natural dullness and slowness and vagueness that they keep me down, though sometimes I wish they wouldn't do quite so much.

I was delighted by your account of Lord Montagu's trial and wish you would tell me . . . We buy a *Telegraph*, read some fascinating case, and then never see another word. This leaves us tantalized . . . With fondest love to you all.

Gerald

CHURRIANA, 8 JANUARY 1954

Dearest Ralph,

... We are certainly coming back to England next summer. I have some reading to do in the B[ritish] M[useum] for St Theresa and want to pack and bring back four more cases of books. Also I would like to get rid of Bell Court by selling it, compensating Hope [-Johnstone] and giving you no more troubles. We should love to come to H[am] S[pray] but it could only be for a few days.

A new American publication starring Lionel Trilling and other big shots has asked me to contribute to their first number. They offer from 150 to 200 dollars for a short article, which *Der Monat* of Berlin will also take at half the same price. Naturally I have accepted and am suggesting for my title 'On Reading Virginia Woolf's Diary' – an appreciation of her work and character, with some reminiscences thrown in. A new venture for me; it frightens me. The professional critics are so insidious. I shall feel like an innocent explorer walking through a jungle full of natives, whom he cannot see, with poisoned arrows. But the change to English or French literature must be made if I am to keep my paraffin stove burning. If by any chance you have V.'s little essay, 'A Room of One's Own', could you possibly lend it me?

We have had icy winds for a week. Temperatures down to 46°. In your nice damp climate you don't know what that can be. We keep warm in the evenings, but my workroom is unheatable and I sit wrapped up in an Arab burnous while my imagination freezes. So I feel in low spirits, as I always am when my powers of work go down. I want to work 8 hours a day for the rest of my life and then drop dead, leaving Gamel sufficiently provided for. It's illness and poverty, I fear, not death. The dead need no doctors or bank balances ...

You are always interested in what people spend, so I will tell you how we have got along. My accounts show that we have spent £870 this last year, but that £250 of this went on furniture, doing up the house and buying our tenant out.[3a] Actually about £50 more than that, as I did not put down small things. But no clothes were bought. So it seems, so long as we don't travel about, we can live here at rather under £600 a year. There are really only two realities in the world – health and money. One discovers that when one's access to either of them is threatened. And, of

---

3a. Not the English tenant, who was still occupying the ground floor, but another, Spanish tenant who had rented the first floor and had the decency to leave when Gerald and Gamel came back to live in the house.

course, the health and prosperity of one's friends. Today I don't live for myself any more; I live for Brenans Incorporated, my personality quite sunk in the business. And most of the time I ask for nothing better.

Gamel has discovered a new vein – writing short stories in Science Fiction. They are surprisingly competent and the last one is very imaginative. I believe she will sell them. She has a new story coming along for which I have provided the plot and I think it will be very good indeed. I used to have a lot of bright ideas, but couldn't write them. A writer is like a plant of ivy growing in a dungeon; till he can find a crack of light and push a shoot through it, all his store of talent is wasted. I have always been starved of chlorophyll.

Howling tiger wind, creaking and groaning of canes, visions of all Spain beyond the mountains covered with snow. An aeroplane has crashed, the mails to Madrid have been held up, I wonder how people manage to live at all. In cold weather all my ancestral memories come back to me – of how a bison chased me, of how my fingers were stiff with cold while I drew the death of the animal in a deep Lascaux cavern. My real self wears a straw boater, sits in a café in the Boule' 'Miche, twirls his moustaches and ogles the girls. I am one of Toulouse Lautrec's *rentiers* . . .

You don't mention your health or how you find your injections. I wish you would, for it's one of the things I most want to hear . . .

Gerald

HAM SPRAY, 4 FEBRUARY 1954

Dearest Gerald,

We're in the ice age – last hot bath 5 days ago, and even the cold taps are sealed up and have to be unfrozen with blow-lamps; over 20 degrees of frost at times; life in the igloo rather like life in the womb, dreamy and thoughtless. You are kind to take an interest in my diabetes, which is more than I can do. I resent it so much. I've been raising my dosage steadily, until now I'm taking twice as much as 6 weeks ago, and still I can't clear my urine of sugar. In addition I now inject Vitamin B_{12} once a week. This is a comparatively new vitamin (4 years old) for counteracting pernicious anaemia. What bearing it may have on diabetes, no one seems to know; the local doctor is obeying the London specialist in prescribing it, without venturing an opinion of his own. I read on the bottle that the dose I'm taking is the same as that for 'sub-acute degeneration of the chord.' Have I got that to contend with as well as diabetes? Mercy on us.

Frances has taken advantage of our suspended existence in the cold to sort out a mass of my old letters. You prove my most consistent correspondent, except for the stretches when we weren't on speaking terms. It's now nearly forty years since our paths first crossed and our lives became entangled, and I wish to say now that the attachment on my side has been one of the greatest pleasures in my life. Whenever I see your handwriting on an envelope addressed to me my spirits rise spontaneously, and I thank you for the long years of friendship . . . Fondest love to you both.

Ralph

CHURRIANA, 12 FEBRUARY 1954

Dearest Ralph,

Thank you for your charming letter. Yes, it is just 40 years since I saw you in that mess-room at Great Totham, immersed in *The Times* and suddenly giving a roar of laughter. It seems that one cannot make deep friendships after the age of 25. You have always been for me in a class by yourself – you and Carrington. No one else near. Gamel – well, she is a part of me, my climate, the air I breathe.

What is the meaning of this new Vitamin B_{12} injection that you take? Have you got some secondary complaint as well? It is most disturbing. You mustn't fail to let me know how you go on . . .

Our cold spell went as suddenly as it came, and now it is deliciously warm. But I can hardly bear to go out into the garden. Everything except the orange trees, the Japanese medlars and the ivy has turned black. Even the young shoots of butchers' broom have withered. Out in the country much of the grass has turned yellow, and the asphodels after all were frost-bitten. Snow fell even in Marrakesh, though I was wrong in saying it fell in Almeria. The road from Granada to Ugíjar was blocked for a week and an avalanche (!) fell on Torriscón. There are reports that many of the orange trees round Valencia have been killed. In Churriana some people who had never seen snow before thought that the North Pole had exploded, and got under their beds fearing that their houses would be buried and they killed. In short it has been a sensation.

I have just heard from Sir Walter Monckton[4] who said that, during an operation he had been having R. A. Butler[5], had lent him my essay on St

---

4. Later 1st Viscount Monckton, he was then Conservative MP for Bristol and Minister of Labour. Gerald had met him at a luncheon given by the British Consul at Malaga.
5. Richard Austen Butler, then Lord Privy Seal and leader of the House of Commons.

John of the Cross. I am flattered, yet I feel that the world must be in a bad way if Cabinet Ministers get excited by mystics. *I* am safe from infection since I can also turn to [H.C.] Lea's *Spanish Inquisition* and get an impulse driving me in an opposite direction. Catholicism is either for simple people or else a thing to be taken *in extremis*, like extreme unction. But people must feel very pleased with themselves to wish to envy their rag-bag of disparate qualities beyond the grave. I find nothing in myself worth such embalming and preserving. Only I would like all perfect things – works of art, scene. *y*, gardens – to live for ever . . . In haste. Love.

Gerald

HAM SPRAY, 14 MARCH 1954

Dearest Gerald,

. . . I saw my Harley Street man a week ago and emerged with credit. My blood pressure is 'like that of a baby'. I need not give up smoking and the dosage of insulin seems to be correctly matched against my diet; so I need not go near him again for another 6 months, thank God. I'm feeling rather well too, which is what doctors hardly bother about . . .

I've been approached to write a book on Homosexuality, which is all the rage. Dare I? And if I dared, could I? I feel my rough methods are hardly suited to such an egg-shell subject. I should want to do my usual covert propaganda, but I don't know how to disarm the ranks of prejudice. It's far easier to say that everyone has a touch of the murderer in him – rather flattering indeed, and impressive – than to insist that hatred of homosexuals derives from a prudish inability to face one's own homosexual tendencies. Besides, how would all one's friends feel when one dragged out into the open all their mother fixations?

We went to Bunny's birthday party at Hilton a few days ago and there met Morgan Forster, looking, I may say, considerably younger than I do. I asked him whether he advised me to proceed with such a book and he wagged his head like a bird in a zoo aviary – a toucan perhaps – and said No. Bunny looked a grand old man of literature with his snowy locks. His four little girls are exquisitely pretty and engaging. Richard, his son, has just become engaged too, to a very attractive dark girl mixed up with theatrical design . . . But I spent most of the evening alongside Baroness Budberg, chatting about buggery and H. G. Wells, whose last hours she consoled. It was a delightful party; and because the average age was over 50 and sex nowhere to be seen, everyone was entirely amiable. Fondest love to you both.

R.

CHURRIANA, 20 MARCH 1954

Dearest Ralph,

Your letter brought the best possible news – that you have found the right dosage and feel well. I am very pleased. I believe myself that there is nothing like having a pet disease, because it keeps others away. It is those people who enjoy perfect health who are liable to feel the tiger's presence when they pass sixty . . .

I hope you will write your book on Homosexuality. I do not know what you mean by your 'rough method', for it was the tact and circumspection of your book on Broadmoor that most impressed me. I think that for this reason you are an excellent person to write on any thorny subject. But if you want to produce a good effect, you will have to resign yourself to a certain amount of hypocrisy. Homosexuality can't be defended in England, or classed as an unavoidable abnormality; it must be blamed like adultery. Toleration of it must be put forward as the lesser evil unless you wish to write for the converted. And I believe that when one wishes to write or speak for immediate effect in any political controversy, one must address all one's arguments to the unconverted. However, you are so circumspect that you will be able to do this without committing yourself to statements that you do not believe in.

One thing that has always struck me about this question is this. Even the most reactionary and conservative people invite to their houses people whom they know to be homosexuals, and only cut them when they get into the papers. Over theft, blackmail, etc. they act differently. This implies an exceptional amount of hypocrisy and I think they should be accused of this. It seems to show, too, that they would be glad to see the act against homosexual relations between adults dropped, provided that a proper amount of moral thunder and manly disgust were used at the same time to salve their guilty feelings . . . With fondest love to you both.

Gerald

HAM SPRAY, 2 APRIL 1954

Dearest Gerald,

. . . Homosexuality has been obsessing me. I'm not yet finally committed to writing about it, but Kinsey[6] is being written to for permission to use his statistics and if he agrees I shall be cornered. The Montagu trial I

6. Alfred Charles Kinsey, author of *Sexual Behaviour in the Human Male* (Philadelphia, 1949).

sat through for eight long days. It was a barbarity – three perfectly
responsible young men hounded to gaol for a little sexual indulgence
nearly two years ago; the grim apparatus of the law crushing them in its
jaws as cruelly and meaninglessly as heretics in other spheres used to
suffer. Voltaire and the Calas family[7] is a precedent for me to follow;
but I am just a puny journalist and my pen is steeped in Quink and not
in the bitter gall of genius. [Michael] Pitt-Rivers[8] was obviously a real
charmer; [Peter] Wildeblood[8] was pathetic; Montagu a trapped animal,
fierce and resentful. The two wretched Air Force boys, saving their skins
at the expense of their bottoms, were just an ignoble sight. The villains
were the police, determined to taste blood and enjoying every minute of
it. They behaved so outrageously in getting their evidence that there is
just a possibility that there will be a row. Kingsley Martin says he's
prepared to take it up once the case is not *sub judice*, i.e. when there is no
appeal to follow or the appeal is disposed of; but just now he's busy on
another tack, trying to make the lives of the Spandau prisoners[9] less
comfortable. I met him for the first time in my life in London; he's a sort
of Left-wing clergyman with a nose for sin whenever the wind's in the
Right direction; fortunately where homosexuals are concerned we sniff
the same breeze . . . Fondest love to you both.

                                                                        R.

                                                      CHURRIANA, 5 APRIL 1954
Dearest Ralph,
    I too was horrified by the Montagu case, so horrified that I sat down
and wrote a letter of protest to the N[ew] S[tatesman]. It was a bad letter,
like all letters written under the stress of indignation; but even if it had
not been it could not have been published, since they are going to appeal.
So I send a copy to you. I am delighted to hear that you are going to write
a book on Homosexuality and this trial will give you something to hang
it on. As you say, it is a Calas case. But on the homosexual acts
themselves, be circumspect. Your book must influence opinion and so
you must not defend the practice.

7. Jean Calas, the eighteenth-century French Protestant merchant who was accused, with his
wife and family, of having strangled his son Antoine (who had almost certainly committed
suicide) to prevent his turning Roman Catholic. They were tortured in order to extort
confession, and Calas himself was condemned to be broken on the wheel. This judicial murder
caused an agitation in which Voltaire played a leading part.
8. Lord Montagu's co-defendants.
9. High-ranking Nazis who had been convicted as war criminals.

I have just been writing another letter to the papers. The *Manchester Guardian* has been bringing out a series of articles on Spain by someone called Jean Creach. In many respects the articles were able, but she overloaded the dice and came out with the statement that farm labourers in Andalusia were paid only 9 pesetas a day. Actually they are paid 30 here, a little less in the villages. There were other false statements of the sort, so I wrote at some length to correct them. It is only a short time ago since the *NS* came out with an even more unjust and ignorant article on the same subject and I spent a whole day replying to it, but then decided not to post my letter. Am I right in thinking that my conscience makes me testify to the truth, or am I merely becoming reactionary?

Louis Wilkinson[1] has been staying at Torremolinos. He is 70 but looks over 80 and his young wife leads him about, as she says herself, like a bear. He kept up his fucking too long. He had a good story about his last wife, Diana.[2] She, with her brothers and sisters, were illegitimate and every spring her father used to say to her mother, 'Now I really must go and spend a few months with Laura. After all, she *is* my lawful wife.' By this Laura he had several children, one of whom was [J.R.] Ackerley, who wrote a famous book on India[3] and now, I believe, edits the *Listener*. Diana had never met him, so Louis brought them together. Then it turned out that Ackerley and his brothers and sisters were illegitimate too, but had always believed Diana and *her* brothers and sisters to be the legal offspring, because every autumn his father had said to his mother, 'Now, my dear, I must go off and spend a little time with Lucy. After all, she *is* . . .' With fondest love to you both.

Gerald

HAM SPRAY, 29 APRIL 1954

Dearest Gerald,

I liked your letter to the *New Statesman* very much; but it couldn't be printed, I suppose, while the case was still *sub judice* and after that it's out of date. That is the cunning effect of the *sub judice* rule – no comment can ever be made on a case until all the steam has gone out of it by the mere passage of time. I see that yesterday the Home Secretary announced an enquiry into homosexuality, solicitation and prostitution. With what object? To relax or to stiffen the law? I don't like the

---

1. The novelist and biographer.
2. The writer Diana Petre, whose book *The Secret Orchard of Roger Ackerley* (Hamish Hamilton, 1975), gives a first-hand account of Louis Wilkinson's story.
3. *Hindoo Holiday* (Chatto & Windus, 1932).

man ever since he allowed Bentley[4] to be hanged out of respect for the police; so I expect he'll pack the enquiry with stooges.

I can't decide whether to have a shot at the book. The reply from Dr Kinsey has come, to say he'll allow permission to quote from him *after* he has seen what it is proposed to quote. That is a little restrictive but not deterrent. I had lunch with Hewitt, alias 'C. H. Rolph', who is the *New Statesman* 'reformer' of penal laws and denouncer of abuses. He's an ex-policeman himself and a member of the Howard League Council,[5] almost too earnest and high-minded; but he told me where to find the material on the subject if I want it. The great flaw in the theory of writing the book remains – that everything one wants to say can really be said in a paragraph, and why should it be spun out into 200 pages? Repetitiousness is detestable, yet how can it be avoided? . . .

We are going to see the eclipse in Sweden at the end of June, and shall look at Stockholm and Copenhagen while we're about it. A party is going – Raymond [Mortimer], Eddie [Sackville-] West, Eardley, Knollys[6] – and we and Burgo are tacking on. Scandinavia is not my idea of foreign travel, but a total eclipse is what I've always wanted to see. We shall be away from Ham Spray for about 12 days in all. When are you coming to stay with us? . . . Burgo has gone back to Oxford for his summer term. He failed in an exam last term and is labouring under a sense of inadequacy in consequence. He'll take the exam again in a few weeks and I hope to God he gets through, or we shall be once more in the old familiar soup. Fondest love to you both.

Ralph

CHURRIANA, 8 MAY 1954

Dearest Ralph,

I have just been reading V.S.P.'s book on Spain[7] . . . Spain seems to draw out a deep and poetic side of his nature that is usually suppressed, and his pages on Spanish painting and architecture, on the bullfight and on the national character are superbly written and, besides that,

4. During the night of 2 November 1952 a policeman investigating a burglary at a London warehouse was shot dead by a boy of sixteen called Christopher Craig. On account of his age Craig was spared the death penalty, but his accomplice, nineteen-year-old Derek Bentley, who allegedly incited him to pull the trigger, was sentenced and hanged. Ralph was not alone in considering this a gross miscarriage of justice.
5. The Howard League for Penal Reform, named after the eighteenth-century philanthropist John Howard.
6. The painter, a close friend of the Partridges.
7. *The Spanish Temper*, Chatto & Windus, 1954.

revealing and true. I think he has never written better and I am full
of admiration . . .

I am recovering from an evening at the Davises where I drank too
much. There was an Englishman called [Emerson] Bainbridge and his
wife – rich, live at Cap d'Antibes, have a White Russian chef who used to
be a landowner, and know the Culme-Seymours. The wife is an old flame
of Cyril Connolly's and came to Spain with him in 1937 as his 'secretary'. I took to Bainbridge very much – a little monkey of a man, fifty,
with a livid face and a delightful friendliness, frankness and vivacity. A
man of the Regency Age – you'd like him. Mrs B. was one of those mildly
querulous women who seek consolation for their ruined looks in social
life, but do not find it. Their palmist tells them they must be chic and
sophisticated but, being self-conscious and Englishly dissatisfied with
themselves, they cannot make the grade. All Cyril's women, I note, age
badly. He chooses them for their lemur-like innocence and sugariness
and pussiness, and these qualities don't last. The bottom layer in him is a
sort of protective tenderness, but there are a *lot* of other layers on top.

At the Davises' house Cyril is always the presiding spirit, even when
absent. Every conversation comes back to him. Mrs D., a very simple,
naive woman, adores him and he writes to her in the kindest, most
affectionate tone, like a brother. Bill Davis admires him, but is cynical.
As for myself, I admire Cyril enormously for his courage in always being
himself . . .

I must end this letter. We shall be home either on 25 June or in early
September. Miranda and Xavier[8] have bought a big new car and
propose to take us either from or to Paris. They come here for August.
With fondest love.

Gerald

HAM SPRAY, 25 MAY 1954

Dearest Gerald,

. . . I have been numb in mind and body for the last fortnight – not an
idea in my head and no particular desire to do anything. Is this a foretaste
of senile decay? The ego wearing thin? I attribute it to a more passing
malaise: my inability to write about homosexuality when it came to the
point. I have had to dismiss the intention to write the book, yet it nags me
although it is dead and done with. Someone could write it, but I'm not
the man; I'm too short-winded, I can write articles of 2000 words but

---

8. Xavier Corre, Miranda's French husband.

not books, and I must resign myself to that. Talking of authorship, Bunny paid us an unexpected visit two days ago. There's a writer for you! He has no nerves whatever; his next volume of autobiography will cover the 1914–18 war and tread on serried ranks of Bloomsbury toes, but he just grins at the prospect. (He's just lost two vital chapters that he's written, but he merely frowns and resumes without repining. The loss reminds him of T. E. Lawrence losing *The Seven Pillars of Wisdom* at Reading station and Mill burning Carlyle's *French Revolution* in the grate, that's all.) His son William lives at home at Hilton tapping on a typewriter; nobody knows what goes on up there, but whenever William witnesses a document he describes himself as 'author'. Bunny says his idea in the new volume is to describe houses like people – Garsington, Tidmarsh, Charleston, etc. – as he thinks they influence the lives of those who live in them more forcibly than do the casual visitors who come there; first you create your environment and then your environment takes its revenge on you . . . Fondest love,

R.

CHURRIANA, 3 JUNE 1954

Dearest Ralph,

It was nice to get your letter. I don't take your depression too seriously; it seems to me simply the usual author's trepidation. The professional grows a hard skin over his sensibilities and plugs away without considering too much whether he can pull it off or not. Yet I see that a book written just now on homosexuality is a ticklish business, because its object must be to produce a certain effect. I advise you just to start on it, but to be ready to tear it up if you decide it will be *counterproductive*. That will give you confidence . . .

I have been full of admiration for V.S.P.'s articles since he returned from the USA. That wonderful essay on Sterne in the *Listener*[9] . . . reaches a new level. The review of Aldington's book[1] in the NS shows, too, a sharp edge to his mind which I had not observed before. He goes on getting more and more mature – and God knows he is mature enough already. I feel an infant by comparison. The qualities I most appreciate in writers – the lyrical gift, the warmth in human matters, the sense of the beauty of the world, of the delight of being alive – he lacks completely;

9. Based on the second of five talks on 'The Comic Element in the English Novel', broadcast on the Third Programme.
1. Richard Aldington: *Pinorman* (Heinemann) reviewed by V.S.P. in the *New Statesman* of 29 May 1954.

but all the same I admire his talent enormously. His intuitive powers, his penetration, equal those of the greatest writers. I place him far above Hazlitt, to whom he is often compared.

My little book on Yegen[2] is now half completed. I have sold the first two chapters for 450 dollars and they ask for more. I am also reviewing a book on Spain for the *Reporter* at a high rate of pay – I'm told they give £60 – and have a *New Yorker* article on the stocks. I want for once to pile up a little sum in the bank out here, as it is not comfortable to live on the edge of nothing. I am also preparing a great assault on the Civil Governor of Malaga, who alone, it seems, has the power to relieve me of my tenant . . . It would give me an unspeakable relief to get rid of him. If I die suddenly, Gamel will wish to go on living here. She has a great friend, very skilled in the running of pensions, who would probably come to live with her, and if they had the whole house they could easily – as they both have some private means as well – support themselves.

In the struggle between parents and children my sympathies always go with the children. It seems absurd to me that our generation, which had such difficulties with their own parents, cannot learn a little wisdom. One cannot treat one's children as though they were one's equals in age and expect a balance in the trade of love with them. As I see it, parents have to do two things: first, love their children very much when they are young, and then, as they grow up, recede into the background. The adolescent must react against his parents if he is to have a character and life of his own, and the parents must allow him to do so. That is, they must present a passive front, be tolerant, never criticize him *or notice him* too much. He is rising, they are delining; and they must recognize this, be old before their time, and let him (or her) bully them a little. Then, in the long run, they will get back all the love which children ought to give to the old nest-birds and will have the satisfaction, for what it's worth, that they will always live inside those children and perpetuate their life in them. One loves one's parents most when they are either old and helpless, or dead . . .

Yes, one must flatter one's children. The young lack self-confidence and we must let them have their first victories over oneself. I let Miranda know that intelligence was just one thing and that high spirits, love of life and sex were equally important. I let her laugh at me. I told her what a foolish youth I had had, how late I had woken up to the pleasures of love

2. *South From Granada*, a little masterpiece, dedicated to Ralph and published by Hamish Hamilton in 1957.

affairs, how I had never been able to dance, how I had always been clumsy and stupid. I told her everything I knew about love-making, not so much to inform her as to excite her. I said, 'It's not enough to be beautiful. You must be so good in bed that no man who sleeps with you will ever forget you.' Gamel looked on askance – wasn't I training her to be a good-time girl? But the good-time girl is a rebel, and Miranda had nothing to rebel against. I knew that she would never refuse the first good offer that came her way. She would fall in love with the man who offered her the settled and happy life (with plenty of good clothes) that she wanted. Reason and my natural inclinations worked together. However, don't think I am reading a lecture to you. Your problem is a much more difficult and painful one. I am talking about parents in general and the folly of their possessiveness . . . With fondest love.

Gerald

HAM SPRAY, 13 JUNE 1954

Dearest Gerald,

Your plans will include us for any time you please, I hope – this is just a renewal of a standing invitation – and you could handle your packing at Aldbourne from here, if you chose to. We are not going to be away in Sweden at the end of this month after all, as a stone has been discovered in my left kidney and until I'm relieved of it it is thought inadvisable to go travelling abroad. The treatment so far is simplicity itself – drinking enormous quantities of water to wash the offending object out from the niche where it is at present lodged. A further X-ray in 10 days' time will show what success, if any, has been obtained by this intensive irrigation.

Renal colic, the symptom which revealed that something was amiss, is a stupendous pain near the navel. It came on late one night, lasted three hours and then vanished. When it returned the following night the doctor was called from Hungerford, who was delighted in a doctorish way with my writhings as they identified the cause so clearly. He at once gave me a morphia injection and a stock of morphia pills to take when the effect of the injection wore off. I had one more bout of pain, which my pills blanketed, and a few twinges that came to nothing. The X-ray showed a little stone stuck in my ureter. The colic is caused apparently by the ureter objecting to its presence by spasmodic squeezing. The afflic-tion of passing a kidney-stone is far commoner than I ever knew before experiencing it myself. From all sides I have heard stories of people who've had it. [André] Gide had one when staying with the Bussys and declared, 'C'est pire que l'accouchement'. How did he know? But no one has ever had to go to a surgeon for the remedy; the chance of that, my doctor assures, me, is one in a hundred. I've got the name and address of a surgeon ready in case of need, but don't intend to call him in unless all else fails. I am rather disquieted that my body has begun to function so badly – first the pancreas, then the kidneys; what next? But I feel perfectly well; after the pain one is as fresh as a daisy, and that makes it *'un peu mieux que l'accouchement'*. Apart from cancelling the journey to Sweden, it has not interfered with the ordinary run of life at all. We went to the Covent Garden ballet last week for a treat and loved it; our ballet dancers aren't Russians, but their performance is very professional and polished and a pleasure to watch . . . We are so looking forward to seeing you both within a few weeks. Fondest love.

Ralph

After a month in England, Gerald hurried back to Churriana to resume his work on *South from Granada,* which was to occupy him for two more years. Ralph, meanwhile, continued to regale him with news from home and accounts from time to time of jaunts abroad.

PART FIVE   1954–1960

Dearest Gerald,

We had a touch of your weather in Italy – as we topped the Simplon pass the clouds unrolled and there was the warm South – and only one day's rain in the Appenines marred our holiday, which was the greatest success . . . Rome was terrific – far too much to see, infernally noisy, and infernally sympathetic. One could live in such a city without a qualm; the women are handsome, with absurdly small waists and a dignified carriage; and the men don't think amiability beneath masculine consideration. The general air of affability shows what the human race is capable of, given a good climate, a capacity for enjoyment and no great preoccupation with morals . . .

Bunny's Vol. 2 of his autobiography[3] has just been here in MS. He sets himself up as a bit of a Casanova, which I suppose he was. That, I don't object to, nor the low-down on some of living as well as dead Bloomsburys (Vanessa and Duncan may well stage a resistance movement) but I find the extraordinary complacency rather trying. He enumerates all his good fortune and clearly indicates that his opinion is that he richly deserved it. So much for the tone; the matter is another ground for criticism. Bunny takes a purely superficial, extrovert and egocentric view of all his experiences – if he cures a cart of squeaking, that is better for the record than lying awake night after night in the torments of jealousy; not that he admits he ever was jealous! Ummh! . . .

Burgo got chicken-pox while we were away and was removed to Oxford Fever Hospital where he spent 3 dreary weeks. We saw him as soon as we got back and he seems strengthened by the experience – very gratifying. We shall bed down now for the winter, and I shall have to take a squint at the sociology of the Public Schools[4] or live in disgrace for ever . . .

When will you finish your Yegen chapter to your satisfaction? The winter migrants will soon be with you, and then back will come botany. The *Times* bird correspondent has a phrase I like – 'These birds require careful watching.' I should add, 'And so do those who go in for

---

3. David Garnett: *The Flowers of the Forest* (Chatto & Windus, 1955).
4. V.S.P. had suggested that Ralph should write on the English public schools 'from an anthropological point of view' for the Turnstile Press.

bird-watching.' Were mammals created to watch feathers fly? It's high time the birds kept an eye on the men, and who knows whether that's not exactly what they're doing on the sly? Vulture to Eagle: 'Do you see that red-faced human taking a peek at us? Hardly the local Andalusian type. Winter migrant from Britain maybe. Wonder how he'd eat.' Fondest love to both.

R.

CHURRIANA, 13 NOVEMBER 1954

Dearest Ralph,

I was very pleased to get your letter and to hear that you had both enjoyed yourselves so much. Yes, Italy is a perfect country to travel in but, remember, cold as a vault in winter unless you find that almost unheard of thing, a house with a fireplace. When I was last at Rapallo the water in my radiator froze, though it was in a closed garage. I agree that Italian women are the most seductive in the world, though whether at our age there is more pleasure than pain to be got from that, I do not know. And that little lonely villa near Ostia that catered for all ages and tastes has, I gather, been closed down. What are the Pope's nephews doing?

. . . At the moment I am describing your visit to Yegen with D.C. and Lytton. You fit badly into my book, I don't know how to present you briefly and discreetly; but if I miss you out I have nothing to fall back on but folklore and scenery, scenery and folklore, spiced a little by a 20-page adventure in the brothels of Almeria and by some dancing in the Seville Kursaal. So please resign yourself to being a writer's poor material.

Bunny is one of the Georgian prose writers, companion of Masefield and Aldington. His smooth, slow style is founded upon a thick, slow bloodstream, never scurried by a fast heart-beat. He should be put in the zoo as the last of the healthy men, or injected into the blood as an anti-Eliot, anti-Prichett, anti-Sartre. I'd like to have a phial for my bad moments on the mantlepiece. In all his life he has never felt anything but natural animal sensations. There can be literature in that, and if he'd been jolted a little he might have written about as well as Hemingway. But no, moral Bloomsbury forbids it, so when he is not either poetic or humorous his writing tastes like a sleepy pear . . .

Well, we are to buy a Vespa motor-cycle and a sidecar. Do you know of any mechanical objections to them? So far as I can see, they will serve our purpose of knocking about Andalusia perfectly. If I am *driven* to it I will then write a guide-travel book. I bought a Rolleiflex camera in England with an eye to this, but care so little for these things that I haven't tried it yet. And now I stop. With fondest love to you both.

Gerald

CHURRIANA, 19 DECEMBER 1954

Dearest Ralph and Frances,

Christmas, and my head is quite empty. We have just had a four days' visit from Trevor-Roper,[5] which has rather depleted my batteries. He is a very intelligent man, and a nice one. A touch of snobbery, very useful in a historian, not a great deal of imagination, but an absolutely first-rate mind which he applies to everything that crops up. Underneath this, a sort of boyish love of adventure, which once led him to spend some very tough holidays alone in the north of Iceland. He had some good stories. One was about the lists the Nazis made for their expected conquest of England. A white list gave the names of those who would be useful in a Pétain-like way; a black list gave the names of those who were to be bumped off. Rebecca West was not on either list. Lady Astor was on *both*.

We met Augustus [John] and Dorelia at the station and took them to their hotel. Yesterday we walked over to see them. They have a bed-sitting room and a private balcony looking over the sea. They are both very tired and Dorelia has a broken arm which still hurts her a bit, but they seemed cheerful and to like the place. I don't think they want to do much at present but lie in the sun and rest; and fortunately the weather has been perfect, as it usually is round Christmas . . . Wonderful weather, wonderful sun, not a breath of air. The roses, but not much else, flowering. I forget if I told you we are thinking of buying a car. They are turning out in Barcelona a two-seater with a dicky and canvas hood, engine British, for £290. After Christmas we shall order it and receive it in May. But in doing so I bank on getting the article I am writing for the *New Yorker* accepted . . . With fondest love from Gamel and myself.

Gerald

HAM SPRAY, 14 FEBRUARY 1955

Dearest Gerald,

. . . Anthony West[6] has never sent me one word since I posted him off my article on Agatha Christie six weeks ago. I shall wait another month

5. The historian Hugh Trevor-Roper, later Baron Dacre of Glanton.
6. The natural son of Rebecca West and H. G. Wells, he had been a staff writer on the *New Yorker* since 1950.

and then pester him, but I'm hoping I shall get a cheque for dollars before that from *Harper's Bazaar*. The rumour is that he is quitting the *New Yorker* and slipping entirely into *Harper's*. He's supposed to be coming to England for 6 weeks this summer, when it will be possible to badger him more effectively, but that's a long time ahead . . .

We've been over to Oxford to see Burgo, who was very cheerful and only wanted some money to go with a party to Norway or Switzerland at the end of term. We aren't worrying about him for the time being. Any indication that he has found friends of his own with whom he wants to associate in vacations is inexpressibly welcome to his fussy old parents . . .

Old Saxon [Sydney-Turner] is coming here for a week. That'll be gloomy. He's in a hopeless financial mess as a result of betting on horses and is reduced to the point where he hasn't a shilling in his pocket and can't cash a cheque. Poverty is the incurable disease of our time; money is the only medicine to apply and that does not grow on trees. Nor is it provided by our Welfare State. What's the good of a bottle of tonic when what one wants is £20,000? Fondest love to you both.

R.

HAM SPRAY, 28 MARCH 1955

Dearest Gerald,

I have received a cheque from *Harper's Bazaar* today quite silently, without a word from Anthony, so I suppose you have probably got one too. The pay is splendid, when it comes! But three months' waiting for it sours the gratification . . .

Bunny's next volume is entitled *The Flowers of the Forest* and is already announced by Chatto's, with Vol. III, *The Familiar Faces*, due to appear next year. So you had better be quick into print or he will draw first blood. I haven't read Virginia again since the war, and now I'm afraid to come to a similar conclusion to yours about her. I never could see her characters as anything but toys for Virginia to play with; even the father in *To the Lighthouse* was a wraith from her memory rather than a sentient being, as Julia [Strachey] likes to call humanity. But if her style is not mothproof her novels are meaningless; they won't date, they'll just disappear. I think she hated all human beings except Vanessa and fell back on literature as a substitute. That's why *The Common Reader* had nothing to hide, while in the novels she was always trying to disguise her essential dislike for people by mooning round the scenery and looking for a mark on the wall to distract her. With such faulty equipment for a novelist, could she ever have written better novels? I don't believe so. Her eye was not in focus, and her ear too deficient; she never heard what people said; there is never a telling conversation in her books ... Virginia chose novels rather than criticism because she was wildly ambitious and wanted to soar as a best-seller in the best of taste – a Flaubert, yes, never a Sainte-Beuve. Ambition was the worm in Bloomsbury, riddling their fine ideals with its insatiable progress.

Talking of Rebecca [West] (as you were) I went with her sister, Miss Letitia Fairfield, to a meeting of the Medico-Legal Society last week to hear the Merritt case discussed. He was the psychopath who shot his mother in Scotland in 1926, and was not convicted, and then went on last year to murder his wife and mother-in-law (who kept an old people's home at Ealing) under the name of Chesney. All the forces of society opposed to crime were at the meeting – lawyers, doctors and policemen – and we were all sworn not to divulge the proceedings to the Press. Chesney was never tried for the crimes at Ealing, as he committed suicide in Germany when he realized the game was up. The police view was that they never had sufficient evidence to extradite him, until he was dead and the German police cut off both his arms and posted them to Scotland Yard for scientific dissection. Under his finger-nails he was carrying a shred of his wife's pink jumper and some hair from patting the chow dogs who guarded the Ealing house. Mrs Fairfield is a high-minded R C who has devoted her life to improving everything, garrulous and a little sentimental, but the kind of magistrate you'd be glad to see on the bench if you were charged with homosexuality. She edited the Straffen case in the *Famous Trials* series – that's how I struck up with her.

F. will have told you that we're taking the Jiménez house near Coruña from 5 August to 25 September. Why don't you cross the peninsula on a visit to us? I believe we're to have twelve beds to dispose of. Fondest love to you both.

Ralph

CHURRIANA, 15 MAY 1955

Dearest Ralph,

We got back two days ago from Almeria and found your postcard. Our first stage was to Guadix. Dust, flies, stinking meat and fish, and a harsh Anatolian atmosphere. But the caves, which we investigated closely, are very extraordinary – some with two stories, one with a patio and bathroom. From there we hired a car – 500 pesetas – over the Sierra Nevada by a very rough road to Ugíjar. On the summit, blue gentians, enormous cowslips and an Alpine buttercup and a yellow *Gagea* that even Frances does not know. In Ugíjar nothing has changed except that the church has been burnt down and rebuilt. At the parador the hostess immediately recognized me and asked after you and 'my sister'. (This was Carrington.) After a bad lunch we walked up by the steep way – 3 hours – to Yegen, Gamel riding a mule. Rosario's brother put us up. The village is now whitewashed and has a church-clock. There is a posada on the road and the girls look better-dressed and the children much healthier and cleaner. Attendance at school is compulsory. Otherwise there were no outward changes. We had a few visits and sat all evening of that day and the next while old friends and acquaintances came to pay their respects. Those I remembered all had white hair, and many were dead. Paco, whom you may remember, died 3 months ago in the Argentine. There was a lot of philosophizing. '*La vida es un soplo. Venimos emprestados. La muerte no para.*'[7] A lot of stories of wolves and lost cows, and comments on my walking prowess.

I thought the place enchanting. Long-branched olive trees hanging over corn four and even five feet high; water running everywhere; above the village, grass of an incredible greenness growing under the poplar trees. And when one turned round, that amazing ochre and lilac tangle of mountains. In the village there was an extraordinary silence. The villagers have low voices. And a sense of being cut off from the rest of the world and from the passage of time. What luck I had in discovering such a place so unlike any other in the world! And yet what an odd thing for a young man to do! I tried to imagine my feelings during my early years there, and yet I could not enter into them. As one grows older one becomes a different person, inheriting by some strange magic a young man's memories.

Then to Almeria. Here it was rather hot, and in spite of the good food my inside gave way. For me travel now means threading a narrow channel between constipation and 'Beethoven'. After an 8 hours' trip on a springless motor-bus we were both glad to get home. Moral – never travel in these latitudes after 1 May unless one is doing so in great comfort. Although my old Marco Polo blood still flows and raises phantasms of new countries to be seen, I doubt if Gamel or I are up to prolonged rough travel. She stands it better than I do, though I naturally can walk better. It is bad food, lack of tea or coffee, long bus drives and even moderate heat that get one down.

7. 'Life is a puff of wind. We are born indebted. Death is never idle.'

We saw two extraordinary but unknown plants from our seats in the bus, and picked another of great beauty. It is *Statice echioides* – long loose sprays of lilac flowers growing out of the baked Almeria soil. In Spain botany gives an excitement to travel, as one never knows what one will come across. Oh for a nice little car in which we could ride about and stop whenever we felt like it!

One annoying thing. The principal object of our trip was to take photos for my book. But when we got to Yegen we found that the Kodak spool we had been using was a shade too tight for the Spanish films we had to use and that the camera would not wind. I have therefore only three of Yegen and may have to go back again.

I have decided to cut some pages of my Virginia chapter – perhaps half of it – perhaps rewrite it entirely. The summing-up of Bloomsbury stands out too much from the Spanish theme. This book is going to be a mess anyway. With fondest love to you both . . .

Gerald

HAM SPRAY, 20 MAY 1955

Dearest Gerald,

We've been away for a fortnight in the Massif Central, which accounts for my not replying to your letter and MS. Janetta came with us part of the way and is a delightful travelling companion. We walked up gorges and had picnics in fields of narcissus and lay in the sun (and Frances sliced up flowers to identify them in three fat volumes of French Flora), and came back 2 days ago feeling much the better for leaving this wretched island. We are extremely pleased, I hardly need say, that you and Gamel will make the journey to Galicia in August or early September in the Davises' car to stay with us; we were feeling sadly neglected when you said it was too far for you and the country too horrid. There are 12 beds in the house, so there should be room for all. Burgo has decided against coming with us, as he says he will be 'otherwise engaged' from July to October. What on earth can he be up to?

Now for your visits of Lytton and Virginia to Yegen. I like them *very* much and I don't think you ought to cut a word of either. The description of Bloomsbury as an orchestra is exactly right. Their minds played together in conversation to produce a work of art there and then, with no ulterior purpose of getting anywhere but just for the joy of playing their own instruments to perfection and creating an intellectual harmony; and, as you say, that accounts for the topics being so limited –

the theme being fixed, each could score his own variations on it, like members of a jazz band.

As for our visit *à trois* in 1920, without more details of the emotional situation at the time, I think your frantic efforts to get the house ready and meet us seem rather unaccountable to the reader; there is a heroic feat for no particular reason – why did you go to all that trouble? It makes you out an unselfish, considerate host but rushing to welcome some rather churlish guests, and looks like a claim for sympathy which I'm sure you don't intend. Only, if you cut out some facts, the picture goes awry almost without your noticing it.

The bit about my rowing is not right as it stands. I'll give you the facts and you can do what you like with them. You need never consider my feelings in writing; diabetes has robbed me of them. The first Oxford v. Cambridge Boat Race after the war at Putney was in March 1920. The Trials from which the final crew is chosen took place the term before, i.e. in November 1919. If you row in Trials you bind yourself to row in the race if required. I knew that, and when sending in names of candidates for Trials from Christ Church I left myself out. I was besotted with Carrington at the time and used to pedal from Oxford to Tidmarsh and back day after day, which didn't allow any time for rowing. Horsfall, the President of the OUBC, was too proud then to press me to row in Trials, but next term, when the final crew was being made up, they couldn't find a decent No. 6 (which was the place I used to row). I had fixed our visit to you in Spain; it was a treat really for Lytton, therefore D.C. liked it, and therefore I could be with her – the tail-chasing that went on in our ménage! – and when Horsfall asked me if I would row No. 6 for them I refused. He asked me to reconsider it and I took D.C. round to see him to explain the situation. There was a scene in his rooms at Magdalen when he made a passionate appeal to her to throw up the trip to Spain to enable Oxford to win the race – 'our only chance', he said with tears in his eyes (or do I exaggerate?); but D.C. was adamant; she was thinking of Lytton; and as I was thinking of her we walked out, and Oxford lost. So I refused to be a Blue – I never was one. I rowed in College Eights in May 1920 after returning from Spain, and we did so well that the crew wanted to go in for the Ladies Plate at Henley. That would interfere with my being with D.C. at Tidmarsh as soon as term was over; but Alan MacIver wheedled D.C. into an arrangement by which I lived at Tidmarsh during training while the rest of the crew were at Henley, and Alan came over and fetched me daily and took me back in his car in the evening. I kept no sort of training, except that I didn't smoke, and had D.C. as much as she would let me, and never felt the least bit the worse for it in rowing. Christ Church won the Ladies (the last time it has ever done so) and my oar now hangs in Ch. Ch. boat-house. That was the end of my rowing career. I was asked to row for England in the Olympic Games at Amsterdam the following year, but naturally refused. When I wore a Leander tie one day to the Hogarth Press, Leonard was impressed; but that was the only appreciation I ever got out of Bloomsbury for my solitary accomplishment . . . Fondest love to you and Gamel.

Ralph

CHURRIANA, 28 MAY 1955

Dearest Ralph,

I am glad you had such a nice trip in France and were able to have Janetta with you. I think the Roman system of adopting adults for one's children is a good one,[8] as then one can be sure of getting one who suits. Then France is delightful, the first and best of countries. Its scenery is varied, its people are gay, and the certainty of finding a good inn and the excitement of looking forward to even a plain meal are wonderfully soothing to one's declining years. I am not sure that I have not more genuinely romantic feelings about *café au lait* and brioches taken in a chair on the pavement than I have about Persia or the Sahara or Syria.

I am deeply obliged to you and Frances for reading my typescript. I was surprised to hear you liked the part about Bloomsbury, as I had come to the conclusion that it would not do at all. The points you criticize shall be attended to. I may say, however, that in writing about your visit to Yegen I had no idea that I could be understood in the sense in which you understood me. Your visit was of the greatest importance to me and I would, if necessary, have gone four times as far to fetch you. The fact that you were all in a bad mood owing to your emotional situation did not much diminish what I got from it. Friends then were not a luxury but a necessity, and I needed your presence and reassurance. Nor was my account of my long marches intended to rouse sympathy; if anything, they were boasts of my youthful toughness and ability to take it. You have forgotten my even today not quite extinct ambition to be Marco Polo. These pages really form an appendage to what is almost the only autobiographical element in my book – the struggle to find a house

---

8. Janetta was not in fact adopted by the Partridges, but since her childhood had been so close to them as to be looked upon as a daughter.

and settle. It was a great struggle – endless walking, acute dysentery, bugs, horrible food, and a perpetual fear that my money would give out. Looking back now I feel astonished at my persistence under such difficulties, but my whole future was at stake and I had to go through with it or fall back on a profession. However, in writing this chapter I did feel that too much stress had been laid on my own difficulties; only, when I considered cutting them out, I saw that the drama of Lytton's journey would be weakened and the whole episode reduced to nothing. Now I will make some cuts and emendations to meet your criticism, for which I am very grateful.

As for Frances's feeling that I have given too slight an account of Carrington, I must answer that I could not possibly paint a set portrait of her. I am far too aware of her complexity. Both you and she are there solely because you were the companions of a public figure – Lytton – and in writing about you I decided to take a flash photo of what you might have looked like in 1920 to someone who did not know you very well or, at least, who hadn't realised all your potentialities. This gave me a definite and necessary limit . . . With fondest love to you both.

Gerald

HAM SPRAY, 8 JUNE 1955

Dearest Gerald,

. . . I hope you didn't take my remarks about the MS. as in any way critical of your intention in describing your forced marches; it was only that the *effect* on a dispassionate reader (which I am not) might not correspond with your intention. But I'm not competent to give a sound opinion – V.S.P. would be better at that – I'm anxious you should do yourself justice.

I'd heard the Turnstile Press was packing up and handing over its authors like serfs to other publishers. V.S.P. came over the other day and said you'd asked him about Max Reinhardt. He thought Rupert Hart-Davis would be better; so do I. Collins is, of course, the great go-ahead publisher of our time; or there's Heinemann, running Secker & Warburg, where Roger Senhouse[8a] still functions . . .

What did you think of John Raymond on Lytton?[9] The epithet 'vulgar' was thrown in, I imagine, to cause the utmost annoyance to Old

---

8a. One of Lytton Strachey's favourites.
9. John Raymond had published a reassessment of Lytton Strachey's *Eminent Victorians* in the *New Statesman* of 16 April 1955.

Bloomsbury (but it fitted John Raymond himself singularly well). All self-conscious writers and artists can be divided into 'vulgar' and 'precious', if you think it worth doing – those who want to please a public and those who think it derogatory to do so. Virginia was 'precious' in that way; Shakespeare was 'vulgar'. But, as science and the Kinsey report have drummed into us, dichotomy is just a human failing – when confronted with a baffling continuum, cut it in two and call one half black and the other white. I should prefer to divide artists up into 'saints' and 'missionaries', to use less opprobrious terms. The saints are too busy with their own devotions to consider the rest of the world; the missionaries wish to spread their gospel, whatever it may be; each runs a trade risk. The saint may be unintelligible and therefore meaningless; the missionary's gospel may degenerate into mere patter and be contemptible and worthless. In the end it is not the trade that matters but the practitioner. I still think Lytton's gospel, the gospel of Candide, is a good deal preferable to T. S. Eliot's or D. H. Lawrence's or John Raymond's, and that the great enemy of mankind is self-righteousness; but whether Lytton packaged it in the most hygienic wrapping is questionable. As you say, there was something spongy in his prose which made one uneasy without quite knowing why; one was never marching on *terra firma* to one's destination. But I must stop jabbering . . . With fondest love to you both.

R.

CHURRIANA, 14 JUNE 1955

Dearest Ralph,

. . . No, the content of poetry, i.e. what one gets out of it, has little or nothing to do with the meaning of words. The purest atheist can revel in T. S. Eliot, the narrowest moralist in Verlaine's homosexual pornography, if they have a true feeling for poetry. Prose is a bit different, yet who cares about *Candide*'s moral, though indeed it happens to be a sympathetic one? What one enjoys is the speed, wit and conciseness of the story. Why is this? I think it is because good literature taps a region of the mind that is more fundamental than that where opinion is formed. When this husk of opinion is removed, every human being can respond and feel in harmony with every other human being. All the arts are rooted in a level where one is not 'engaged' in actuality – that is, all the arts have something of music.

We've been spending an evening with the Duquesa de Valencia. You may have heard of her as a lady who has been 17 times imprisoned for her monarchist opinions. She is the great-grand-daughter of General Narváez, first Duke of Valencia, who was Isabella's reactionary Prime Minister and who made the famous dying remark: 'Forgive my enemies, father? That is impossible. I have shot them all.' The Duquesa is a little slip of a chestnut-haired girl, rather worn as to the face because she is forty. Mental age 14, but very lively and *simpática*, in the style of Jan Woolley. She wears trousers and *alpargatas*[1] and smokes continually. Her man is an Austrian count known as Ali – an Albanian, brought up in Vienna, cousin of King Zog and a Moslem. He made a huge fortune in South Africa, since when he has lived in New York where he met Bill Davis who was, it seems, in love with King Zog's sister whom Ali married. Now he is living with the Duquesa and hopes to marry her and become a duque, but unfortunately there is a husband in the way. The Duquesa, though reputed to be a virgin, did once marry another grandee and lived for a few years with him. Ali is a splendid man of 50, a real *Roi des Montagnes*,[2] loud, handsome, forceful, egoistic, domineering. He had just bought a yacht in Belfast and, though seasick all the way and knowing nothing of navigation, had sailed it here through three storms against the advice of the British Navy. The Duquesa seemed enraptured with him and sat on his lap in the car like the pure little girl she is. But she was amusing about her prison experiences. She had to sleep on the floor without a mattress and eat prison food – I imagine because she refused to send out for her own, as the other prisoners do. Her companions were prostitutes and thieves. 'Charming people,' she said. 'One hasn't really lived till one has been in prison and met them.' They had taught her among other things how to pick pockets. 'Stand up,' she said to me. 'Imagine we're in a tram.' I did so, she held up a newspaper as though reading it, and in a moment my fountain-pen and wallet had gone. However, her social views were not enlightened. When I told her there was dreadful poverty in the Andalusian *campo* on account of the seasonal unemployment, she denied it and said, 'If they don't work, it's only because they're lazy.' So prison doesn't teach one everything. Her trouble seems to be love of a father who died when she was a child and hatred of her mother and sister. We were invited to visit her at her big palace at Avila and I daresay we shall go. I want to see a wolf-hunt. After driving to the harbour to see her very luxurious little yacht, we got home to bed at 2 a.m. With fondest love to you both.

Gerald

1. Espadrilles.
2. The hero, or villain, of Edmond About's novel of that name.

HAM SPRAY, 18 JULY 1955

Dearest Gerald,

A long delay in writing to you, for which I beg forgiveness. My excuse is that our plans for going to Galicia have been in chaos, one way and another, and we've only just got them comparatively straightened out. We cross with the car to France on 25 July and take up our residence on 4 August after a turn round the Picos de Europa on the way. Address: Quinta de San Victorio, San Fiz, Betanzos, Coruña ... We'll stay at San Fiz until 24 September, and hope to entertain you and Gamel there for as long as you can stay with us. Janetta (who has just been to Greece and hopes to be in Mexico in October) will be with us throughout ...

We've been having weather for the last ten days which makes it ridiculous to think of leaving England – perfect sunshine and warmth, and bathing in the pool 3 or 4 times a day. Even Julia and Lawrence[3] couldn't complain of it when they were here for the weekend. At Lawrence's picture show last month he sold 13 out of 42 pictures and made over £1000 – the fruit of seven years' work. Somehow none of his paintings stirred me to reach for my cheque-book; I prefer the Gowings I have already, particularly my apples. The Euston Road Group are out of fashion; [Roderigo] Moynihan only sold ¼ of his pictures and poor Victor Passmore can't sell anything at all in his abstractionist blind alley. Lawrence received some crushing reviews as well, but shrugged them off; he didn't even bother with press-cuttings in his indifference. The upshot of the show will be that he goes on at Newcastle.[4] If it had been a terrific success, they would probably have thrown up the professorship and he would have gone in for whole-time painting in the South. Trevor-Roper bought one Gowing and he has asked Lawrence to paint his wife.

Saxon [Sydney-Turner] has been moved from his flat by little Barbara [Begenal] and put in lodgings; it was an excellent thing, but he felt it like a nail in his coffin. He now can watch cricket on television to his heart's content and will adapt himself to living in Hendon in good time. I think you'd better write next to San Fiz. Fondest love to you both.

Ralph

---

3. Julia Strachey had separated from Stephen Tomlin in 1934, three years before his death, and married the painter Lawrence (later Sir Lawrence) Gowing in 1952.
4. Gowing had been Principal of King Edward VII School of Art in Newcastle since 1948.

My dearest Ralph,

After five days of rather laborious travelling we have reached Madrid. Astorga, Zamora, Toro, Medina del Campo, Olmedo, Segovia. Zamora and Toro are rather extraordinary places, full of Romanesque churches and still reeking of the Cid and Queen Urraca and early Medieval history, whereas Medina and Olmedo are pictures of decay such as one scarcely finds anywhere else in Europe. Segovia, which I have been to before, is enchanting; and its cathedral by Gil de Hontañon, Gothic of the early 16th century, is, I think, architecturally one of the finest cathedrals in Europe. Roger [Fry], I remember, had a high opinion of its originality.

And now we are here in a very pleasant and cheap hotel, and Gamel is in bed with a cold. After the usual first flutter at the beauty of the women I have settled down to the exhausting business of museum-trotting. And the Prado has given me a cold too.

I lunched yesterday with Pío Baroja.[5] He is a very quiet, serious man with a fine, solemn forehead and a grey beard, and he impressed me very strongly. He talked very quietly and simply of Paris in 1890, which he remembers. He had nothing of the intellectual, but one felt he was a man who was incapable of saying anything he did not feel or think. He was truth itself. Talking of travelling he said he had been all over Italy in a car, but at the end of the journey he could remember absolutely nothing of what he had seen; but when I told him of my method of seeing the small towns in Spain – getting stranded in one and feeling the monotony and boredom of their life in one's bones – he only said, 'Qué pena! How sad to think such places exist!' He is, I think, a man with such a penetrating moral sense of life that nothing else but morality – that is, how people live – exists. No sense for history and no *conscious* feeling for beauty, but a very keen feeling about the way in which people live. I think that you and Frances would enjoy his books now that you know Spanish better and can read it faster; only one has to make allowances for his complete ignorance of, and contempt for, the art of novel-writing. To encourage you I may say that he is greatly admired by V.S.P. He was pessimistic about the future. Speaking of the Paris, the London and the Madrid of 50 years ago, he said that they had had a character and a mystery which today they appeared to have lost. The world was becoming duller and more uniform, and the sense of adventure was

5. The distinguished Basque novelist, then aged eighty-three.

being lost. Making allowances for the prejudices of age, I feel that that is true.

Today I met a poet who edits the Spanish *Times Lit. Sup.* Like almost all the writers, he is a Liberal. He spoke with regret of the increasing power of the Church and of its bad effects on literature. The ecclesiastical censorship was so severe that they even objected to words like *seno*, breast, in poetry; and all the old classics, which had passed the Inquisition, were being re-edited. Some of his clerical friends were against this: 'Last time they killed a third of the priests in Spain; next time they will not leave one of us alive.'

I don't know when I have enjoyed a holiday more than these last weeks at Betanzos. It was delightful seeing you and Frances again. There is really nothing in the world to compare with the pleasure of seeing old friends, and I have so few. Anyhow you are my only Waterloo vintage. You are also perfect hosts and I enjoyed enormously seeing and getting to know Janetta and her children . . . This visit has renewed me and made me feel less old and dull and stodgy than I was. Now I look forward to getting back to my work again. We take the Tuesday-afternoon plane to Malaga. With fondest love from us both.

Gerald

HAM SPRAY, 30 OCTOBER 1955

Dearest Gerald,

. . . Kitty[6] brought us Anthony West's new autobiographical novel, *Heritage*, published in America where it is said to be a best-seller. As it describes his bastard childhood with Rebecca [West] and H. G. Wells with the minumum of disguise, Rebecca has been thrown into a frenzy and is trying to get a legal injunction against its being published in England – either that, or launching a libel suit against any publisher who takes the risk. Kitty thought it particularly mean of Anthony because he begged or borrowed £200 from Henry Andrews[7] just before the book was published. I cannot share all this righteous indignation; the book is very readable and will be a great success if it appears here. Rebecca is turned into an actress instead of a writer; H. G. Wells appears as himself except in name . . . As all novelists exploit their own experience, why such a fuss? Is straight autobiography better (which of course cannot be true, because the memory distorts) than fiction (where the distortion

6. Anthony West's wife Katherine, *née* Church.
7. Rebecca West's husband, a merchant banker.

is deliberate but may be truer than the author thinks, because the subconscious may take its revenge)? Anyway there's the making of a fine literary rumpus. I'm sending *Aspects of Love*[8] under separate cover. Love to both.

R

CHURRIANA, 15 JANUARY 1956

Dearest Ralph,

This is a short note written by a smoky oil stove after a night spent in composing epitaphs for my tombstone. Since you're my executor I enclose two which I think might do. But no marble please, only local limestone . . .

I see nothing the matter with Burgo. He seems a perfectly normal youth and his wish to be very rich, do no work, and live on his parents, is just every young man's day-dream. As a rule the father makes it clear that he can't do this and so in the end the son gives in. But I must stop. With fondest love to you and Frances.

Gerald

Two epitaphs for my tombstone

1. Pray for the unwritten works of G.B., b. 18 . . , d. 19 . .
    Silently, in secrecy
    his death-wish grew and grew.
    Life still seemed almost beautiful when
    the ice cracked, he fell through.

2. RIP
    G.B.
    He lived, he loved, he corrected every word he wrote, he altered everyone he loved, he regretted every word he said, he died everything he lived, he ceased to exist long before he died. Here he lies, here he doesn't lie, he wasn't himself, he wasn't his opposite, he was always travelling between one and the other; call him an egoist without an ego, call him a decyrilized Conoly starved of an 'n' and an 'l'; he was always emptying himself of himself and always finding himself full of something or other very like a self again.

    Drop, stranger, a polite tear and refrain from reading the books which his alter ego, who was his enemy, wrote in his name.

HAM SPRAY, 21 JANUARY 1956

Dearest Gerald,

Your epitaphs are in the metaphysical mood that baffles me, so I won't try to expound them; but you must be dissatisfied with your present state

8. David Garnett's latest novel.

to write like that. Have you just finished your Yegen book and fallen into writer's despond in consequence? Or are there other troubles? . . . Death has been busy. Barbara [Bagenal]'s old mother died at the age of 97 and has left her some money, which was what B. has been waiting for for the last 20 years; she is beaming from ear to ear with delight and doing up her kitchen at once on the strength of it. Maroussa has died in Paris and Boris is badly shaken and miserably lonely at losing her, although they spent much of their time apart. Helen has probably told you all about it. I saw her in London 3 days ago; she is still tottery and uncertain in her walk, and her new teeth have so changed the shape of her mouth that her whole character looks altered – a very determined jaw confronts one and she hardly opens her lips when speaking. Then Saxon has had a slight stroke and has been put to bed with his right arm and leg affected. Bad news all round . . . Fondest love to you both.

Ralph

CHURRIANA, 30 JANUARY 1956

Dearest Ralph,

It is sad about Maroussa and Saxon. I only hope Saxon won't fret or take a lot of nursing. And I am sorry Helen is getting so shaky. We are all deteriorating fast, as I expect you've noticed – losing our pleasure in ourselves, our splendid life-long egoism, as a prelude to relinquishing the rest . . .

I have been reading *The Quiet American*.[9] I wonder what you think of it. I admire its force and drive and its brilliant, imaginative, modern style. But of course it's totally false to reality. Characters, feelings, episodes (did you spot the brilliant falseness of some of the war passages?) all come from the author's strong but schoolboy imagination. The book is a thriller, with everything in it shaped and distorted by the violent streamlining which a book made for speed and thrust must have. Then he has done a thing that some of our novelists do for us – shown us the 'modern hero' and the 'modern mode of feeling' for us to imitate. This is a book of fashion plates. I think that both Stendhal and Hemingway have in their time done much the same thing. Carmen Laforet, on the other hand, whose last book[1] I have just been reading, seems to me to deal with real people and feelings. I thought that the first half of her book – in spite of the rather fumbling plot technique – was very good, with

9. Graham Greene's latest novel.
1. *La mujer nueva*, Barcelona, 1955.

some fine scenes and a superbly written dawn scene in the train, but after that it became too Catholic for me to bear with. I wonder what was Frances's feeling.

But this letter is long enough. It would be nice if you and Frances quietly popped into a plane and flew to Gibraltar. Is there any chance of that happening? . . . Fondest love to you both.

Gerald

HAM SPRAY, 11 APRIL 1956

Dearest Gerald,

. . . The life of [Sir Roger] Casement by René MacColl preoccupies me and Robert Kee. We want to blast the Casement diaries out of the Black Museum at Scotland Yard[2] by making a public uproar, but neither the English nor the Irish Government wants to stir up the mud. So far it is just literary sniping at the Home Office, but the hanging debate has put Lloyd George[3] on the defensive. You no doubt followed the attack on Koestler[4] in the House of Lords that backfired. I'm rather anxious about the Silverman Hanging Bill;[5] it'll be in great danger in Committee. One way to stop hanging is to drop this private Bill altogether and leave the Home Secretary in a predicament; if he does not reprieve everyone automatically he is defying the twice expressed view of the House of Commons, by whose authority he is in office, and would expose himself to a vote of no confidence. Keep hanging on the statute book and abolish it demonstratively – that's what has been the Belgian practice for 100 years.

Our own plans are to go to the Spanish side of the Central Pyrenees in a fortnight's time and look at the flowers; we shall be away for 3 weeks

2. At the time of Casement's arrest on a charge of treason his diaries, which contained a voluminous and detailed record of homosexual activity, were seized by the police and taken to Scotland Yard. During his trial passages from them were 'leaked' by the Government to a carefully chosen public – certain Members of Parliament, important newspapermen, etc. – in order to blacken his character and discredit him personally. This smear campaign ensured that petitions for mercy should come to nothing.

Subsequently the authorities denied the very existence of the diaries, but in 1959 they relented and placed them in the Public Record Office, where, however, no one is allowed to see them without permission from the Under-Secretary of State at the Home Office.

3. Gwilym Lloyd George, later 1st Viscount Tenby, was then Home Secretary.

4. An anti-hanging article by Arthur Koestler in the *Observer* of 4 March 1956 had been the subject of several debates in the House of Lords.

5. Mr S. Silverman, MP, had just introduced a private member's bill in favour of total abolition of capital punishment.

and back here in time for the night-flowering *Cereus* to open on 17 May. With fondest love to you both.

Ralph

CHURRIANA, 24 MAY 1956

Dearest Ralph,

This is only a short letter to catch you before you leave for the Pyrenees. I suspect you are starting too soon. Everything is late this year and I doubt if you find the lilac or the elder out, much less the alpines . . .

Since you mention politics I will say that I feel the sooner Labour returns to power the better. Weak governments are always dangerous and the stupid way this one has been throwing its weight about in the Near East seems to presage worse things. It should be the most elementary sense that we cannot follow a 'strong' policy anywhere without the backing of America. Not that I am in love with either [John Foster] Dulles[6] or Daddy Eisenhower. Politically speaking, we are back in the brainless days of between the wars.

No, I want hanging formally abolished. Everything about it is disgusting and repulsive. Then, when happier days come, we can look about for some quiet and painless way of disposing of our sub-humans. The definition of 'criminal' might then go and more meaningful words be substituted. The whole prison system, the whole judiciary process horrify me; they are brutal, stupid and almost pointless. Something infinitely better could be devised tomorrow . . .

Some time I would like to have your advice on whether I should sell out my Government securities. I thought of investing in South African mines or industrials, which are priced low at present. I do not anticipate serious political trouble there for ten or twenty years, but I have some doubts as to whether one should invest in a country whose government one detests. What do you say to that? We should be nicely caught here if the pound were devalued, unless of course I can really get rid of my tenant. With fondest love to you both, and may you enjoy your botanizing.

Gerald

6. On Eisenhower's election to the Presidency in 1952, Dulles had been appointed Secretary of State. His attitude on Eastern affairs clashed with that of Britain on several occasions.

HAM SPRAY, 31 MAY 1956

Dearest Gerald,

I haven't an idea when I last wrote to you or what I said. We've been back here for 2 weeks and are obsessed with the anxieties of Burgo's final exam. He has worked himself into a neurotic panic over it and is trying to refuse to go through with it, so our heads are spinning and we wait for the telephone to ring with leaden hearts. Within a week we shall know, for better or for worse, whether his three years at Oxford have been a waste of time or a preparation for life.

My Judas tree is in exquisite flower for the first time since it was planted; is this an omen, or the result of the cold winter? When I saw Ham Spray again, coming back from France, the spring green was so beauiiful that all thought of looking elsewhere for a better home evaporated. When English weather is kind there is nothing more comforting and maternal . . .

What did we see in the Pyrenees? At Benasque we were a month too soon, but even in early May the grass where the snow had melted was blue with gentians, the tiny spring ones, and the Pyrenaic fritillary hung its dark head by the streams among the narcissi. The *fonda* there is to be recommended, cheap and well run. The owner was busily engaged throughout the war in running fugitives of all sorts over the high passes from France; he said the Spanish Government did not try to stop this traffic in spite of its Axis leanings. To get back to France in May one has to drive through a five-mile tunnel in Spain (which I had never heard of). One had to show one's passport to go through it – what on earth for? Do they expect Casals[7] to blow it up? Or smugglers to have burrowed into it from France twenty miles away?

Robert Kee has been here for 6 days translating away from the German; he is in a very contemporary state of mind, i.e. he hasn't the faintest idea what to do in a topsy-turvy world. The young are all like that, utterly sceptical of all values, and facing the future with a wry, defiant grin. I wish I had some good news of any kind; perhaps you will send some. Another landmark of Old Bloomsbury will go in June, when James and Alix [Strachey] leave 41 Gordon Square for ever to reside in Bucks. Poor old Saxon still lies in Hendon, paralysed down his right side and waiting for the next stroke to carry him off . . .

Have you read the American book on Dylan Thomas?[8] An odious

7. Pablo Casals, the famous Spanish cellist, was still living in exile at Prades, on the French side of the Pyrenees.
8. J. M. Brinnin: *Dylan Thomas in America* (Dent, 1956).

man, the writer, but informative and revealing all the same, I thought. Facts should always come out, even if people like Edith Sitwell call the process betrayal. There is another book by Mrs Thomas to come,[9] they say – a panegyric of herself and her suffering life, at a guess.

There is no thread to my rambling, so I must stop. Would you say that adultery was the cement of modern marriage or the solvent? The question has arisen with some vehemence and an urgent answer is required. Fondest love to you both from this moribund old boot.

Ralph

CHURRIANA, 6 JUNE 1956

Dearest Ralph,

Your letter sounded sad. I hope that Burgo has now finished and passed his exam, though does it really matter so very much if he hasn't? Neither you nor I ever passed any exams, yet here we are.

May in Malaga is a delicious month. Every afternoon I have sat in the garden reading Racine, which I think must be one of the purest and most refined pleasures of which literary-minded man is capable. Classical art? In the feelings and attitudes I see Pascal, Baudelaire, Eliot, even Sartre, that is to say, remorse, angst and melancholy. Only the organization is classical – but then that is everything.

My spirits are not particularly high. Since Christmas I have been finishing my book, yet the end never arrives. I write slowly, badly, and with increasing effort, and do not know whether this is old age coming on or the languid Malaga climate . . . A week ago I was on the track of some caves in our sierra, escorted by a young shepherd boy and lass who knew the way. The day was hot, the slope was abrupt, and they were as light-footed as goats. After I got back I felt a mild pain over the heart. I still have it, extremely mild, but it has been a warning – needed perhaps, for my body gives me none when I am climbing. Unless I run I am never out of breath and my legs carry me, not merely without effort but often with a sort of exuberance, up hill. I fear my real talent was for climbing Everest before breakfast, not for this impossible thing – writing.

I know little about modern marriage, so I cannot answer your sweeping question about adultery. I have always taken it for granted that it contained dangers best avoided (if possible) for those who do not like risking their own and their partner's happiness. But since you tell me that the young are almost professionally unhappy, I think that perpetual

9. Caithin Thomas: *Leftover Life to Kill* (Putnam, 1956).

adultery must be the best thing they can go in for, as that will keep them in the proper, fashionable state of mind – 'wry, defiant, Sartre-ish, without values,' and so forth. Only I feel little sympathy for this disease of one crop of intellectuals and, rightly or wrongly, see a good deal that is unreal and phoney in it. What is it that tends to make the modern intellectual a *mauvais clerc*, a fifth-column man, an exile from his age and society? Most other people have their values, are happy or unhappy, and live their lives without striking attitudes. I must say that in a world where there is so much real, unavoidable misery and unhappiness I feel little sympathy for the synthetic product. If I were a dictator – this is becoming one of my favourite phrases – I would condemn them to a year in an Arab or an Andalusian slum to teach them what life can be. And that they should, as writers, be allowed to go on poisoning the wells – well, that's another thing Dictator Benito Brenanini would put a stop to. But one may well moralize – other people's lives are inconceivable and I feel I understand my cats better than I do any human beings except myself. The novelists only skim human nature and, if one must tell the truth, very few people show any aptitude for life at all. The animals have a lot to teach us.

But I will end these desultory, old-fogeyish remarks and also this letter . . . Our lawsuit with our tenant will come off in the autumn and decide our fate. With fondest love to you.

Gerald

PS *Vive l'amour, la joie, la gaieté et la félicité*, and down with their opposites.

HAM SPRAY, 28 OCTOBER 1956

Dearest Gerald,

I'm very sorry to hear of your *again* developing flu; it must be endemic in Southern Europe, or are you sure it's not Maltese fever recurring? I, in my way, have struck ill health. I'd been getting a pain in my chest since August occasionally when out walking; when I saw my diabetes expert a week ago on my annual visit he said, 'classical', and rubbed his hands. I went to Oxford for an electro-cardiogram and a barium meal; the digestive tract is exonerated but the EC reveals an inclination to thrombosis, 'which we don't want to run into,' as he put it kindly. So I must reduce my weight, eat no fat or fry, walk slowly, pause often, and ponder on my prospects rather gloomily. Fortunately, again they say, my sedentary habits come in useful; it would have been more cruel if I'd wanted to go swimming or play golf. So much for me. Frances is watching over me like a guardian angel – the one with a flaming sword – and reconciles me to any fate that may come. She has resumed her orchestras and proposes to translate from the French this winter, if she can't get any more Spanish. We shall live quietly. Burgo's inability to respond to any stimulus has taken him to a Dr Dicks, a psychiatrist. He lodges in London, in Chelsea, and is looking for a job with the British Council; he comes down for weekends when he feels like it. Until Dr Dicks can effect some change in his disposition, I can't see him getting any pleasure out of his life . . .

Ralph

CHURRIANA, I NOVEMBER 1956

Dearest Ralph,

I somehow had a presentiment that you had not been well, and now comes your confirmation. At first your letter depressed me a good deal, but on talking it over with Gamel I see it in a better light. For you have only the *tendency*. Eisenhower, who has the malady itself, is standing for a second term and Gamel's brother Bill, who had it for 6 or 7 years and is past 70, never moves except at a snail's pace and feeds on bacon rind and avocado pears; yet has been through a motor accident that killed his wife, has married again, motored two years ago all over Europe, and never stops talking for a minute. All you will have to do is to be very careful and avoid emotions. Wouldn't you do this better if you came out here for part of the winter? I am getting pretty decrepit too, have put on a lot of weight, taken to cigar-smoking, and we both notice that we walk less. Also I am suffering from two cancers – one, which at the moment is under control, at my bank, and the other in my tenants downstairs. It is they alone who prevent me from asking you to come and spend every winter with us.

This Anglo-French invasion of Egypt[1] is a terrible thing. It seems even worse now than if it had been carried out a month or two ago, because the excuse is so disingenuous. I could not imagine that any British Government was capable of acting like this. And, apart from the sheer wrongfulness, it seems to me a gamble of the most dangerous kind, with unpredictable consequences. Some blame, I think, must be attached to that bungler Dulles, who began well by condemning Nasser and holding us back but who then very cynically made it clear that the Suez Canal did

---

1. Following the seizure of the Suez Canal by the Egyptian President Colonel Nasser.

not concern the USA. If violence is to be avoided, it seems to me that moral and economic sanctions must be employed against nations who forget themselves. Here America failed to show that she stood with us and meant to see us through. Must we see the hand of the Texan oil-grabbers in this? I read recently in *Time* that at a recent meeting of the Anti-Slavery Commission, which is a UNO organization, it had been shown that the slave trade had been increasing rapidly in the Red Sea area. The slaves were kidnapped in Africa and taken to Saudi Arabia, and the Arab states defended slavery as beneficent. There was a vote on this *and the USA abstained.*

It seems to me that if Eisenhower wins the election our relations with America will become much more distant. NATO will break up – if the Russians really retire to their frontiers it will be unnecessary – and Britain will sink back into Europe with a diminished reputation. But, as I listened tonight to the BBC report of British planes bombing Egyptian airfields, I felt very sad. The sheer stupidity of it!

Two very sad things: Juan Ramon Jiménez, the greatest living Spanish poet, aged well over 70, has been given the Nobel Prize. His wife was dying of cancer at the time and died two days later. They had intended to return to Spain from Puerto Rico; now I do not know what he will do. Then Pío Baroja died two days ago in Madrid, with an offer of the next year's Nobel Prize dangling over him. [Ernest] Hemingway flew over from Cuba to pay his homage, though he scarcely knew him personally, and walked weeping in his funeral . . . With my fondest love to you and dear Frances.

                                                                          Gerald

                                                    HAM SPRAY, 6 NOVEMBER 1956
Dearest Gerald,

Your letter that came this morning brought a ray of sunshine to pierce the encircling gloom. I agree with every word you say about our beastly, silly, reckless invasion of Egypt; we are just about to develop the pains of indigestion that invariably follow such gross appetite. I've never liked surgery either; the knife cuts more than it proposes to. Have we cut our own throats in one bold slice? By the time you get this, the mushrooms may be sprouting and civilization vaporized. The future is utterly unpredictable now the shot's been fired.

We saw Ulanova dance in *Romeo and Juliet* – a miracle of impersonation by a woman of 47 of a girl of 14. *That* is the Russia that deserves to survive, but it is Genghis Khan sitting on his mound of skulls we have to contemplate.

I still have a vestige of private life; my reducing diet has taken off 10 lbs. weight in a fortnight and I've not had a return of the angina. In another fortnight I may know where I am, if the world still exists. One has to go on as if it will.

We *long* to come out to Spain this winter, say January–February, but I must wait for a medical OK before making definite plans. Could you look in the local paper for a flat or small house for us provisionally? As I shall be on a diet, it's much easier to cook for ourselves – with a maid, if such exist . . . I heard that your tenant was obdurate and made no room for you to take anyone in. It would have been a rare pleasure to stay with you, but we shouldn't have wanted to impose ourselves for weeks on end, and somewhere nearby would suit us best of all . . . Fondest love.

Ralph

CHURRIANA, 12 DECEMBER 1956

My dearest Ralph,

So you really had a thrombosis! I am very glad to hear at any rate that you are making a good recovery and that you still intend to come out here. As it happens, I have been following a little in your tracks – that is, having quite severe pains over the heart. I went to a doctor yesterday and he told me that there was nothing physically wrong with me, except that my blood pressure had gone up since last year, but that if I was not careful I might develop something unpleasant. The reason? Apparently reading the papers during the Suez crisis. Our post comes in at 9 p.m. and this is followed by a little orgy of hating Dulles, Eden, Nasser and (since his whitewashing of the Russian behaviour in Hungary)[2] Nehru, and all the cooks who concoct our daily dinner for us. My doctor then uttered words of wisdom. After the age of sixty never have any disturbing conversation or read any agitating book or periodical after sundown. If you are prone to politics, choose a paper that does not set itself to arouse the emotions. In the evenings only think of pleasant things. For, he went on to say, strong emotion is one of the commonest causes of death among sexagenarians, though it operates indirectly. 'As I went through the Civil War as a doctor,' he said, 'I know.'

I shall certainly try and take his advice and will begin by not reading

2. Growing discontent in Hungary had culminated in an anti-Russian rising, which in November 1956 was ruthlessly crushed by Soviet forces.

the *New Statesman* or the *Observer*, which batten on the emotions and are, I am sure, great killers. But I shall continue to read (after lunch) the weekly *Manchester Guardian*, which is never hysterical, and the American press which has been most balanced and impartial over Suez. And of course I have to follow a régime. One may as well tread this minefield of our elderly years seriously, and that is why I pass on my doctor's advice to you . . .

I've been doing proofs, buying a house for a Spanish friend, and have been having too many visitors. A bad fortnight altogether and that's why I haven't written before. Life has been one long rush and hurry; and I, you know, and Gamel too, need a lot of emptiness and calm. Now I must stop. With fondest love to you both.

Gerald

CHURRIANA, 28 MARCH 1957

Dearest Ralph,

We have just got back from Morocco . . .

Just before starting I heard from the Cambridge [University] Press office in New York that *The Spanish Labyrinth* was coming out in an American paperback and that I should get for this 1250 dollars in three instalments. With the first instalment I opened an account at Galliano's Bank in Gibraltar and at the same time cashed a large English cheque in Tangier. This has given us the idea that next spring we might go to Greece . . . I have always wanted to see it; yet I must say I have scruples about going off with my novel unfinished.[3] I never *really* want to leave Churriana for more than a few days, because I am obsessed by the desire to write. Although my mental faculties are obviously failing, I do feel that I have at last reached such maturity of mind as I am capable of. Still, as this will be my last chance for seeing Greece, I shall take it if I can, especially as the symptoms in my heart have suddenly disappeared. Who knows if they weren't in fact due to a guilt-sympathy complex concerning you? Now that you are so much better, I can recover too. That anyhow would be the proper hypothesis to make in this psychological age.

And I am *delighted* to hear that you have so greatly improved. Now that you know what your medicine is – a winter in Churriana – you should be safe for another ten years . . . With fondest love from us both.

Gerald

3. *A Holiday by the Sea* was not finished until the end of the year.

HAM SPRAY, 4 APRIL 1957

Dearest Gerald,

. . . It is excellent news that *The Spanish Labyrinth* is to bring you in a wad of dollars and that you propose to visit Greece next spring in consequence . . .

Your book[4] came out 6 days ago; I had an advance copy from Hamish Hamilton. I think it is characteristic, with what Cyril calls *brenanismo*, and perfectly splendid. To misquote a *copla*, your pen is like a sharp nose singling out the most delicious ingredients from the kitchen smells of our life's cookery. I've not heard a hard word said of it, and much rapturous praise. Raymond read it here last weekend and was properly impressed. The illustrations are wretched – done on the cheap, one can see – and the jacket reflects no credit on the publisher either. Now all that remains is that it should sell, and Cyril's review on Sunday may rouse the general interest if he's as celebrated a pundit as I think he is . . .

My health has recovered pretty well (as a result of Churriana, I like to think) and I'm very pleased that your symptoms have relaxed too. I rather agree with you that there must be some affinity between us. Certainly your state of mind affects mine, as my state of body may influence yours. Your enterprising look towards Greece makes me want to go to Asia Minor, where the spring flowers ought to be as luscious as in Spain but different in some Asiatic way.

What can I tell you of our friends? I saw Helen Anrep with her terribly changed face . . . She had been to *Phèdre* and witnessed Edwige Feuillères's first performance in the part. We too saw her, and came away amazed by Racine but unmoved by the actress; there should be tears, or something in the throat, when she dies; but there were no moist eyes anywhere that I could see, and I felt as cold as a fish. I compared that indifference to the surge of emotion I felt when Ulanova in *Romeo and Juliet* started as she felt the poison beginning to work in her. History informs us, however, that the great Rachel was a complete flop when she first played Phèdre . . .

Alix [Strachey] has a book out on psychoanalysis – a disaster of desiccation; we read it in MS. some time ago. Clive [Bell] has sold a Vlaminck for a large sum at Sotherby's. Julia is writing a play in the London Library and eating raw carrots for her lunch. Lawrence is touring USA for the English-Speaking Union . . . With fondest love to you and Gamel . . .

Ralph

4. *South from Granada.*

CHURRIANA, 20 APRIL 1957

Dearest Ralph,

The miracle that broke over me less than three weeks ago is becoming consolidated.[5] Joanna and I have come to a perfect understanding. Although there is always some uncertainty to be expected in the lives of beautiful girls, she has said that whatever happens she will return here in August or September and spend the autumn, winter and spring with us, painting enough pictures to allow her to have a show in London. In spite of the horrible precariousness which everything takes on when one is in love, I believe that this will happen and that we shall settle down to a fairly calm and productive life without much agitation for anyone. It is wonderful in some ways to be 63. I love her in every way and yet, because age moderates the physical passions and reason tells one that the young are made for the young, I do not feel jealousy or possessiveness. I have been able to test myself over this, for we invited a very lively young Englishman to spend a day or two with us and I did not mind in the least leaving them alone together.

There has been a certain ironic influence of Bunny's *Aspects of Love*. I had just finished reading it when she arrived and it irritated me by its calm assumption that elderly men could make a stronger appeal to girls than young ones. I jeered at it so much that she took it to bed with her and read it, enjoying it more, I think, than my book. And now what Bunny said has come true. An unhappy girl, tired of the wear and tear of life, of the egoism and immaturity of young men, and wanting above everything the security that is given by love and affection, can feel deeply and not solely in a daughterly way about a man of my age. For me it has been a miracle, more miraculous even than the collapse of all my ideas and life before Carrington at Watendlath. And the way is clearer.

Being in love has always been to me a dangerous and precarious thing, more charged with unhappiness than with happiness. I was rarely able to enjoy Carrington's society because time was always so limited, because everything was always hedged in with difficulties, and because I was so prone to agitation. I couldn't listen to anything she said because I was so possessed by the idea that in an hour or two she would leave me. I wanted love, expressions of love, all the time. Lily [Holder or Connolly][6] was a hangover from this in a Baudelairian setting and therefore, I

5. In the spring of 1957 Joanna Carrington, D.C.'s niece, came out to stay at Yegen. A flirtation began between her and Gerald which soon carried him out of his depth.
6. See note to letter from Gerald dated 13 May 1929.

suppose, quite vamped up and phoney, whereas with Juliana I was 'in love' – if that is the word to use – in a much more physical way. The poetry lay in the fucking, and I gave her a child deliberately because that seemed a more complete and thorough way of fucking her. Then came Gamel, but she was always so strange, not of my clan or family, not a girl of robust mind or body or health; and besides, from the first everything went wrong. During the war two other girls – a young actress and an ex-schoolgirl – made my heart beat a little, but there was no future in these episodes, and I didn't want a future for them, so they rapidly petered out. But with Joanna I feel I have met the girl I ought to have met 30 years ago. I feel completely and utterly at ease with her; I am entirely charmed by her conversation and company; I am moved in every sort of way by her beauty; and I see that she completely and unreservedly responds. Now I have to make of this what my age and my unalterable relation to Gamel will allow me, and above all I have to contribute to her happiness. It seems to me that I have never desired the happiness of another human being completely, utterly, unselfishly before, and perhaps it is this consciousness of my own freedom from egoism that makes me so confident and so happy.

Well, I have written enough. The awful rain we have been having has gone and the sun has come out. I hope you will remember to be discreet about what you say. Later on this will come out – I can't and don't even want to conceal my feelings – but it must come out in the right way. And of course not a word to Catharine and Noel[7] or their friends . . . And now my fondest love to you and Frances.

Gerald

CHURRIANA, 8 JUNE 1957

Dearest Ralph,

Some friends of Bunny's who live at Hilton came to tea yesterday. They told me two things that have amused me. The first was that Bunny's copy of *South from Granada*, which he lent them, had all sorts of emphatic annotations in the margin such as 'Nonsense!' and 'Gerald will say anything!' I gathered that these were principally written in the chapters on Lytton and Virginia . . . If you hear any Bloomsbury repercussions of what I said, I should like to hear them.

The other story was about the origins of *Aspects of Love*. I said, 'I understand it came out of some rather dramatic episode in Bunny's life.'

7. Joanna's parents.

'Oh yes, he went off to Paris with a rich American woman and stayed in her flat with her, living on the best of the land.' 'An affair?' 'Oh, naturally.' 'And this American woman was of course quite young?' 'Not at all. She must have been Bunny's age.' So the food and the drink got into *Aspects of Love*, but the lady's age was more than halved! That's the way to write novels.

I've been pulling myself together lately and with the help of a lot of argument and a little cynicism have definitely got rid of my obsession. So you won't hear of me leaping off the Leucadian promontory if J. does not come out. And if she does come I shall be much better equipped to play my cards, if playing cards is what is then going to interest me. I think myself it will always be cards with her. But I am still very, very fond of her and shall be very disappointed indeed if she does not return. Yes, life will become very flat, which it can never be for a moment if she is around. But will she come? Her latest letter is all frenzy and agitation. . .

All these events have excited me and made me feel I cannot live as I have done for some years without women. Perhaps I shall go off soon for a few days to Tangier. I have pleasant recollections of a young Jewess who danced naked for me in a small room – her own house – and of little boys who say, 'You want see my sister age 18 dance Arab dance?' I can't take crude sex, I can't feel any attraction in women who have passed 30. I think what I need is a little of the mystery of the Orient, even if that mystery lies only in my own head. I think, too, that almost every sexual relation is improved when you give money. Even when no sex is involved, giving it can be so very nice. And I am always touched by the poor, by those who want, for I have lost the desire for anything that money can buy. Wanting is a talent I have lost, except only wanting love and its imitations. Women who have *no* streak of the mercenary in them, women who tell the truth like men, are sexually slightly repugnant to me. They lack an important sexual characteristic. They are *terre à terre*, good only for marriage. I see you bridling under these statements, so I will stop. With fondest love.

Gerald

CHURRIANA, 13 JUNE 1957

Dearest Ralph,

I was shocked and amazed to hear that James [Strachey] had said that my description of Lytton was 'very bitter'. I have always been divided about him as a writer. I am perhaps excessively sensitive to fineness in style – so much so that when I read Newman's *Apologia* I almost feel I am a Catholic. Now Lytton's writing in my opinion was crude and without fineness; the set, rather dead, schoolmasterish side of his mind came out in it; but as he seemed to me from his manner and conversation to have another very different side, a much more subtle and spontaneous one, I tried to say so. Then I spoke of his appearance – a curious mixture of the ugly and the distinguished, and quite fantastic to anyone who had not come to know him well – and of what I guessed to be his shyness and diffidence with ordinary people and of certain things that you had told me that seemed to throw a light on his character. I thought I had written kindly of him, with appreciation of his brilliance and warm feelings towards his friends. I suppose that in some phrase of mine I trod on a Strachey corn; but to speak of bitterness is preposterous. Any jealousy I ever had of him – and that was never much – has long vanished. And I think that that jealousy was merely my refusal to take him as Carrington did – as a God . . .

Joanna hasn't written for a week. The day of long confessional letters is over . . . I have quite given up expecting her to come out in September, though there are always very good reasons why she may do. She herself can't decide, and of course there is at present no point in her trying to do so . . . But I've recovered . . .

It is poetry that has saved me. In 1923, when Arthur Waley handed me back some sonnets I had written with the words, 'No, I can't see any promise in them,' I decided that I would write no more of it. I set myself to learn the less rewarding and altogether less delightful art of prose. Book followed book and I kept poetry out of my mind. I almost gave up reading the English poets. On only two or three occasions, when I was on a holiday, did the muse break out, and never with any encouragement or preparation from myself. Then, on 8 May 1957, I decided to drop prose and take up poetry . . . So I made a sweep of everything – all prose, papers, periodicals – and began to explore the one branch of modern poetry I did not know – the American. (English poetry is non-existent.) But the main thing was the decision – 'I am going to write poetry'; and write it, I have. Poem after poem has flowed from my pen, some of them incomparably better than anything I have ever even approached before. Love poems, satirical poems, a 'Portrait of Joanna', a dirge, an autobiographical poem, and now a long ambitious poem on the sea. It's a way of life, poetry. When I can't read it or write it or talk to Gamel about it, I just lie in bed and do nothing. Am I mad, am I very conceited – but I feel I may end by being better as a poet than as a prose writer? I owe this entirely of course to Joanna. She seems to have turned me completely inside out. And writing poetry has been my cure. When I think of the years I have wasted on books I never finished – that endless Spanish novel, that dismal biography of St Theresa – and on stuffing myself up with idiotic information, I could kill myself for my stupidity. At last I've found my true, though still uncertain, vocation. At sixty-three!

I had got ready a large envelope of typescript poetry to send you, when I started off again, yesterday, and have been writing ever since. But as soon as this new burst is over and typed and corrected, I'll send it and you can cast your eye over it, if you have the patience . . . I am glad to hear of you taking walks and botanizing and feeling well. I do long to see you and Frances out here again. With fondest love.

Gerald

Joanna came out to Spain in September and stayed with Gerald the whole winter. But things did not work out as he expected. The strain became too much for him and when she left, in January 1958, he was not sorry to see her go and from then on he wrote no more poetry.

HAM SPRAY, 23 JUNE 1959

Dearest Gerald,

Your p.c. from Tangier tells me that you will be home by now.[8] I really think your expedition was splendid. To see the Dra and the Blue Men was one of my day-dreams – I can't say it is any longer as I'm so enfeebled – and I feel I've done it by proxy and take a rather ridiculous pride in your performance. When I told Cyril you'd been to Goulimine, he at once felt a surge of resentment (which delighted me) and tried to spell the place differently, i.e. Goulemine, in order to restore his self-respect. He'd been to Agadir and had funked the discomfort of going on to G. I fear I shan't hear of the Dra from you, as you'll be reserving it for the *New Yorker* or *Holiday*. Well done and bravo!

While you've been in the Sahara, Wiltshire has been taking things easy. Personally I'm more active and on the mend. After 8 weeks from the date of the attack I went last week to have another cardiogram taken by Geoff[9] and heard him say 'Good' when he compared it with the previous one. 'And what's my expectation of life?' I said. That's the question the profession doesn't like to commit itself upon. 'Five years?' 'Oh, yes, I should certainly think you could count on that,' he replied. So count I shall, which I hadn't been doing lately . . .

8. Gerald had just spent several weeks in Morocco.
9. Geoffrey Konston, the heart specialist.

Gossip, gossip! There's never a shortage, but I can't think of any that will interest you. There's a printing strike on and the *New Statesman* has to· be printed in Düsseldorf, *The Economist* in Brussels, and the *Spectator* won't say where, while the local papers won't be printed at all. What difference does it make to everyday life? None at all, so far. The weather is far more important, and there can be no quarrel about that – hot and sunny for nearly a month and already gardeners screaming for rain. Frances has two new botanical squares for the Botanical Society,[1] so we drive off to the Woodhays[2] and potter round lanes and downs and woods trying to pick up an occasional novelty. This constitutes my daily exercise and I reckon that I can now walk two miles slowly without distress. F. is busy from morning to night, translating, cooking, botanizing, gardening, and seeing that I don't eat too much or run upstairs. Her latest task is secretaryship to the old Memoir Club, started by Molly MacCarthy and now sadly aged and almost paralysed. Vanessa used to run it but could no longer be bothered. So far Charleston, i.e. Vanessa, has resolutely blackballed anyone but Charleston loyalists – Vanessa, Leonard [Woolf], Clive [Bell], Duncan [Grant], Bunny, Quentin [Bell] and his wife Olivia constitute more than half the club. Now a new list is going out and we shall see if Vanessa lets anyone in but Sir Dennis Proctor,[3] whom she has fastened on as a trustee of the Tate. She has had a heart attack like mine and been flat in bed for weeks. If she lets in any intruders it will mean she is very ill indeed, to my way of thinking. People only change their characters at their last gasp, when nobody minds if they do or not. Poor Raymond [Mortimer] too has had an attack – not heart. He fell unconscious on the croquet lawn when playing with Lady Churchill. Sir Winston, he said, was almost dead on his feet but showed his appalling paintings to his guests, and when Onassis[4] liked one Winston gave it to him and Onassis kissed his hand in gratitude with tears pouring down his cheeks. Hero-worship! With love always.

Ralph

---

1. The Botanical Society's *Atlas of the British Flora* was made up of reports sent in by enthusiasts like Frances, who recorded every species found in the various 'botanical squares', on the National Grid one-inch map, which had been allotted to them.
2. East Woodhays and West Woodhays, two villages near Newbury.
3. A civil servant, later Chairman of the Tate.
4. Aristotle Onassis, the Greek millionaire ship-owner, on whose yacht Churchill was a frequent guest.

CHURRIANA, 18 AUGUST 1959

Dearest Ralph,

The summer is passing by, this summer which is so different to last summer and to the summer before . . . Miranda and Xavier are here with their charming children, so our patio is often full of callers, though I don't usually go down. Most evenings they go dancing and drinking in Torremolinos . . . But you'll be more interested in Ken and Elaine Tynan's[5] visit. We've seen quite a bit of them and like them better than we did last year.

They know the Hemingways well and went to see them last spring in Cuba. H. said to K., 'What's this fellow Bill Davis like? I used to know him a bit long ago and now he's asked me to spend the summer with him.' Ken Tynan made a favourable reply and the Hemingways came. Then, after the first day's fight at the Malaga *feria*, they ran into the Davis party in the lounge of the Miramar Hotel. Hemingway, very drunk, crossed the room to the Tynans' table and asked Ken what he thought of the performance of a certain torero. Ken's opinion was less favourable than H.'s, on which H. in a loud voice insulted him again and again. At the end he said, 'Come on, where's your *esprit d'escalier*?' The argument had been about whether stabbing three inches from a bull's heart was a big miss, and Ken replied, 'Your wife might find three inches an important factor when she's in bed with you . . .' Next day the Tynans and the Cónsula group found themselves in the Miramar lounge again. Hemingway got up, crossed to Tynan's table and said in a loud voice, 'I owe you an apology because I was very rude to you yesterday. I was very tired, I was drunk, and my tongue ran away with me. I'm sorry.' But too much had been said and the Tynans weren't asked to the Cónsula.

We've seen quite a lot of Annie D. and Mary H. in the absence of their husbands. We like Mary very well. She is amusing about Ernest, who, she says, is just a schoolboy and who has completely lost his head this year over bulls. Apparently he only sleeps three hours a night, suffers a good deal from his crushed kidney and does not expect to live long. He never misses a morning's work; has on hand a novel and several stories. Ethel de Croisset,[6] who has actually been staying at the Cónsula, says that every morning Ernest gives his orders for the day – cars to be round at such and such an hour; the women to go here, the men there; and so

5. Kenneth Tynan, the dramatic critic, was then married to the novelist Elaine Dundy.
6. A rich and extremely generous American lady, who had a house built for herself near the Cónsula.

on. Bill has fallen under the bullfighting spell, but Annie is looking tired. She has felt the quarrel with the Tynans and being cut off from her friends . . . Miranda leaves a week from today and then a great peace and boredom will descend on our world. With fondest love.

Gerald

The correspondence between the two friends came to an end with Ralph's sudden death on 30 November 1960, six days after his sixty-sixth birthday. Here are the last letters each wrote to the other.

HAM SPRAY, 14 NOVEMBER 1960

Dearest Gerald,

I write, without any real news, to keep the lines of communication open. Your last letter seemed to come out of what used to be called 'the dumps' – I expect the name's been changed – although your book[7] had been sent off and I'd have thought that would have brought an 'Ouf!' of relief. Someone in Marbella says it's never stopped raining there – and nor has it here – so all the European spirits are low.

We lived on Lady Chatterley[8] for a fortnight – splendid jury; the Judge has retired from the bench in dudgeon. Pritchett was asked to give evidence, but was in Turkey at the time. Bunny Garnett, rather piqued, wasn't asked. Allen Lane only read the book for the first time when the case was on, and was quite shocked to see what he was publishing. His 18-year-old daughter thought it 'rather old-fashioned'.

Bunny came here with Angelica [Bell][9] and his eldest girl Amaryllis, who has gone to Crichel School at the age of 17 and was being taken out for half-term. (As we are fairly close to that school in its new premises, we are handy for parents.) While here a telephone call came from William Garnett[1] to say that another daughter had had her neck dislocated by a third daughter; fortunately this has happened before and the Cambridge hospital fits a sort of collar. But what a life such a patriarch leads! When the whole family were in Ireland this summer, the catamaran was always being capsized in the middle of the lake and the two twins [Frances and Nerissa] took to disappearing at night to camp on islands. Amaryllis will not be a beauty like her mother, but is a

---

7. *A Holiday by the Sea*, on which Gerald had worked off and on for thirty-five years.
8. Penguin Books had been committed for trial at the Criminal Court for publishing an unexpurgated edition of D. H. Lawrence's *Lady Chatterley's Lover*. The jury found the book was not obscene.
9. Bunny had married Angelica in 1942; they had four daughters.
1. Bunny's younger son by his first marriage to Ray Marshall.

friendly, long-legged girl with a jutting nose, who would have liked to caper about if anyone under 40 had been around. Bunny has taken up with a Rumanian elixir of youth – he's been having it for a fortnight – and says he feels wonderful as a result. It is so powerful it practically grows hair on the soles of your feet. I imagine his purpose is to retain – regain? – his potency, but for whose benefit? He made allusion to an Indian lady living in Hampstead, separated from her husband, and I draw conclusions. Angelica has a furrow between her brows from cooking and tending seven in the family – a noble character as well as very fine to look at. Her relations with Bunny? Did one see occasional daggers being looked? Honestly I have no idea, but I think he goes his way and she hers.

I actually saw my son when I was in London and had lunch with him, and I believe he quite liked me and I liked that. He had no complaints of his manner of life at all and was in high spirits and so talkative that I could hardly edge in a word. In a few weeks he proposes to go to North Africa with Simon Raven[2] – Tunisia and Libya, and perhaps Algeria and Morocco – quite undaunted by the civil war in progress. If he does, that lets us off the horrors of Christmas in England and we shall probably start out ourselves on Christmas Eve. Burgo's book[3] still sells like hot cakes; the Japanese love it, the Portuguese translate it, and the American edition has brought him in a packet . . .

Frances is in a state of suspense. From fear of not having anything to do, she wrote round the publishers for translation, got a nice non-committal reply from Hamish Hamilton and an urgent message from Weidenfeld – would she consider translating the new edition of Casanova, 12 vols., coming out in France? Would she not! She's to submit a sample chapter, and, if the American co-publisher agrees, there's 3 or 4 years' work dumped in her lap!

I see from the Papers that the Mag.[4] is to have a new editor and that Kingsley Martin retires. High time too! John Freeman, the new man, I met once in the office and thought him a very cool customer – not at all a left-wing enthusiast. We shall see when he takes on after Christmas. Perhaps I too ought to retire, but if I haven't a book upstairs in the library nagging at me I shan't know what I'm supposed to be doing in the world. I'd rather said to myself that as long as Agatha [Christie] went on writing

2. The well-known novelist.
3. *A History of Orgies*, published by Spring Books in 1958.
4. i.e. the *New Statesman*, to which Ralph was still a regular contributor.

detection – and she's over seventy – I'd go on reviewing it unless the Mag. sacked me first . . .

Your proofs won't be ready, will they, before Christmas? If they were I'd ask to correct for printers' errors, as a supplement to your own corrections, but I can't believe the book can be set up so soon in type. With fondest love from us both to both.

Ralph

CHURRIANA, 22 NOVEMBER 1960

Dearest Ralph,

Yes, we are all in rather low spirits. Gamel had an attack of sciatica, which was intensely painful for one night and has left her leg rather stiff. I have had a bad cold, which has been followed by a sinus infection which has to be kept down by aspirin . . . My autobiography depresses me a lot. One third of it was quite appalling, but even when I have cut this I can't see that it amounts to much or that anyone will want to read it. I am completely bored by the whole subject and would much prefer not to publish it. However, I shall plug on and by April will have it completed down to 1919. Much more fun to translate Casanova.

The University of Michigan has asked me to write a book on Spain for their Modern Historical series. Two years ago they made an offer, which I turned down at once. But they say I will get a sale of at least 40,000 copies, so I have written asking them for further particulars. If they give the usual royalty I should make, say, £4,000, less tax, for what is presumably a short book. If I can count on even half of this I propose to go to London next April for 3 months to read in the British Museum . . . Gamel would stay on here for a bit and then go on her usual visit, as I want to be independent. I should work hard and see few people; but I expect that a period in London, with something to do, would do one good. If the book is to be short, as I suppose, I could write it quickly, for I know the underlying framework of this century and only need to fill it in.

A little bird has whispered that you and Frances are taking a house in Marbella for December or January. Can this be true? It sounds almost *too* good news . . . Our fondest love to you both.

Gerald

Less than three years after Ralph's death Frances was dealt another shattering blow – Burgo, her only child, also died suddenly, likewise of a heart attack. He was barely twenty-eight years old and had been married only a few months to Bunny Garnett's second daughter, Henrietta. By this time Frances had moved from Ham Spray and settled in London. She lives there still, intellectually more active than ever, having produced in the last eight years four volumes of biography and autobiography[5] which, as complements to this edition of Ralph's and Gerald's letters, are essential further reading.

Death has taken its toll in Gerald's family too. In July 1967 Gamel was found to have cancer, emanating from her left breast and spreading down the lymphs through her body. There was no hope of her living more than a few months. The pain began to increase after Christmas, but mercifully the end came very quickly, on 18 January. Some years later Gerald's daughter Miranda also died.

By then he had sold the house in Churriana, having at last got rid of his tenant, and built himself a smaller one further up the valley, just outside the little town of Alhaurin el Grande. Here he lives today, honoured and cherished by the Spanish authorities, who have not only named a street after him but also undertaken to keep him in comfort for the rest of his days.

5. *A Pacifist's War* (Hogarth, 1978); *Memories* (Gollancz, 1981); *Julia* (Gollancz, 1983); and *Everything to Lose* (Gollancz, 1985).

Brenan, Gerald, *South from Granada* (Hamish Hamilton, 1957)
– *A Life of One's Own* (Jonathan Cape, 1962)
– *Personal Record* (Jonathan Cape, 1974)
Carrington, Dora, *Letters and Extracts from her Diaries*, ed. David Garnett
  (Jonathan Cape, 1970)
Garnett, Angelica, *Deceived with Kindness* (Chatto & Windus, 1984)
Garnett, David: *The Flowers of the Forest* (Chatto & Windus, 1955)
Holroyd, Michael, *Lytton Strachey*, 2 vols (William Heinemann, 1967, 1968)
– *Augustus John*, 2 vols (William Heinemann, 1975, 1975)
– *The Familiar Faces* (Chatto & Windus, 1962)
Partridge, Frances, *A Pacifist's War* (The Hogarth Press, 1978)
– *Memories* (Victor Gollancz, 1981)
– *Julia* (Victor Gollancz, 1983)
– *Everything to Lose* (Victor Gollancz, 1985)
Woolf, Leonard, *Downhill All the Way* (The Hogarth Press, 1975)
Woolf, Virginia, *Diaries*. ed. Anne Oliver Bell, 4 vols (The Hogarth Press, 1977–82)
Woolmer, Howard, *A Check List of the Hogarth Press*, 1917–1938 (The Hogarth
  Press, 1976)

INDEX